'*How to Win Friends and Influence Peopl[...]* read (and a re-read) for any organisa[...] to find new, interesting and practical ways to succeed, in life and business alike.'

Emily Drew, EMEA director of sales enablement, Box

'A Malcolm Gladwell-style page-turning guide to success. I could not put it down. I found myself laughing, then grabbing a pen to jot down tips I could use in the office.'

Belton Flournoy, director, Protiviti

'This book had me from page one! I learned shed loads whilst laughing out loud. Anyone who wants to be a better version of themselves should read it, anyone who wants to be a confident communicator should read it, anyone who feels sick at the thought of doing improv definitely needs to read it.'

Sherilyn Shackell, founder and CEO, The Marketing Academy

'This book, and the practical steps in it, make "becoming more creative" a reality.'

Ian Priest, founder, VCCP; former president, IPA; founder and CEO, Grace Blue

'I didn't realise how fundamental improvisation is to everyday life until I read Max's book. Max makes the concepts relatable by "speaking your language" and bringing ideas to life with his stories, humour and wit. You can feel his personality oozing as you giggle your way through the pages. I came away with a feeling of freedom – a freedom to be myself, a freedom from needing to control everything, and a freedom to not take things quite so seriously.'

Alice Ter-Haar, former Deliveroo EU marketing lead

'In a time where emotional intelligence and "soft skills" are increasingly valued alongside technical knowledge, *Improvise!* should be essential reading for anyone heading out into the professional world.'

Ben Tyson, CEO and founder, Born Social

'Unlock those barriers you didn't realise were holding you back in your work life with practical and engaging know-how from the world of improv. You owe it to yourself and others to rediscover the curiosity and play already inside you. Yes and ...!'

Kate Diver, head of people operations, Transferwise

'*Improvise!* is a book that will help you see a new ways of doing things. It makes total sense and is packed full of tricks to help you work confidently with your teams. It's a lovely balance of great examples, some really good case studies and is written in a way that won't make you want to weep. Who knew we should all be using improv in business?'

Tash Walker, founder, The Mix London

'A refreshing read. I can't wait to put the lessons into practice.'

Jack Westerman, digital strategy manager, Accenture

'The perfect antidote for the volatility of an unpredictable year. Through a series of well-crafted anecdotes, social observations and genuine laugh-out-loud moments, Max is able to transport the reader into a world of new and better possibilities through the art of improv.'

Seun Shobande, consumer marketing lead, Facebook

IMPROVISE!

IMPROVISE!

USE THE SECRETS OF IMPROV TO ACHIEVE EXTRAORDINARY RESULTS AT WORK

MAX DICKINS

ICON

This edition published in the UK in 2021
by Icon Books Ltd, Omnibus Business Centre,
39–41 North Road, London N7 9DP
email: info@iconbooks.com
www.iconbooks.com

Sold in the UK, Europe and Asia
by Faber & Faber Ltd, Bloomsbury House,
74–77 Great Russell Street,
London WC1B 3DA or their agents

Distributed in the UK, Europe and Asia
by Grantham Book Services, Trent Road, Grantham NG31 7XQ

Distributed in the USA
by Publishers Group West,
1700 Fourth Street, Berkeley, CA 94710

Distributed in Australia and New Zealand
by Allen & Unwin Pty Ltd,
PO Box 8500, 83 Alexander Street,
Crows Nest, NSW 2065

Distributed in South Africa
by Jonathan Ball, Office B4, The District,
41 Sir Lowry Road, Woodstock 7925

Distributed in India by Penguin Books India,
7th Floor, Infinity Tower – C, DLF Cyber City,
Gurgaon 122002, Haryana

Distributed in Canada by Publishers Group Canada,
76 Stafford Street, Unit 300
Toronto, Ontario M6J 2S1

ISBN: 978-178578-687-7

Typeset in Baskerville MT by Marie Doherty

Printed and bound in Great Britain
by Clays Ltd, Elcograf S.p.A.

This book is dedicated to Naomi Petersen,
the best improviser I know.

CONTENTS

FOREWORD

'Everyone's got a plan until they get punched in the mouth.'
—Mike Tyson

My editor signed off the first edition of this book for publication in January 2020. It was due to be published on May 7th that year. Ah, January 2020! Remember then? A time when, for most of us, the idea of a global outbreak of a deadly virus was just that, an idea. Something we'd see in a Bruce Willis movie. It would never actually happen, right? And then, it did. Publication of this book was pushed back till late August. The global economy imploded. Hundreds of thousands of people lost their lives. Millions of us totally changed how we lived and worked overnight. In fact, most commentators say that the COVID-19 outbreak sped up technological transformation by a factor of roughly five years.

Yet. The COVID pandemic is just one of many upending crises humanity has faced over recent years, although they seem to be coming thicker and faster. The Dot Com crash. 9/11. The Credit Crunch. And so on. Change, seen over this timeline, is the norm. We are losing our scripts. They are burning in our hands. The roles we are used to playing are being lost. Our lines are no longer relevant. So what do we do when we have no script? We improvise. Given the state of things, I would argue that the ability to improvise is perhaps *the* crucial skill in the modern world.

I have re-written this book to incorporate the consequences of the COVID pandemic and our new ways of working. You'll also find an in-depth guide to virtual communication in the appendix. The world of improv comedy offers not just a useful metaphor for these times, but also a practical methodology we can apply offstage to move through it with creativity and optimism. And I think that's what we need at the moment. Hope. Confidence. A sense of humour. You will find all of these things in these pages.

However, this book is relevant far beyond the coronavirus. The thing I am most proud of in my life is not this book or others I have written. It is not the business I have built. It is my relationship with my (now) fiancé. This has been an act of improvisation. I have had to be flexible in how I live and love. To bend around her values, her idiosyncrasies, her vision of the good life. I have had to listen more profoundly, both to her and my own inner world. To become aware of my own patterns, my own buttons, so that I discover new choices in how I relate to her and myself. I don't think I could have built such a strong relationship without improvisation. That was one positive I took from the COVID outbreak: I proposed!

If you get half as much out of improvisation as I have, it will be transformational. Good luck.

Max

INTRODUCTION

'All the world's a stage.'
—William Shakespeare, *As You Like It*

I am flustered already and I haven't even started my first improvisation class. Rushing down Brick Lane in East London, glued to Google Maps on my phone, furtively looking up at street names: I'm running late. One minute behind schedule becomes five, becomes ten. I have no good reason for being late. My tardiness is almost certainly a subconscious act of self-sabotage. Being late gives me plausible deniability. *I'm not a chicken for quitting,* I think. *It's common sense. After all, I've missed the first ten minutes of the workshop.* But I don't give up. Not yet.

My heart racing and my back sweaty, I finally find the turn-off. I can see the entrance, 100 yards down the street on the right. The urge to quit suddenly grows more urgent. I suppose those of an artistic bent would describe the venue as bohemian. Less forgiving folks might opt for shanty town. Officially, it's a converted fabric factory. The little voice in my head becomes louder still: *This is obviously a ramshackle operation. Come on, cut your losses and let's go home.* But still I don't throw in the towel. I check my watch: fifteen minutes late. *It's rude to go in now,* I conclude, and finally I turn to leave. That's when I'm spotted.

'Are you here for the improv class?'
Shit.

1

'It's quite hard to find, isn't it?' The man who has just emerged from the factory entrance is dauntingly cheerful. 'It's a bit hidden away. Don't worry. We haven't started yet; everyone's running a bit late. We're all upstairs.'

I smile weakly, my heart sinking. There is no escape now. Before I know it, I'm climbing a rickety outdoor staircase up to a converted attic. Inside are fifteen people sat on chairs in a circle, like some sort of therapy group for people addicted to damp. Except everyone's chatting jovially; laughter fills the air. One lady is even handing out home-made brownies. 'I've appointed myself Snack Captain,' she explains, with such an easy joy that it makes me feel worse about myself.

I am not as nice as these people, I think, *and I never will be.*

I put my bag down and search through it, pointlessly – anything to avoid making small talk with the person sat next to me. Soon enough the class leader announces the beginning of the workshop. The chairs are pushed to the back of the room and we all gather in the middle again. It's a real mix of people: a hotchpotch of actors, accountants, management consultants, housewives, students and more. The actors have all taken their shoes off. 'This is a really lovely space,' says one of them, quixotically. (I will eventually learn that 'space' is what actors call a room.)

Our cheerful teacher asks us to suspend judgement of everything in the workshop: to suspend judgement of the exercises we'll do, of each other and most importantly of ourselves. *What a wanker,* I think, before realising that maybe I'm the wanker.

'OK, we're going to start with going around the circle and sharing our name,' he says. *Simple enough,* I think, already practising saying my name in my head, as if it's the solution to a particularly difficult equation rather than a word I've said a million times before. 'But the twist is,' he says, 'you're going to add a word

2

before your name, but it must begin with the same letter. And you'll combine it with an action. So, for example, Chris, you might be Clapping Chris.'

At this point I genuinely think of feigning a heart attack. But before I have the chance to throw myself moaning onto the floor, we begin to go round the circle, everyone coming up with their alliterative names, and then all of us repeating them back, all while doing the matching action. We have Jumping Jenny, Karate Kate and Digging Daniel. When it's finally my turn I panic and designate myself 'Manky Max', choosing an action which is sort of a spasm-cum-fit of no discernible form. It feels offensive but in a way that no one can really put their finger on. But everyone joins me in my mistake, leaping into their own version, as if I've just choreographed the most wonderful dance in the world. Seconds later we're on to Raging Raj.

'OK, everyone, so this next exercise is called Bunny Bunny.' The teacher, 'Stirring Steve', is grinning like a loon. It's hard to know if he's grinning because he's having a great time or because he knows how stupid we're all going to look in a few seconds. We begin the game and immediately I want the ground to swallow me up. The person to my right, Graham, an enthusiastic divorcee in a Hawaiian shirt, is facing me, making bunny ears with his fingers. 'Bunny Bunny!' he says, gleefully, miming the actions with every word. 'Bunny Bunny!'

I promise myself that this first improv class will also be my last. I smile unconvincingly at the delirious Graham, before turning to face another member of the group. 'Bunny Bunny,' I say, no louder than a whisper. 'Bunny Bunny …'

The blizzard of eccentric exercises continues. At various points over the following hour I am pretending to be a dog, a shopping channel presenter and a sentient fridge, until finally and mercifully we take a break. The Snack Captain goes back on patrol. I mutter that I'm going to the toilet, but really I am about to sneak out of the building and never come back. But as I pick up my bag, Stirring Steve corners me, as if he has a sixth sense for people who are thinking of doing a runner.

'Manky Max really made me laugh!' he says.

I bashfully look at the floor. 'I'm not great at thinking on my feet, so ...'

Steve asks me what has brought me to this workshop. 'Oh, you know, just fancied doing something a bit different.'

I cringe when I hear myself say this because this is a lie – a lie I don't have to tell but which I tell anyway, presumably because I am too embarrassed to tell the truth. On the face of it, I am a confident and adventurous person. I make my living from doing stand-up comedy. For most people, this is the epitome of swagger and spontaneity. But appearances can be deceiving. Because anyone who has done stand-up will tell you that 'confidence' and 'spontaneity' are con tricks. You can learn to look confident without feeling it at all. It's a simple matter of presentational technique. Similarly, spontaneity is a stubborn myth of the art form. The truth is, almost every syllable of a stand-up's act is pre-planned, pre-written and pre-rehearsed. Even the so-called 'mistakes' are repeated on cue, every night of the week.

They say that people start doing comedy because it allows them to control why people laugh at them – *control* being the operative word. As a stand-up you are the most powerful person in the room. You are the only one with a microphone. You are the only person lit up, the only one with a script. While it might look dangerous and terrifying to the layperson, if you are competent, being onstage is the safest place in the world. I had started stand-up because, on some level, I felt insecure. The laughs I got were affirmation of my self-worth. Onstage I was King. But I wanted to feel confident for more than twenty minutes a day. I felt that improv might help me feel it offstage too.

But I don't tell Stirring Steve any of this. Instead I say something glib, something to deflect, something to stop the conversation in its tracks. I don't leave the workshop.

Steve's small act of kindness means that I come to the next session, and then the next, and then the next. After I complete my eight-week beginners course, I sign up for another. And then another. Eventually, I form my own improvised comedy group, The Committee.[1] Over the subsequent years we perform hundreds and hundreds of shows. It still feels surreal to say it, but I am now a professional improviser. And Stirring Steve is my business partner!

* * *

WHAT IS IMPROVISATION?

I'm lucky enough to travel the globe sharing improvisation concepts and skills with amazing clients like Google, Facebook and Unilever. Demand grows every year as the world wakes up to the power of improvisation to make us more effective communicators, more flexible collaborators and more creative thinkers, whether we are working online or off. In fact, improvisation is now part of the curriculum of all the major business schools worldwide. So, whether you're a product manager in a global technology firm, run your own small business, are starting out in your career, or are developing a side hustle, improvisation can help you to tackle the challenges you face every day at work – and in life. Think of this book as both a beginner's tour around the key concepts and a practical user's guide. You'll discover that improvisation offers brilliant new perspectives in tackling some of life's oldest challenges:

- How do we overcome our fear of failure?

- How do we build meaningful relationships with other people?

- How do we speak confidently in front of an audience?

- How do we effectively overcome conflict?

- How do we come up with new ideas?

- How do we lead people with authenticity and charisma?

Improvisation can help you deal with the new and the unexpected too. Improvisers know how to hit curveballs out of the park. Later we'll explore the techniques they use to do it, so that you can use them too. Imagine the power of facing the world with the belief that you can handle anything it throws at you. This is the seductive potential of improvisation. It's a confidence I've enjoyed using onstage countless times – and the stage *is* where most people's associations with improv lie. When you think of the word 'improvisation' you probably think of comedians like Tina Fey, Steve Carell or Paul Merton. You probably think of TV shows like *Whose Line Is It Anyway?* or movies like *Spinal Tap* or maybe even jazz.

But improvisation isn't just for comics, actors and musicians. Improvisation is for everyone. In fact, we all improvise every single day. We just don't realise it. After all, life isn't scripted. When we have a conversation, we improvise. When we miss the last train home, we improvise. What is parenting but one long improvisation? And don't get me started on global pandemics!

Improvisation is the art of acting without a plan. Or, more commonly, the art of acting when your plan turns out to be incomplete or even completely useless. This is an essential human capacity because few plans survive contact with reality. What you do when that happens will determine whether you succeed or not.

Improv teaches you that, although you can't follow a plan for every scenario, you can be equipped for every scenario. While we have no control over whether life gives us lemons or not, we can develop a mindset that allows us to turn them into lemonade as and when required. Improvisation training, therefore, is preparing to be unprepared. Of course, some things in life are planned in detail. But even within well-defined plans we often improvise too. A great example of this is when we follow recipes.

If you're the sort of person who is able to follow a recipe to the letter then I salute you. I am genuinely in awe of both your discipline and your precision. I comfort myself with the knowledge that you are a rare breed. Most of us are much more laissez-faire in the kitchen. When cooking a dish, we look down at the endless list of herbs, spices and condiments, and we panic. *What the hell is harissa?!* we think. *The guests are coming in 40 minutes!*

So, what do you do? You think of substitutions. You look in the cupboard, venture to the spice rack, pick up the curry powder and think, *I'll lob some of that in.* Onwards and upwards with the dish. It's not the same colour as the photo in the book. You did things in slightly the wrong order. You didn't chop the sweet potatoes thinly enough, so now they're taking ages to cook through. Plus, half-way into proceedings you had to go wipe your four year old's bum. And now the sauce has caught on the bottom of the pan. So you stir in some cream, load it with salt and pepper – anything to make it taste less burnt. The point is, while the plan was useful to an extent, the unpredictable demands of the present moment required you to adapt as you moved in order to reach your goal. *This* is improvisation.

Of course, when you've cooked for a while, you don't need recipes anymore. An experienced and confident cook can get home in the evening, open the fridge and combine whatever resources they have at their disposal to create something delicious. Rather than moaning about what they *don't* have, or fantasising about what they *could* have, they improvise a solution that is a celebration of what is actually available to them at the time. This is fundamentally the great joy of improvisation. It doesn't require you to have more time, more money or more resources, of any kind. Improvisation helps you get better results with the same ingredients. All by using small shifts of mindset and behaviour.

WHAT IMPROV IS NOT

The idea that improvisation is comedy, theatre or music is just one of many popular misconceptions. Improvisation is also not about being good at 'bullshit'. Nor is it merely 'making it up as you go along' or 'flying by the seat of your pants'. Yes, good improvisers are often best-in-class bullshitters. But the point of learning the art of improv is not so you can fake expertise when you haven't got it. Nor is it about making up for a lazy lack of preparation. Instead, we improvise at the point where our preparation and expertise become irrelevant. When do they become irrelevant? It depends on the nature of problem we are facing.

As we will explore in more depth later in the book, there are three sorts of problems we commonly face in the world: simple, complicated and complex. An example of a simple problem is frying an egg. There is a proven best practice method of frying an egg. It makes no sense to improvise here; we just need to follow what works. An example of a complicated problem is fixing a car engine. Again, experts in the field have a proven best practice approach for fixing cars. No improvisation required here either, just expert knowledge. But a complex problem does require improvisation.

A complex problem is one we have never faced before, or certainly not in its current guise. We can't just learn all the rules or study how someone else has solved it before, because no one has. An example of a complex problem is pivoting to an online offering, starting a disruptive new business or designing a marketing campaign for a new product category. There is no recipe for success here, at least not a precise one. Knowledge, therefore, is only partially relevant. Instead, we have to create the recipe ourselves by trying stuff and responding to feedback as we move. In other words, we have to improvise.

But improvising is not the opposite of knowledge or expertise. When an improviser is onstage, they use everything they already know, everything currently available to them in the environment and everything provided by their colleagues to create value. Improvisation is not about the creation of something out of nothing. *Improvisation is about the creation of something out of everything.* Rather than falling back on a plan, or on their knowledge, improvisers use everything at their disposal in the present moment to define and respond to the unique challenge in front of them.

Improvisation is also not the opposite of planning. As improviser and author Bob Kulhan puts it: 'Improvisation thrives where planning meets execution, and the art of improvisation is really about making fast decisions and adapting when faced with unanticipated situations.'[2] As the old adage goes, plans are useless, but planning is essential. Even improvisers prepare for shows. The cast of *Whose Line*, for example, will practise the games they will be playing onstage on the evening of the performance. But what they say in those games on the night will entirely depend on audience suggestions and on the responses of their fellow performers. Improvisers are not against plans, but the reality of the present moment trumps all.

Improvisation is not merely an emergency measure either – although it certainly can be useful to dig yourself out of a hole. (For example, you've forgotten your daughter's school play and now you've got to make a Shrek costume by 7am the next morning – using only black bin liners, some green spray paint and some old ping pong balls.) In this book we will focus on a much more positive conception of it that focuses on noticing resources you may have previously overlooked and using them to pursue your most meaningful goals.

Finally, improv is not just for wacky, archetypally 'creative' people. It also has a lot to offer those of a more analytical bent, those people who work in jobs that are tightly regulated or perhaps overtly technical. Clearly, not everything in life should be improvised. For example, nobody wants you to spontaneously make decisions around risk management. But, no matter what sort of job you have, there are hundreds of situations where improvisation is relevant to you. Everyone has to solve problems, to collaborate with others, influence colleagues, overcome conflict, or bounce back from failure. The domain of improvisation is the myriad tiny encounters we have every single day with other people and with ourselves. It is self-improvement on a granular scale, tweaking our responses to these encounters so we can extract more connection, more confidence, more creativity and – most of all – more joy from life. Introvert or extrovert, improvisation is for everyone. Because *life is improvisation.*

WHY IMPROVISATION HAS NEVER BEEN MORE RELEVANT

I like to think of improvisation as yoga for your soft skills. If yoga makes your body more flexible, then improvisation makes your thinking, your behaviours and your communication more agile. And never has agility been so essential. We live in what has been termed a VUCA world: defined by volatility, uncertainty, complexity and ambiguity. The speed of modern life is incredible. Of course, there has always been change in the world. But it seems to be happening faster and faster. The reasons for this are well known and they all centre around technology. Things aren't going to slow down, either. In fact, they're likely to accelerate even more.

You only need to consider Moore's Law, which says that the processing power of our computers doubles every two years. We've had the Digital Revolution – personal computers, the internet and so on – but now the Fourth Industrial Revolution is upon us. Robotics, artificial intelligence and other new technologies are bringing their own disruptions. The statistics are inspiring or terrifying, depending on your point of view. But they all point to the same thing: the nature of the work we do is undergoing a radical transformation.

Let's start with the most controversial aspect of the future of work: job losses. Throughout human history there have been endless bleak predictions about machines making human beings economically obsolete, including a recent report by the University of Oxford which suggested that 47 per cent of jobs in the US were at risk of automation. However, subsequent research by the World Bank and World Economic Forum predicts that, while technology is certainly going to destroy millions and millions of jobs, it will also create millions of jobs too. In fact, the World Economic Forum suggests that technology will have comfortably provided a net benefit in terms of job creation by 2022.[3]

For most white collar workers, the question is not whether or not there will be enough jobs but what the jobs will be like. Currently most jobs are mix of both simple routine tasks and more complex non-routine tasks. For example, scheduling a meeting is a routine task, whereas building a relationship with a potential new client is a non-routine task. But as our jobs are augmented by technology, more and more of these routine tasks will be automated, meaning that the non-routine, more uniquely 'human' tasks will become much more central to our roles.[4]

In many organisations this is happening already. Our jobs are less about delivering tried and tested 'off-the-shelf' solutions and much more about co-creating innovative solutions with clients in the moment. As our job tasks change, so will the skills required of us at work. According to that same report by the World Bank, the top three skills of the future are: complex problem-solving, teamwork and adaptability. The World Economic Forum also rates complex problem-solving as the most important skill for future workers (a skill we will address in Chapter 6). Their research shows that the following skills will also be highly rated:

- Creativity

- Persuasion

- Resilience

- Flexibility

- Emotional intelligence

- Leadership

- Social influence

- Service orientation.

You'll notice that all of these are so-called 'soft skills,' best understood as social, emotional and thinking abilities (as opposed to job-specific technical knowledge, or 'hard skills'). The clear takeaway is that, in a world dominated by technology, to stay relevant we must learn to be more human than ever before. We will never beat the robots at their own game. We must focus instead on being better at our own. Over the next six chapters, you'll learn how to excel at each and every one of them.

CASE STUDY: Sarah McKinless, head of product

I've learned more about myself through improv than any professional training course. I've always known that listening is important. But improv was the first time I was taught how to do it effectively. I learned that listening isn't about waiting your turn in a conversation; nor is it about focusing solely on the words you hear. Improv taught me to pay attention to everything, which is particularly helpful when coaching my direct reports. I learned to identify key information, themes and biases in people's communication, which helps me to navigate sales conversations to understand the stakeholders' needs and wants. I learned to think critically about the status of the speaker and its effect on those listening, which I use when working with regional teams to influence change.

I have always held myself to high standards, which previously went hand-in-hand with a deep-rooted fear of failure. Improv has taught me to take risks and embrace situations when something goes wrong. I learned to manage my emotions in these moments and move forward in a positive way. This is critical to my current role heading up a department: when something fails, people look to me for calm leadership. Beyond this, improv has taught me to read a room and adapt whatever I am doing based on the audience response. I use this every day, whether I'm presenting at a conference or introducing a new idea to my team. I've learned to quickly reflect on the effectiveness of my language, tone and expression, then make necessary adaptations to better engage my audience. This is especially helpful when I am upward managing and trying to influence change at the highest level in my organisation. ∎

MEET THE CAST

I've argued above that learning how to improvise is a 'must have' in the modern working world, but the gifts of improvisation are relevant far beyond the workplace. In fact, the origins of improvisation show its inherently social purpose. The modern incarnation of improv can be traced back to the seminal work of Viola Spolin in early 1940s Chicago. Inspired by the ideas of sociologist Neva Boyd, Spolin created a drama programme in order to help migrant women and children assimilate into Chicago culture.

This programme eschewed the traditional formal teaching style and was instead made up of a series of experiential exercises structured like games. Boyd believed that play was integral to the human experience. In structured play, a group needs to be aware of the constant adjustments that all the players make during a game. It puts the focus, therefore, on the group and not the individual. Boyd believed that: 'The spirit of play develops social adaptability, ethics, mental and emotional control, and imagination.' In short, play helps make us better people.

Improvisation is still learned through games today. I will share many of the classic exercises in this book. I encourage you to take them, use them and make them your own. Improvisation is inherently democratic. No one owns it. Certainly not me. I stand on the shoulders of giants. We'll hear from many of these historical pioneers of improv throughout the book – people like Viola Spolin, Del Close and Keith Johnstone who helped create the simple set of principles and 'rules' that improvisers still use even now.

It seems strange to talk about rules in the context of improvisation. After all, improvisation is about making it all up, right? Aren't rules the antithesis of spontaneity? Here lies the paradox of improvisation. It isn't about untrammelled spontaneity at all. For example, let's briefly return to the cooking analogy from earlier. Say you get home from work, open the fridge and try to improvise a pasta dish using whatever ingredients you find. This doesn't mean that anything goes. Sure, you have a huge amount of freedom over what you make the pasta sauce from – but not total freedom. You still fall back on your knowledge or experience about which ingredients roughly go with what, not to mention the basic principles of cooking. You improvise within these broad walls, and the results are all the better for it.

Not only do rules help us achieve a degree of consistency in our performance, they also provide a necessary balance between freedom and structure. Because, while too many rules are stifling, having no limitations at all would be overwhelming. The rules set us free: they provide a structure within which we can play. Each chapter will be structured around one of these rules.

Before we look to applying them offstage, let's see them in the context of an improvised scene. It's a technique we'll return to many times in the book because, although this isn't a book about how to do comedic improvisation, it is useful to see these rules in the context in which they were originally conceived. So, without further ado, ladies and gentlemen, I take you to a comedy club in London.

8:31 PM AT A COMEDY THEATRE IN LONDON BRIDGE

The MC finishes her duties, introducing the next act. Warm applause and whooping fills the room. An improv group goes onstage. They are about to perform an improvised comedy sketch show. The first scene will be inspired by an audience suggestion, and every scene after that will be inspired by what has come before. Nothing has been planned or pre-prepared. Up goes the trademark call: 'To start our show, can we please have a suggestion of anything at all?' The audience erupts. The word that's yelled first, and that etiquette demands the group take, is 'ball'. The troupe thank the audience for their suggestion and assemble on the 'back line' ready to begin the show.

What do you associate with the word 'ball'? Onstage, every member of our improv team has their own answer, each as idiosyncratic as they are. There is no right or wrong choice. This is the nature of free association. One player thinks of a literal ball, such as a tennis ball. Another thinks of a ballgown. The third thinks of the phrase 'having a ball', as in to enjoy oneself. Of course, they have no idea what the others are thinking, but they proceed regardless. Two actors come onstage to begin the first scene, one slightly before the other.

Convention dictates that the first actor out gets to make the '*initiation*' (the first line of the scene). The second actor waits to hear what this line is and then responds. This is the heart of improvisation: the giving and receiving of '*offers*'. An offer is simply any piece of information that is added to the scene. It might be verbal or nonverbal, a line of dialogue or simply a shrug. Offers are the currency of improv – the bricks from which any scene is built. The audience wait hushed for the scene to unfold. Neither they nor the performers have any idea what will happen next. Here are the first two lines of the scene:

> **A:** 'Melon baller? Melon baller? What sort of wedding gift is a melon baller?'
>
> **B:** 'It's not important, darling, is it? What's important is we had a wonderful day and we love each other.'

Notice the various different offers in Person A's line. First, the subject of the scene is clearly the melon baller. Second, this melon baller is obviously a wedding gift. But there's another offer in there too: the tone in which she says it. This person is clearly not a happy bunny! In order to respond to this line effectively and entertainingly, Person B needs to listen very closely to his scene partner. We'll discover that this is one of the counterintuitive aspects of improv: it's about listening more than it is about speaking. We'll explore the art of listening in Chapter 2.

Let's pause to consider for a moment that Player B will have walked onto the stage at the beginning of this scene with his own idea as to what the scene should be about. Yet as soon as Player A gives her idea, Player B throws his away in order to focus on making her idea work as best he can. Notice too how he not only accepts Player A's offers (melon baller, wedding gift, irritation) but also adds some offers of his own (they have just got married and it is *their* gift!). Improvisers call this fundamental principle the philosophy of *'yes, and'* (it's the subject of Chapter 1). Let's see how the scene continues.

> **A:** 'We had an expensive day, certainly. A hundred pounds a head, it cost. What do we get in return? A fucking melon baller.'
>
> **B:** 'Johnny and Phyllis are nice people. Perhaps they're a little hard up at the moment?'
>
> **A:** 'The cheek of it. Do you remember what we got them for their wedding? An ice-cream maker. It cost 200 quid.'
>
> **B:** 'We might find a melon baller useful, darling.'
>
> **A:** 'I've got an idea how we could use it – to ball his stupid eyes out! I'm going to call him! I'm going to ring him, right now!'
>
> **B:** 'NO! Darling. Please don't …'
>
> **A:** *Mimes dialling a phone.*

Notice how collaboration works in this scene. Nobody controls it. Player A can't control it because the meaning of her line is only confirmed by how it is *received* by Player B. Similarly, Player B can't take control of the scene with his response either. Each offer is not left alone but embellished and (mis)interpreted by either player at every turn. Thus, they genuinely co-create the scene, while maintaining their own individual voices. No one dominates the conversation, no one steamrollers the other person with their idea, and yet in just eight lines the scene quickly builds to a moment of drama. We'll explore in depth how you can *collaborate* in this way offstage in Chapter 5.

Notice too how, despite being under so much pressure, both Player A and Player B trust themselves completely. They commit to their ideas, banishing any self-doubt. Of course, like the rest of us, they have an inner critic, but they have learned how to control and act despite it. We'll look at how you can do the same in Chapter 3. Finally, we can also see how, despite not knowing what the response of the other player will be, neither Player A nor Player B is fazed at any point. They are flexible in the moment, reframing the unexpected offers thrown their way as opportunities rather than roadblocks, as if they were always part of the plan, all the while working at great speed. We will explore how you can approach life with the same *agility* in Chapter 6.

FREEDOM IN YOUR OWN IMAGE

Earlier I told you the story of why I attended my first improv class. It was confidence I sought, and it was confidence I (thought I) got. However, as I reflected on my journey into improvisation while writing this book, I realised that improv has given me something more nuanced and valuable than confidence: it has given me freedom. Freedom from the need to look cool or be perfect. Freedom from needing to know what happens next. Freedom to learn by doing. Freedom to play and to make mistakes. Freedom to be myself. And, even more blessedly, freedom from *myself*.

When I improvise, I am totally absorbed in the moment. One hundred per cent of my focus is on my scene partner. Nothing else exists apart from me, them and the sound of the audience. I may have entered the theatre fatigued from a stressful day; I may have just had a blazing row with my girlfriend; I may have just read an email full of bad news. All that disappears when I step onto stage. I lose myself in the show and enter what psychologist Mihaly Csikszentmihalyi calls a state of 'flow'.[5]

My reward for entering this flow state is that I lose track of time. A show may last an hour but, once it's over, seems to have flashed by in the blink of an eye. Yet, while I am in a scene, time seems to slow down. Choices that to an audience look like millisecond decisions feel deliberate and thought through. I experience a feeling of profound control. This may seem paradoxical, given the nature of the artform. After all, there is no script and I am at the mercy of the choices of my fellow improvisers. But it is an experience of total efficacy – a feeling of having access to unbelievable skills.

It's not just skills but creativity too. I access ideas that were unreachable offstage. I use words that I had no idea I knew. At the best moments, it's like I have a direct line with God. This is not to say that I'm a godlike improviser! Far from it. But that's how it feels when I am improvising well. It's as if information is channelled through me. It doesn't have to be found or invented; it's just there. My scene partner says something, and I respond with words that only register to me as they leave my lips. I am myself, only better, and it is all effortless.

This book is about how you can gain the same sort of freedom. And while you can't achieve it without putting in some effort, unlike many models of personal and professional development this book doesn't ask you to make a sea-change in behaviour. Instead, the principles of improvisation slot seamlessly into what you are already doing. This is about tweaks in mindset and methodology. You need no new resources to begin. In fact, I believe that thinking and acting like an improviser can help you achieve extraordinary results with what you've already got. The improv mindset is not 'What's missing here?' Instead it's 'What do I have?'

You might think that, as a former stand-up comedian, I fit into the perfect cliché of the improviser: an extrovert, a show-off, a clown. It might be said that it's easy for someone like me to feel free in this way. Does improv offer anything for the shy introvert? The answer is an unmitigated *yes*. If you visit your average improv class, you might even say it was weighted towards the introverts over the extroverts. They sign up not just because they want to have some fun, but to learn to be more confident and sure of themselves. Improv is a community that emphasises repeatedly that it is OK to be yourself, that it's OK to make mistakes and not be perfect, that what we build will be weaker without you. If improvisation is about anything, it is about inclusivity. Improvisation really is for everyone.

But whether you are an extrovert or an introvert is beside the point. The point is not about where you *start*. The point is about where you want to *go*. If we are to get different results in life, we need to take a different approach. That much is obvious. We need to break out of our old ways of doing things, throw away our old scripts, be brave enough to act without them. But you don't need to be an adventurous person to take this leap. *You become adventurous by taking the leap.* To put it another way: we are never ready for change. We become ready through the process of changing. It is in this spirit that we begin.

So, come to the edge. Look over a while. Then jump. You'll realise that you could fly all along.

Chapter 1

'YES, AND'

'There are people who prefer to say "yes" and there are people who prefer to say "no". Those who say "yes" are rewarded by the adventures they have. Those who say "no" are rewarded by the safety they attain.'[6]
—Keith Johnstone

Yes. And. Two short, simple words which, together, define an entire approach to living, working and playing. 'Yes, and …' is the beating heart of all improvisation. It is the elixir that allows improvisers to create something out of nothing. There is magic in these words. Except … it's not magical at all. It's a simple rule of thumb that anyone can use to build almost anything. In this chapter I'll show you how 'yes, and' can help make you more creative at work, have better conversations at home and be more adventurous everywhere.

But what exactly is this 'yes, and' concept? For improvisers, it is many different things. First, it's a practical technique: a tool we use to build scenes or ideas together as a group. Second, it's a way of thinking that will set us on a path to every other key concept in improvisation. By the end of this chapter we'll see that the best way to think of 'yes, and' is as more than either a methodology or a philosophy, but as a Tao: a way of being in the world. You're either a 'yes, and' sort of person or you're not – but 'yes, and' people are made not born. That's what this book is all about. Ready to start? It all begins with 'yes'.

ALWAYS THINK 'YES, AND ...'

The best way to understand how this works is through example. So, here's how it looks onstage. Say you and I are doing a scene together. I get the first line. I crouch on my haunches, pat the stage with my hand, and say:

> 'It's been a hot summer, Jack, too hot. The damn
> fields are like concrete. Who'd be a farmer, eh?'

You listen carefully to this blistering piece of dialogue. Then, having basked in the warm light of my celestial talent, it's your turn to speak. How might you respond to my line? Here are two options. Choose the one you think is better for the scene:

> 1: 'Aye, Ted, it's been the hottest summer I've ever
>   known. I'm sweating in places I didn't even
>   know I had.'

Or:

> 2: 'Farm? I think you've been smoking something,
>   mate! We're on a spaceship! And who are you
>   calling Jack? My name is Barnabus, King of the
>   Uber drivers.'

Which line did you go for? Line 1 is a 'yes, and' response, whereas in improv parlance line 2 is a '*block*'. Admittedly, 'My name is

Barnabus, King of the Uber drivers' is an amazing line. It's just not an amazing line *for this scene*. In fact, it's a terrible line for this scene. Because, first, you've thrown me under a bus by denying the reality of my 'offer'. (I told the audience we were on a farm, not a spaceship!) And, second, you totally ignored my idea and steam-rollered it with your own. As improvisers we now have two totally different ideas of what's going on in the scene. Without agreement we're not building anything, we're moving sideways. A hard job has suddenly got harder and the audience is not impressed.

This disaster is very easily avoided. In improv, instead of blocking or negating other people's ideas, we accept and build on them. This is the meaning of 'yes, and'. By saying line 1, you have accepted all the details contained within my initiating line (the 'yes'): your character's name is Jack; we're on a farm; it's hot. You've also built on them by adding some information of your own (the 'and'), which allows us to move the scene forwards. First, you've endowed me with a name, adding that my character is called Ted. Second, you've intimated that your personal hygiene is a disgrace. This fun offer is something that I can now build on with my own 'yes, and' response. For example, our scene might grow like this:

> **ME:** It's been a hot summer, Jack, too hot. The damn fields are like concrete. Who'd be a farmer, eh?
>
> **YOU:** Aye, Ted, it's been the hottest summer I've ever known. I'm sweating in places I didn't even know I had.
>
> **ME:** I've been meaning to talk to you about that actually, Jack. I think it's about time you started wearing deodorant.

Now, admittedly, we're hardly at Will Ferrell levels of zinger yet. But we do have the acorn of a fun situation. By accepting each other's offers, we've established a platform from which we can build the rest of the scene together. We've established that there are two gruff farmers, one of whom has a body odour problem, which the other thinks he needs help with. What's more, to the audience, we look telepathic, when really all we are doing is paying close attention to each other's offers and then responding in kind with our own. You might continue this scene as follows:

> **YOU:** I don't believe in male grooming. A woman
> likes a man who smells of himself.

And so on. You'll have your own views about the comedic potential of this scene. But the point stands that we would never have got to this level of complexity and fun without the simple practice of agreeing with, and then building on, the established reality. We certainly would not have got there this quickly. We'd obviously need to push things on further in order to reach comedy nirvana. But this simple process of 'yes, and' will get us there eventually.

APPLYING THIS OFFSTAGE

You can see that the philosophy of 'yes, and' is crucial for improvisers because it is an effective and efficient way to develop action onstage and therefore satisfy an audience. But not everyone treads the boards. So, let's turn our attention now to offstage applications. Why should *you* care about this 'yes, and' thing? We'll discover that 'yes, and' thinking can help you:

- Lead happier and more collaborative teams.

- Be more creative.

- Overcome conflict and negotiate effectively.

- Own the room (or screen) in meetings.

We're going to explore all the above in depth as we move through this chapter. But, as before, let's begin with an example. I'd like you to imagine you are part of a communications team at some glamorous marketing agency. It's the sort of creative company where the floor is carpeted with AstroTurf. You can write on the walls. There are no chairs; everybody just sits on obsolete washing machines. The Creative Director doesn't wear shoes, and there's an office turtle. A meeting has been called because your team needs to come up with innovative ways to communicate a new company strategy internally. The email goes out. Everyone assembles – including you.

All the meeting rooms in your trendy office are named after former members of the Spice Girls. You're in 'Posh'. Behind the door, the leader of the team goes through the usual platitudes: 'Let's brainstorm guys'; 'Come on, think outside of the box'; and 'All aboard the creativity train! Next stop, Ideas City.' The table is caked in Post-it notes, highlighter pens and Haribo. Things are looking good. Your boss looks expectantly at his battalion. Silence.

Sixty painful seconds pass. Your boss writes the word 'Ideas' on the wall in bright red pen and surrounds it with a cloud shape, as if this might help. Another minute passes. The wide-eyed intern James suggests a coffee run. Another minute passes. Finally, mercifully, your colleague Sindy bravely sticks her head above the parapet.

'Why don't we do a short YouTube video explaining what we want to do? We could stick it on the company intranet?'

Your boss laughs. 'A video! Thank you, Steven Spielberg. Be realistic, guys. Let's face it. No one's going to bother watching a video.' Sindy bows her head, her face turning as red as the Fizzy Fangs on the tabletop.

Another colleague pipes up: 'And I'm not being funny; I'm not having a go, Sindy, but when are we going to have time to film and edit a video?'

A chorus of agreement rings out, a mumbled elegy: the idea is dead. Resting in pieces on the meeting room floor.

DELAY JUDGEMENT

The example above might seem extreme. But episodes like this play out every day in workplaces throughout the land. This blocking behaviour, anathema to improvisers, has serious short-term and long-term consequences for teams. We'll look at the longer-term damage a bit later, but first let's see the immediate problem that blocking has caused. The idea that Sindy pitched has been killed before it was even explored. The team has denied themselves a potentially useful solution by judging it immediately. This is a huge waste of potential because new and challenging ideas – ideas that change things – don't often come out fully formed. They are incomplete and ugly, newborn foals stumbling around bewildered in the light, trying to work out who they are.

A central part of the 'yes, and' mindset is to delay judgement. This means hearing an idea and not immediately deciding if it's right or wrong, useful or useless. It requires you to look for all the potential in an idea before you look for all the problems. This doesn't require you to agree with the idea. (You don't have to become some sort of inane, grinning yes man.) But it does require you to unconditionally accept the idea in a spirit of play, to decide to explore it for a while. 'Yes, and' doesn't require you to *believe* a given idea will work, just to *suppose* that it might. The difference between supposing and believing is small but profound. Improvisers quickly learn that supposing can open up the world in thrilling new ways. But what exactly does it involve?

Supposing is the central skill of an actor. If I am an actor playing a milkman in a scene, I don't need to believe that I actually am a milkman. That would be absurd. Instead, for me to convincingly play a milkman, I just need to temporarily suppose that I am one. I simply act as if it were true that I am indeed a milkman. So, I ask myself: *What would I do, think and feel in this situation if I were, in fact, a milkman?* In the same way, when you interact with an idea, you don't have to believe in it. Your interaction with that idea is not contingent upon you believing it to be true or brilliant. You just have to act as if the idea were brilliant, and ask yourself: *If this were a great idea, how could I explore and develop it?* It's a mind-widening business.

Although I said that we should delay judgement, that doesn't mean we should abandon it entirely. It is simply a matter of timing. Clearly, selecting the best ideas from what we generate is crucial in getting the outcome we want. However, we often jump to criticism too quickly, at the expense of genuine exploration. After all, analysis makes us look clever. We are especially inclined to do this if we bring significant expertise and experience to the problem at hand. Experience supplies us not just with insight but also with intellectual baggage. In short, experts bring with them assumptions of what will and will not work. These assumptions can shut down their thinking and also the thinking of everyone else too. After all, who are we to question them? They're the experts!

Just as bodybuilders maintain their physiques by working out in the gym, if we want to stay creatively flexible we need to constantly work our 'yes, and' muscle. This is because, just as being enormously muscular is not natural, saying 'yes' actually goes against some fundamental human instincts. We have evolved to hate uncertainty. Studies have shown that people would rather *definitely* get an electric shock now than wait to see if *maybe* they might get shocked later on. Although this seems irrational, it's borne out in our experience of life.[7] We only need to think of the calmness that comes over us when we've resigned ourselves to being late for a meeting, as opposed to the anxiety of rushing like mad when we know we could just make it.

Because we loathe uncertainty, we instinctively move to block ideas that would force us to embrace it. Rather than going for the innovative option, we fall back on what we've done before. We stick to what is routine or 'safe'. We shut down new ideas by saying, 'No thank you. This is the way we do things round here.' Of course, doing what you've always done might still be the 'rational' or best choice. But perhaps it just *appears* to be the best choice? Although we like to think we choose rationally between well-defined alternatives, growing evidence in behavioural science suggests that our decisions are in fact driven by unconscious biases which skew our judgement.

For example, research shows that human beings exhibit a 'status quo bias'.[8] This means that we stick with what we know, even when it is optimal for us to do something different. Why? Psychologists think this bias towards the same old, same old might be caused by what's known as 'loss aversion'. Put simply, we fear losing what we've got more than we desire getting something new. Our status quo bias has also been explained by reference to another cognitive bias, commitment bias, which suggests that when we've nailed our colours to the mast by saying we think something is good or right (often the 'status quo' option), we will defend our position even in the face of obvious evidence that our conviction is total cobblers.

You can see that there are a number of reasons why embracing a new or disruptive idea is emotionally difficult for people in team environments. The tricky thing is that, because we're often totally unaware of the biases we bring into these meetings, this *emotional* reason for shutting down innovative ideas can appear to us instead as the authoritative voice of *logic*. We often delude ourselves. So what can we do about it? First, while we will always be uncomfortable with uncertainty, we can build our endurance to it. That's exactly what improvisers do.[9] Essentially, they manage their phobia through exposure therapy. Second, we can bring awareness of our biases with us into the room because while saying no to ideas is not bad in itself, we need to check we're doing it for the right reasons. And fear is rarely a good reason to say no to anything.

FRIENDLY FIRE

Let's go back to our scene in the brainstorm meeting at the trendy city firm. If you recall, Sindy opened up proceedings with this idea:

> 'Why don't we do a short YouTube video explaining what we want to do? We could stick it on the company intranet?'

And her lovely boss immediately responded with this massive block:

'A video! Thank you, Steven Spielberg. Be realistic. Like anyone's going to bother watching a video.'

What are the consequences of blocking behaviours? Do you think Sindy is likely to suggest an idea at this company ever again? Of course not. Why would she, if this is her reward? More than that, Sindy's colleagues are now unlikely to suggest ideas either. After all, they've seen what happens when you do. In this team, speaking up is pointless. Actually, it's worse than pointless. It's dangerous. Presenting an idea is a supremely vulnerable thing to do; it exposes the ego. To shoot someone down like that not only kills their idea, it's humiliating, an act of social violence.

The use of the word 'violence' seems hyperbolic until you consider the fast emerging field of social neuroscience: the study of what goes on in our brains when we interact with other people. Social neuroscientists have discovered that we register social pain in the same brain circuits where we register physical pain. Not only that, threats to our ego are felt as intensely as threats to our life.[10] This means that when we're shot down in a meeting, when we're made to feel stupid or inexperienced or naïve, we react as if a lion had just walked into the room and roared at us. If this seems extreme, then consider frequent findings that show people rating public speaking as scarier than death!

We learn to regulate our behaviour in light of psychological pain, just as we do with physical pain. For example, when a child scalds her hand touching a hot hob, she learns never to do it again. This is because she's now formed an association in her brain between the act of touching a hob and a great deal of hurt. The pattern is set to avoid that behaviour in future. Conversely, say she gets into bed on time and is rewarded with a bedtime story. This child now forms an association between getting to bed promptly and the pleasure of a story. The behaviour is suddenly attractive.

How do you get people in your team to associate speaking up with pleasure rather than pain? It's pretty simple: you suspend judgement of their ideas rather than blocking them, and you aim to accept and build on what they've just said. Let's jump straight back into the meeting scenario and see what this looks like in practice. A 'yes, and' response to Sindy might look like this:

> **SINDY:** Why don't we do a short YouTube video explaining what we want to do? We could stick it on the company intranet?
>
> **BOSS:** Using video is certainly an engaging way to communicate. And we do want our messaging to be as accessible as possible.

Notice the boss didn't literally use the 'yes, and' language here. The specific words aren't important. What's important is the mindset and behaviour he's showing. *Improvisers try to make their fellow players look good.* This is what the boss is doing to Sindy here. He is collaborating with her, not competing with her. Sindy now feels listened to and supported. Her idea is being fleshed out and moved forward. It doesn't stop here. In a 'yes, and' culture, ideas are springboards, not landing mats. Other members of the team now chime in with their own 'yes, and' builds. Everyone is trying to make Sindy look good (or at least trying to make her *idea* look good). For example:

> **GREG:** Sindy makes a good point. We need to be more modern in how we sell these messages internally. We could make the videos personal to each department, so it feels more relevant?
>
> **RAJ:** A video could work. Perhaps the MD might be part of it? This would add real credibility.

Notice how the 'and' is as important as the 'yes' in 'yes, and' thinking. While the 'yes' validates the idea as something worthy of examination, the 'and' helps us explore and deepen the idea to maximise its potential. What's more, the 'and' is itself a new offer which we can then 'yes, and' in turn. It's a chain reaction of creativity.

CASE STUDY: Kate O'Connor, advertising creative

It's easy to dismiss ideas. People are scared of looking silly; so if an idea isn't immediately brilliant, it's easier to dismiss it. But by doing that you often miss out on the little nuggets of a good idea buried in a half-baked idea. Improv has taught me to persevere and find the hidden magic in something a bit weird, daft, unusual or obtuse. When my team and I sit down to talk about a project in its early stages, 'yes and' is the golden rule. That way we can explore a concept and really work out if it could be fleshed out into a fully-fledged ad campaign. It's an art, not a science. Often a brilliant advert ends up being greater than the sum of the brains that dreamed it up. ■

TO BE MORE CREATIVE, CREATE FROM ABUNDANCE

How do you work out how creative someone is? This was the question that NASA posed to Professor George Land in 1968. To stay ahead in a hyper-competitive space race, they had to optimise their resources, and Nasa wanted to match their most creative men and women to their hardest challenges. An expert on innovation, Professor Land gladly accepted NASA's challenge, and he and his team developed a test for creativity. It measured an individual's capacity for what's known as 'divergent thinking': the ability to evaluate a problem and then come up with different solutions to it.

While divergent thinking isn't exactly the same thing as creativity, it is an absolutely central part of it. Divergent thinking forces you – as the renowned creativity guru Edward De Bono would say – to think 'laterally', that is, to come at the problem from angles you hadn't considered before; to think 'outside of the box'; to see multiple answers, not just one or two.

If you want to try a similar test at home, you can. All you have to do is take an object, for example a paper clip, and see how many uses you can think of for it.

Professor Land's test turned out to be brilliantly effective at identifying the most creative scientists at NASA. And that could have been that. But now Land was curious. He realised that the test he'd created for NASA was so simple that even kids could do it. So Land and his team decided to give the same test to children. He wanted to know where creativity came from. Is it innate? Or is creativity learned? Land and his team of researchers tested 1,600 five year olds involved in a government Head Start educational programme in the United States, a programme which provides early childhood education, health, nutrition and other services to low-income children and families.

Ninety-eight per cent of these children scored in the genius category for divergent thinking. Which is inspiring news: we are all born creative geniuses! Amazed at this result, Land turned the experiment into a longitudinal study: his team set these same children an identical test when they were ten years old and then once more at fifteen. As you can see from the chart, only 30 per cent of those same children scored at a genius level at ten years of age. This fell to just 12 per cent five years later. The implications of this data are depressing enough, but it got worse. Land has gone on to test more than 1 million adults over the age of 25 since the initial study. On average, only 2 per cent of adults score at a genius level for divergent thinking.[11]

Creativity scores at genius level

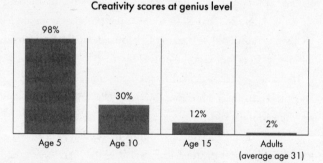

Based on data from George Land's 1968 study, as reported in his book with Beth Jarman, *Breakpoint and Beyond* (Harper Business, 1993 reprint edition).

It seems that we get a lot less creative as we get older. The question is, why? In his analysis, Land called upon two different sorts of creative thinking: divergent thinking and convergent thinking. One acts as the accelerator on the brain, one acts as the break. As we've seen, with divergent thinking you aim to come up with as many solutions to a posed problem as possible. You are in an open mode, focusing on using your imagination to generate a volume of ideas. You are thinking about possibilities, not limitations. With convergent thinking, you bring a much more critical, closed mode. You are looking to analyse, evaluate and test ideas, to narrow down the options based on certain criteria, whatever those criteria may be (for example, budget or timeframe).

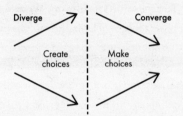

Diverge   **Converge**

Create choices   Make choices

Adapted from Tim Brown, designthinking.ideo.com

Of course, human beings need both sorts of thinking. If we only thought divergently, we'd end up doing a lot of crazy things all of the time. If we only thought convergently, life would be very dull indeed. It most definitely wouldn't be creative.

The problem with schooling, Land would go on to say, is that we teach children to do both types of thinking at the same time. As we come up with new ideas, we are taught to start criticising them, shutting them down immediately if they aren't 'right'. By the time we reach adulthood, we've perfected this skill. For example, how often do you hear phrases like this in your workplace?

> 'That sounds a bit bizarre.'
> 'We've already tried that.'
> 'That's too expensive.'

Defaulting to this sort of convergent thinking is the reason why our creativity levels fall through the floor as we age. Instead, if we want to be more creative, we should bring a 'yes, and' mindset to create an abundance of ideas before we enter that more critical mode. It may well be the methodology of a five year old, but a weight of research now backs up the link between volume and originality. For example, it turns out that your first twenty ideas in response to a problem are significantly less original than your next fifteen. Further research suggests that quality doesn't tend to fall off until 200 ideas are on the table. Psychologists call this the 'serial order effect'; we tend to splurge out the easy to reach, mundane ideas first and then get to the more creative solutions later. It's one of the oldest and most robust discoveries in modern creativity research.[12]

How can you apply this in your life? As I've outlined above, you need to bring a 'yes, and' mindset to your idea generation. But you also need to spend longer in the divergent phase. Often, we quickly run out of patience in brainstorms and settle for those early, mediocre solutions. Finally, you need to be able to tolerate an awful lot of failure along the way. For example, according to Ed Catmull, Pixar co-founder and former president, it takes roughly 12,000 storyboard drawings to make one 90-minute Pixar movie. But, due to the iterative nature of their development process, the Pixar story teams commonly create ten times that number of drawings to get it right. Pixar is one of the most creative organisations on the planet and they throw away 9/10 of their ideas. The takeaway is clear: volume wins, waste is normal, and creativity starts with saying 'yes, and'.

WHEN TO SAY NO

You might be thinking at this stage that 'yes, and' is all very well in the perfect, simple environment of an improvised show where the only cost of a bad idea is an awkward three-minute throwaway scene. It's easy to say yes under these conditions. But what about in the real world, where costs are much more real? *Do you really have to say yes to all ideas?* Absolutely not! First, saying 'yes, and …' does not constitute agreement; it is about delaying judgement in order to explore ideas. Second, saying no is clearly essential at times. If you said to me, 'Hey, Max! Jump out of that window,' I wouldn't respond: 'Yes, and set me on fire first!' That would be madness. Some ideas, whether physically dangerous or morally wrong, should be dismissed instantly as non-starters.

Third, and most importantly from a creativity point of view, 'no' is also a useful word. As I said above, creativity is not exactly the same as divergent thinking. Although creativity cannot happen without it, it's about more than simply generating ideas. Creativity also requires us to select the best ideas (by saying no to most of them) and then to develop them through feedback and testing. It is in these phases of creativity that the word 'no' comes in. I'm not saying that we should never be in a 'closed' (convergent) mode, only that we should be in a closed mode with intention and mindfulness – not simply because it's our default option, as can so often be the case in life.

In order to avoid this when facilitating creative meetings, we need to communicate clearly to everyone in the team which specific phase of creativity we are in. How do we want people to behave in this meeting? Are we in divergent or convergent mode? This labelling of the phases for everyone attending really helps keep your brainstorms productive. In the idea generating phase, we want people to say 'yes, and …' and avoid 'no'. In the convergent thinking phase, criticism and analysis is welcome. You'll find that, as long as people know the phase for criticising ideas is coming, the more analytically minded people in your team will relax and happily contribute with their own 'yes, and' suggestions when required.

So, in summary, 'no' is an important word, and we need to say it. But we need to say it at the right time, for the right reason, and in the right way. Which leads us on to another application of 'yes, and': how to overcome conflict.

OVERCOMING CONFLICT WITH 'YES, AND ...'

In the introduction, I said that improvisation is based on some simple rules. In an improv group all the players play by these rules in order to efficiently and reliably create comedy onstage. However, in the real world things are a lot messier and other people don't always play ball. Perhaps your manager always shuts down your ideas. Maybe your client can't see the potential in your pitch and doesn't even try. Or perhaps you're at a party trapped talking to the 'fun sponge'. Situations like these, where we appear to be improvising alone, beg the question: are these rules of improv still relevant?

Far more than just remaining relevant, I would argue that they are more important than ever. Difficult conversations are a fact of life. We live in a world full of different perspectives and personalities. It's one of the reasons life is so rich and interesting. But it also means that conflict is inevitable. If we are going to have happy, productive personal and professional lives, we are going to have to negotiate these difficult conversations with dexterity and, hopefully, joy. The rules of improvisation offer invaluable tools to help us do exactly that.

As we'll explore in depth in Chapter 2, improv teaches you that resolving conflict with another person is much more about listening than it is about talking. Disagreements are so often based on a lack of understanding rather than on genuinely incompatible positions. Before we flip into lawyer mode and start defending our position in a disagreement, it's much more productive to get genuinely curious about the other person's point of view. Listen without judgement and ask open-ended questions in order to build understanding. You'll often discover your positions are not as far apart as you think.

Improvisers are trained to listen amazingly well onstage because it's one of the few things they can control in such an uncertain environment. Offstage this principle holds too. Clearly, you can't control how other people communicate. You can't control if they are rude, grumpy or objectionable. But you can control how you respond to that. For example, you can control your body language, your vocal tone and the quality of your energy. The most crucial thing you can control when it comes to your response is how you frame the actions of the other person in the first place.

It's easy to read sinister motives into someone's behaviour – as if it's a deliberate and personal attempt to trip you up. An old sparring partner does something and we think, *That is typical of you!* But it's much more productive to invoke the improv principle, 'Make the other person look good.' For example, if my scene partner comes onstage clucking like a chicken, I trust they intend this as a gift rather than as a curse. Assuming their intention is always to make me look good allows me to respond to their suggestion with positivity rather than irritation. Now, I can watch them cluck for a little while and then say: 'Darling, this isn't what I had in mind when I said "role-play".'

This positive framing of an originally rather tricky offer is enabled by trust. Our common understanding of trust is that it's something which has to be earned, but in improv trust is something you give as the default. Trusting your fellow players is an active choice you make. Of course, if people repeatedly betray that trust, you don't let them play with you anymore. But trusting others as the baseline for interactions helps you see their ideas and behaviours in a different light; it helps you approach them with curiosity rather than cynicism. Try the following exercise to see how you might apply this principle in your own life.

▶ Exercise

BENEFIT OF THE DOUBT

I used this exercise with a group of account managers at a major advertising agency recently, in order to help them break out of the same old scripts they fell back on in their communication.

Agencies are often a hotbed of conflict – classically between the account 'suits' and the creative department. It's the job of the suits to keep the client happy. They have to sell the ideas of the creatives to the client and then take the client's (often negative) feedback to the creatives for review. You can see how resentment might breed. The creatives think the client has no imagination and wouldn't know a good creative idea if it punched them in the stomach. The client thinks the creatives are more concerned with being 'original' than actually responding to their brief. The suits are stuck in the middle.

In the workshop, I got the so-called suits to work through the following questions. You can do the same in relation to anyone you find yourself butting heads with.

1. **Who do you regularly come into conflict with?**
   For the account executives, it was the creative department.

2. **What assumptions do you make about them? What assumptions do they make about you?**
   The account managers assumed that the creative department was more concerned with making 'cool' ads,

as opposed to ads that the client would actually buy.
They assumed the creatives didn't understand how hard
it was to present the more 'out there' concepts. They also
assumed that the creatives were 'precious' artists who
couldn't take feedback.

3. **If you assumed this person had good intentions,**
   how might that alter your response to them?
   How might you overcome their assumptions
   about you?
The account managers realised that many of their
assumptions could be false or at least heavily
exaggerated. *What would happen,* they wondered,
*if they gave the creatives trust and reframed their
defensiveness as an offer?*

They concluded that the creatives' job is to push back
on anything that waters down 'the product'. After all,
the aim is to make the most outstanding work possible.
This doesn't just benefit the creatives; it benefits the client
and the entire agency. The reluctance and dissent of the
creatives are signals of passion. And who doesn't want
to work with passionate people? In fact, it's a sign of a
high-performance culture.

In light of this, the account managers decided
to alter how they communicated with the creatives.
Fundamentally, it was to do with their feedback style.
They resolved to communicate not just the problems with
the creative concepts, but what was great about the
ideas too. Most of all, they resolved to show that they
would fight the creatives' corner, that they appreciated
the importance of brave creative ideas and wanted to

protect them as much as possible, while also giving the client what they were paying for.

▲ ▲ ▲

In life we tend to get back the energy we put out. If you respond to negativity and aggression with negativity and aggression, the doom loop continues. Reframing the intentions of others offers a practical way out.

In their training, improvisers quickly learn that conflict isn't fun. Nor is it enjoyable for the audience to watch. A scene full of conflict doesn't go anywhere. So to avoid conflict, improvisers focus on what they can control: listening to understand, trusting their fellow players, and saying 'yes, and'. Using these words is a small language shift that can move you from butting heads to bumping fists – even when the other person doesn't return the 'yes, and' favour. Before we explore how exactly, I'd like you to try another exercise.

▶ Exercise

'YES, BUT ...' VS 'YES, AND ...'

Ideally, you'd do this exercise with a partner, but if you can only do it alone that's OK too. You'll just have to play both parts!

1. **Imagine you're having a conversation coming up with ideas for the work Christmas party with a colleague.**

   For example, one of you starts: 'How about fancy dress? Everyone loves fancy dress!'

2. There's a twist! I want you both to respond to everything your partner says with the phrase 'Yes, but ...' (and then fill in the blank).

For example:

A: 'How about a fancy dress party?'

B: 'Yes, but getting a costume together can be very expensive. Our guests won't want to spend the money.'

A: 'Yes, but it's Christmas. I think people would make the effort.'

B: 'Yes, but some people will always take it too far and it might get offensive.'

Try to keep this conversation going for a minute or so.

3. OK. Now try the same exercise, but this time I want you both to respond to everything your partner says with the phrase 'Yes, and ...' (and then fill in the blank).

For example:

A: 'How about a fancy dress party?'

B: 'Yes, and we could have a theme.'

Try that for 30 seconds or so.

4. Reflect for a moment: how did the character of the conversation differ?

▲ ▲ ▲

I return to this exercise again and again in workshops. Participants find that not only are their conversations more creative when they say 'Yes, and ...' (compared to when they say 'Yes, but ...'), but they avoid conflict too. The immediate objection you might have is that saying 'yes, and ...' only works when you agree with the other person's position. We're going to address this objection in depth very shortly. But first, let's look at how often in life we default to a 'yes, but' approach, and how doing so can entrench and cause conflict, while also creating a negative energy which undermines collaboration.

The trouble with saying 'Yes, but ...' is that, although you have at least nodded towards acknowledging the idea at hand (the 'yes'), you then immediately negate it (the 'but'). 'But' is inevitably followed by a rebuttal of what you've just heard. This not only pits two concepts against one another, it also raises one above the other. When you say 'but', what the other person hears is: 'I hear what you are saying, but *this is much cleverer* ...' This almost inevitably causes an equal and opposite emotional reaction as the other person defends their viewpoint to save face. Status is a fundamental and much overlooked part of communication (and something we explore in depth in Chapter 5).

Using the word 'and' instead of 'but' equalises the concepts in a way that doesn't diminish the status of your conversational partner. The difference is subtle, but the emotional response it engenders is significant. Simply put, 'and' is inclusive whereas 'but' is competitive. Of course, some concepts may be objectively superior to others. Sometimes saying 'But you're wrong!' is a correct and rational response. However, we often forget that the root of conflict is not intellectual but emotional. It's not about the objective facts of a situation; it's about how each party *feels* about the situation.

'Yes, and' takes this crucial point into account. It affirms the other person's feelings before you present your perspective. 'Yes, and' says: 'I have listened to you and I have understood you.' Although you're not saying that they are right to feel that way (necessarily), you are saying that you appreciate that they *do* feel that way. It communicates respect. Let me give you an example from my home life to illustrate.

I'd recently moved in with my partner for the first time. Her flat was a new build and everything was box fresh, including the granite kitchen surfaces. Consequently, my partner was concerned with keeping everything as beautifully maintained as possible – especially those luxurious kitchen tops. This manifested in a strict 'no drips' policy, where any residual water droplets were to be wiped off immediately to avoid them staining the surfaces. It's fair to say I was less bothered about this than she was. I had moved from an old flat I'd shared with two flatmates in which we had, ahem, slightly lower standards of hygiene.

Water droplets were not just something I didn't consider important; they weren't even visible to me. Years of being a slob had blinded me to everything but the worst stains. This eventually led to an almighty row when, one evening, my partner found a small pool of surface water around the sink. 'You never clean up after yourself!' she said. 'You're going to stain the worktop. It's selfish!'

'Who cares?' I snapped back. 'It's just a bit of water. What are you getting so annoyed about?'

From here the argument escalated and escalated until it ended in tears.

Admittedly, the movie rights to this dispute are unlikely to be picked up anytime soon. But notice how my reactionary communication style poured petrol on the flames. This argument could have been easily avoided if I had used a 'yes, and' style response. I should have said, 'I can see this has really upset you,' thus affirming her feelings, 'and I'll remember to make sure I clean up in the future,' thus showing direct and specific engagement with her objection. This would have quickly defused things – perhaps not in one fell swoop, but soon enough. Because it's almost impossible to stay angry at someone who relentlessly 'yes, and's you.

'YES, AND' DOES NOT MEAN YOU AGREE WITH EVERYTHING

When I introduce the idea of using 'yes, and' to overcome conflict in workshops, people sometimes push back. 'This might defuse arguments,' they say, 'but it's a pretty hollow victory if it's achieved simply by agreeing with the other person.' This *isn't* what 'yes, and' requires you to do at all. 'Yes, and' doesn't necessarily connote agreement. It simply says: 'I accept that you think and feel this, AND here is my perspective on things ...' You don't drop your point of view; you simply offer a more collaborative and less emotionally provocative bridge into it.

Let's look at an example of a 'yes, but' response versus a 'yes, and' style response to see this in action. Notice that in both versions, a similar viewpoint is expressed by Person B. Yet the emotional effect it produces for Person A is totally different, and therefore conflict is less likely to arise.

> **A:** 'We've had a brilliant quarter. It would be great to get the whole company together for some celebratory drinks after work next week.'
>
> **1B:** 'Yes, but that excludes working mums who have to leave at five.'

2B: 'Yes, a celebration would be brilliant. And it
would be good if we could do something that
everyone can get involved in. I know a lot of
the mums struggle to stay late after work.'

The second response allows Person B to put forward her point
of view in a way that both connects to and validates the idea of
Person A. She doesn't drop her objection, just presents differently.
Also, while she doesn't accept and build on the idea of 'drinks after
work', she does accept and build on the *intention* behind the idea.
This illustrates another nuance of 'yes, and': you don't necessarily have to build on the specifics of someone else's idea. After all,
that sort of agreement isn't always possible. Instead you just need
to bring a general mindset of: what can I authentically get behind
here? 'Yes, and' simply requires you to be solution-focused rather
than problem-focused.

OK, you might be thinking, *but what about times when there is nothing I can authentically get behind in what the other person is saying? Not even
the intention.* This is certainly a trickier conundrum. The improviser's
response here is to ask: How many conflicts in life genuinely fit into
this category? How often are disagreements based on fundamental
things like opposing ideas about values, vision or strategy? Usually
our disagreements are smaller-scale. Most of the time we want the
same things, but we disagree on how to go about getting them. In
these cases, there is usually an island of agreement we can reach
if we look hard enough.

However, conflict is occasionally unavoidable. In these cases,
you have two options. First, you can say: 'I disagree, but I am
prepared to support you regardless.' This happens all the time in
improv. Improvisers believe an average idea with support goes a
lot further than a good idea with no support. And so, if I don't

like an offer you give me in a scene, I don't decide to simply sit that scene out. I do my best to make it work. After all, it will soon be my turn to have my idea supported. Offstage, Amazon call this concept 'disagree and commit'. They consider it so important they made it one of their fourteen leadership principles. This is because if you aren't prepared to disagree and commit, you end up debating things to death and nothing gets done. Much better to push on with things and let the proof be in the pudding soon enough.

As for the second option, perhaps you need to consider walking away? Sometimes in life positions are simply irreconcilable, and a parting of ways is the best way forwards. But let's not throw the baby out with the bath water. These sorts of conflicts are rare. What we are looking for more generally when it comes to having hard conversations is to find mindful disagreement. To listen well enough, to explore an idea long enough, that our disagreement with an idea or initiative is expressed through a thoughtful response and not an emotional reaction. In this sense 'yes, and' thinking slows you down enough to keep conflict productive rather than destructive. While you aren't expected to drop your perspective on things, what 'yes, and' requires you to do is drop your agenda. That is, you must drop the script running in your head of what the truth is, or what the idea or solution should be.

This requires bringing humility to proceedings: accepting that you are fallible in intellect and limited in knowledge, and that there *may* be another, better way. Rather than asking yourself, as we so often do when we engage with a conflicting position, *How can I find proof that this is nonsense?*, ask yourself instead, *How can I find proof that this is right?* The author F. Scott Fitzgerald once memorably wrote: 'The test of a first-rate intelligence is the ability to hold two opposed ideas in the mind at the same time and still retain the ability to function.' How often are we flexible enough to allow ourselves to consider an opposing point of view?

The sci-fi author Robert Anton Wilson also put it well when he wrote: 'Belief is the death of intelligence. As soon as one believes a doctrine of any sort, or assumes certitude, one stops thinking about that aspect of existence.' Act like an improviser and throw away your old scripts. What it costs you in certainty it will gift you in adaptability. Because when we hold on to our beliefs too hard, conflict is impossible to overcome.

HOW TO SPEAK UP IN MEETINGS

You might be wondering whether or not it's possible to use improvisational thinking without the involvement of other people? Could you say 'Yes, and …' to yourself? Now we're going to look at how you can do exactly that. Rather than dealing with the offers we receive from other people, this time we're going to focus on the offers we give ourselves. All day, every day, as we go about our daily business, our internal monologue chatters away. Of course, most of what it proffers is inane or superfluous: *I must renew my MOT. That person looks like Auntie Maude. How do they get milk out of a nut?*

But sometimes these musings are genuinely useful, whether creative ideas, suggestions for hobbies to try or even goals we might like to pursue. In a moment we're going to explore how saying 'Yes, and …' to these musings might help you live with more adventure and, ultimately, meaning. But before we do, let's see how this relationship with our inner voice is relevant to the workplace – or more specifically, to standing out in meetings.

Meetings can be difficult environments for many people. While not all team cultures are the same, meetings can be dominated by certain extroverted alpha types, and it can be hard to get a word in edgeways. In this competitive environment, a meeting can pass us by if we let it, especially on virtual platforms where there is what I call a 'monologue effect'. Simply put, only one person can speak at a time, and certain sorts of people are likely to dominate the airwaves.

It's not that we don't have things to say in meetings, it's just that we don't say them. Instead we ignore or shut our ideas down, or else we try to perfect them in our head until the moment passes and we can't share them anymore. The longer this goes on, the harder it becomes to contribute. This has the effect of making us less visible in the room. We figuratively take up less space, only for other people to take the credit for the ideas we had first but never put forward. The result is that, while our colleagues' reputations are enhanced, we look both less engaged and less informed.

Why don't we share these ideas as they come to us? The obvious answer is that we lack confidence in them. If we are liable to rush to judge other people's ideas, we are even more prone to harshly judge our own. We worry that our idea is stupid, that it's half-baked or naïve or too obvious. We're treating ourselves unfairly. No idea comes into the world fully formed. Improvisation teaches us that, if we want to discover our confident voice, we need to lose our attachment to perfect.

The phrase improvisers use to represent this principle is *'bring a brick, not a cathedral'*. In improvisation, we aim to produce amazing cathedrals of ideas onstage – that is, beautiful, complex and hilarious scenes – but we do this by bringing one brick at a time. Our focus is on gradually adding small bits of information together as we move, rather than on providing the whole answer all at once. Whether we bring the name of a character, the location we're in, or a short line of dialogue, the emphasis is on the gradual development of the scene rather than on giant leaps of the imagination.

Suddenly improvisation isn't as intimidating as it seems. While each offer alone is unimpressive, when all these offers are connected in collaboration with others, they can become brilliant. What's more, in an improvisation show the pressure isn't on one person to solve everything or bring *the* big idea. It is a team effort, which frees you up to think out loud with your half-ideas and gut reactions. This is important because, for others to build on your ideas, they need you to share them first. *We need your brick.* Because who knows what your suggestion might inspire?

How can you apply this principle in your next meeting? The first thing you need to do is trust yourself. This is easier said than done, I know, but the next time you feel the impulse to speak up with an idea or a question, 'yes, and' the thought and share it. Improvisers call this being 'front-footed'. You'll often see beginner improvisers on the side of the stage, wanting to enter a scene with an idea, playing Hokey Cokey with their feet. They are in–out, in–out, almost joining the action but never going through with it. They have the instinct to join the scene but don't quite do so because they're judging their ideas. They don't make a choice because *what if their choice is wrong?*

Eventually these improvisers learn to trust their impulses and to let their feet lead them. And they soon discover that their feet know when to enter a scene before their brain does. Similarly, if you have an instinct to speak, then speak. If you are brave enough to make that choice, you'll discover that you don't need to know how your sentence will end in order to start it. Your brain is amazing; it will help you find the answer if you let it. As movie star (and former improviser) Tina Fey puts it: 'Just say yes and you'll figure it out afterwards.' It is by making the *choice* to speak that we find our voice, not by knowing the answer. To paraphrase the great Martin Luther King, Jr., you don't have to see the whole staircase, just the first step.

CASE STUDY: Zoe French, assistant TV producer

I work in digital TV content – think apps, quizzes, games and all that stuff that sits alongside TV shows. A lot of my job revolves around pitching new content ideas to clients, but before improv I was always the kind of person who would tail off in the middle of a sentence because I didn't have the confidence in my own idea. Or I just wouldn't share an idea at all unless I'd 100 per cent fully formulated it in my head. Which, of course, is not how creative ideation sessions work. Since I've been improvising I've learned to follow the impulse to speak in those sessions rather than meticulously planning out what I'm going to say. I trust that I can start a sentence without knowing exactly where it's going to go, and that I will find an ending for it – even if it's not perfect.

For instance, working on some Halloween content for a kids TV channel, I started with the idea of a 'selfie filter where you open your mouth and ...'. The end of that sentence by the time I got to it turned out to be '... thousands of tiny spiders crawl out'. Not super appropriate for a channel aimed at eight year olds, but it did provide a jumping off point for what turned out to be a really cool augmented reality game idea where pointing the phone camera at the TV screen during a show made weird spooky skulls appear that started moving towards you, and you had to swipe them away before they got you. A million miles away from the weird place I started in, but it couldn't have happened if I'd been filtering myself. ∎

No matter how it feels sometimes, nobody has all the answers in life. Despite the confident badinage of certain slick individuals, meetings and conversations are not scripted. Everyone else in that room is improvising the same as you. What makes them look so assured? It's what improvisers call *commitment*: the second crucial part of making choices onstage. Improvisers are taught to commit to a choice when they make it, by which they mean, to play it like it's real. For example, if you play a crusty old headmaster onstage, the audience want to believe that he's in the room. There's no room for half-hearted pretending. They want you to play the headmaster with full intensity and conviction.

In the context of a meeting, commitment is about not second-guessing yourself. We sometimes do this because we are worried we aren't 'making sense'. But there isn't one perfect way to express an idea. The same meaning can be communicated in any number of ways. Also, it's a myth that you have to get it right first time. If people don't understand your point, they'll ask you to clarify and you can have another go. Or even better, you can check in with them to make sure your point has landed. So stop trying to be perfect! You are fully committing to the choice to speak up in a meeting if:

- **You take focus with the volume of your voice.** Commitment is making yourself heard.

- **You don't ask for permission to speak.** (Not: 'Do you mind if I add something?')

- **You don't apologise for contributing or for the way you express your idea.** (Not: 'Sorry for interrupting.' Or, 'Sorry, that didn't make much sense, did it?')

- **You ask people who interrupt you to let you finish.** ('I haven't finished, thank you.')

- **You make statements rather than asking questions.** (Instead of saying, 'Do we need to reconsider our approach?' say: 'We need to reconsider our approach.')

- **You avoid qualifiers or 'soft' words that undermine the credibility of what you say.** (Not: 'This is just a suggestion and I might be wrong. But is there something perhaps we aren't quite getting at? Which I suppose is that maybe the presentation could just be polished up a bit?')

- **You literally take up space.** This is especially relevant when you are presenting. Improvisers are told to 'play forward', which means to perform their scenes at the front of the stage close to the audience. This raises your status in the room. How often do you see people presenting miles away from their audience and slowly backing further away from them as they speak? They are giving away authority.

If we don't fully commit to speaking up in meetings, it's often because we're afraid of how we'll come across to others if we do. We worry that we'll be seen as 'taking over' the conversation. But committing to a choice to speak doesn't mean you have to bulldoze your way through a conversation or be aggressive and dominant. It just means being assertive in making your point before you give focus to others.

Sometimes we think that not speaking up is somehow more collaborative and generous. But it can be selfish if it forces all the decision-making onto other people, putting them under pressure. It's important that you don't just support ideas in meetings but initiate them too. We can make room for others not just by staying silent but by speaking up: you may have asked a question that others were too afraid to ask. Or, by taking a risk, you've given other people permission to speak up too. It also shows leadership. After all, what is a leader but someone who had the thought one day, *Hey, I think I could help here*, and then said 'Yes, and …'.

SAYING 'YES, AND …' TO YOUR OWN LIFE

This ability to make and commit to choices has applications far beyond the meeting room. In life we can sometimes find ourselves stuck in a rut, drifting sideways, uninspired and unchallenged. Maybe we want to change careers, leave a long-term relationship or move to a different city. However, although we want to make a change, we might be waiting for the perfect moment to do so. Or we won't act until we have the whole plan mapped out. To take the leap, we need to be sure it's going to work out. In this situation, it's much more comfortable to fall back on the same old script and do what we've always done – anything to avoid the fear of not knowing what's going to happen next. And life slowly passes us by.

When faced with these sorts of life decisions, improvisation offers a useful perspective. Because, clearly, improvisers have no idea what's going to happen next. They make it all up every night. And yet they happily jump decisively into the unknown. They say 'Yes, and …' to their impulses. Which begs the question, how do they find the courage to do so? But courage has little to do with it. Frankly, improvisers have no alternative. If I'm in a scene and I don't make a choice, then nothing happens and the scene dies. This is clearly terrible to watch for an audience. For example, no one wants to see a scene like this:

> **A:** 'Shall we go to the shop?'
>
> **B:** 'What do you think?'
>
> **A:** 'I don't know.'
>
> **B:** 'Are you sure?'

Awful, right? These improvisers are doing anything they can to avoid making a choice. Therefore the scene is circular, anodyne and pointless. But is this not the same in life? As heroes in our own stories we need to make choices because, just like an improvised story, without change or growth our lives wither too. The only way out of the dreariness is to make a choice. An improv adage helps us here: *The only bad choice is making no choice at all.* Because even if you make a bad choice onstage, at least the scene is moving forwards.

Of course, we'd much rather make a good choice. But, as you can never be entirely sure which choices will work out and which won't, you have to risk making bad ones in order to get the good ones. So, if you find yourself overanalysing what choice you *could* make, stop wasting time and just make a choice. Not at some point in the future, but now. For improvisers, there is no such thing as the perfect moment. There is only the next moment. Onstage, if you stop to consider whether a moment is perfect to say what you want to say, it's already gone. The scene has moved on. Just as life does.

When I look back at my life so far, all the things that have given me the most meaning have arisen from making bold choices before

I was ready. They came from saying 'Yes, and …' to the offers life threw at me. When I met my now partner for the first time I could easily have said, 'Yes, but I've just come out of a long-term relationship.' When I was offered my first stand-up comedy gig I could easily have said, 'Yes, but I don't have any material.' When I was asked to facilitate my first business improvisation workshop I could easily have said, 'Yes, but I don't know anything about business.' But I didn't. Instead, I said 'Yes, and …' The rest is history.

▶ Exercise

'YES, AND' YOUR OWN LIFE

Where in your life could you say 'Yes, and ...' to yourself in order to embrace a new adventure?

1. **What is an idea you have been putting off acting on?**
   Remember to create from abundance! Brainstorm to come up with a list of multiple options, then pick the one that is most important to you at the moment.

2. **What would it involve to start? What is the smallest step you can take now?**
   Remember, you can only get to step 2 if you take step 1.

3. **Take a small action immediately that commits you to the decision to start.**
   For example, if you want to move jobs then email one recruiter with your CV.

Not many of the decisions that change our lives feel as if they might be life-changing at the time. They only become so in hindsight. In fact, in the moment we make most decisions, they often feel mundane and insignificant. They get lost in the blizzards of choices we make every day, swiftly forgotten, decisions in response to questions like:

> 'A place has come up on this morning's training. Would you like to take it?'

> 'Do you want to come to the party?'

> 'Would you like to speak at the conference?'

The results of most decisions do indeed turn out to be mundane. But some turn out to be extraordinary. This means that, as you rarely know which decisions will be significant or not in advance, you need to get into the habit of saying 'yes' more generally. Accept the offers that come your way as much as possible. Who knows where things will lead? The training course might give you a skill that eventually leads to a promotion. You might meet someone at the party you fall in love with. Perhaps speaking at the conference helps you make a connection that soon leads to a transformative collaboration. Or maybe not. You'll only find out if you start saying yes.

CONCLUSION

By the way, don't worry if you struggled with the exercise on the previous page. One of the cruellest cultural doctrines of the modern world is this idea that we should all know what we want. Many people don't. Maybe you don't know exactly what you want, just that *something* is missing. And that's OK. But you're much more likely to stumble on what you want if you keep saying 'yes' to things. Who knows? You might realise that you are doing what you love already. But our life means a lot more when we have deliberately *chosen* it. This is why it's important to disrupt yourself: to throw away the same old script and to try something else, so that when you return to it, it's because it's genuinely what you want, and not simply what life bequeathed you. How many of us live life accidentally?

Which brings me on to the final benefit of being a 'yes, and' sort of person. *You start seeing more opportunities everywhere.* Improvisers see the world as a patchwork of offers, camouflaged as life. We filter out so much of the world. Scientists estimate that our brain receives around 11 million bits of data at any given time, yet it can only process around 40. In short, we 'see' very little of the world around us. There's a good evolutionary reason for this: our attention is a finite resource. If we paid attention to everything, our brains would become overwhelmed and we wouldn't be able to function. So, we take shortcuts. The consequence of this, however, is that we miss much of what is right in front of our noses.

This propensity is what cognitive psychologists call 'inattentional blindness', a phenomenon most famously illustrated in the 'invisible gorilla' experiment by Daniel Simons and Christopher Chabris in 1999. In this experiment, participants were asked to watch a video of a game of basketball and count the number of passes made by the team wearing white t-shirts. Halfway through the game, a person in a gorilla suit enters the display and thumps their chest. Despite the boldness of this interruption, more than 50 per cent of participants failed to notice the gorilla.[13]

While the limits of human attention apply to improvisers as much as anyone else, they have trained themselves to notice that little bit more. This is because they walk around with the mindset of: *What's here?* And: *How can I use this?* They are both more present and more curious than non-improvisers. They wander the world expecting to find interesting and useful things. More than that, they expect to find interesting and useful things right there in front of them in that moment, wherever they are. This is an improv principle drilled into you again and again. In the rehearsal room, practising scenes, the coach will say to you: 'Everything you need is already there.' Repeat after me, *everything you need is already there*.

It's an empowering way to live, and an inspiring way to lead others. You both notice more and choose to do more. Because where 'yes, but' thinking says, 'It probably won't work out,' 'yes, and' thinking says, 'It just might, you know. We should try …' Of course, 'yes, and' people are more likely to be disappointed than 'yes, but' people. Perhaps they are more likely to be proved wrong too. But, as Keith Johnstone put it, their reward is a life of more adventure, meaning and – in the end – success. Is that not worth the risk?

Chapter 2

IT ALL BEGINS
WITH LISTENING

*'In the beginner's mind there are many possibilities,
but in the expert's there are few.'*[14]
—Shunryu Suzuki

Listening isn't glamorous. Perhaps that's why there have been no movies made about great listeners. There's no superhero called Super Listener. Most people think listening is boring. Perhaps it's because, for many of us, our associations with the word are bellowed warnings by teachers to 'Listen!' If not that, we take listening for granted. After all, listening *just happens*. It feels passive, unworthy of analysis. But listening is one of the most complex and beautiful things we do as human beings.

If you cultivate your skill as a listener, you'll be the sort of person people will cross the room at a party to chat to. You'll be the first person your friends call for advice. You'll be more influential, more inspiring and more collaborative at work. (Especially when you communicate online.) Effective listening promotes growth in you as the listener, in the person you listen to, and, ultimately, in the relationship between you. Become a better listener and you'll be a better colleague, parent and spouse – all without saying a word. Perhaps listening really is a superpower, after all.

As we've already explored, a common misconception about improvisation is that it's about making something out of nothing. Instead, improvisation is the process by which you can create something out of *everything*. But before you can do that, you need to notice what's actually there in the first place. Listening, therefore, is the foundation of all improvisation. In this chapter, I'll show you how the best improvisers listen so that you can learn to listen more empathetically in your own life.

WHY IMPROVISERS NEED TO LISTEN

When improvisers are onstage they have no script. All they have is each other. Improvisers are tasked with collaborating in the moment to create comedy word by word, sentence by sentence, in front of the audience's eyes. As we've already seen, agreement is crucial to this. If I am doing a scene with you and you announce we are cowboys, then *we are cowboys*. But I can only accept your offer that we are cowboys if I've heard it in the first place. So far so obvious. Say that you've opened the scene with this line:

'Howdy, partner.'

This sentence contains a lot more than the suggestion that we're cowboys, depending on *how* you say it. For example, say it in a child's voice and I'll deduce that we are children *playing* as cowboys. Say it in a depressed manner and the context is suddenly very different. This cowboy is sad! Which begs the question: why? You get the point. Hearing the words your scene partner says is clearly only one half of the equation. Correctly understanding the meaning of what they've said is the other. *This* is real listening.

However, while listening can be tricky, it takes all the pressure off me as an improviser. I don't need to think of anything clever or funny to say. I just need to listen to your small idea and respond honestly to it in the moment. Suddenly, improv isn't about comedic acrobatics at all. It's about human beings staying present to one another and then doing their best to make the other person look good.

I remember what it was like when I first started doing improvisation. I was terrified. Whenever I was in a scene onstage I'd think to myself:

> *What am I going to say?*
> *What do the audience think about me?*
> *Why am I so stupid?*

It was a horrible sinking feeling. Performing improv was an out of body experience. I wouldn't be present with my scene partner but looking down at us from above, judging everything I said or did or, even worse, everything I couldn't think to say or do. But there was a ladder out of this self-consciousness. As veteran improv coach Jill Bernard says: 'If you want to get out of your head, get into something else.' That something else is our scene partner. I slowly learned to put all my focus on them.

When I realised, *It's not about me!*, the anxiety and self-consciousness went. Rather than thinking about what I should say or do, I concentrated on being of service to my scene partner instead. It's a mentality that has served me well offstage too. I was never tongue-tied again. Forget 'having nothing to say'. I learned that the inspiration I needed was always right in front of me.

EVERYTHING YOU KNOW ABOUT LISTENING IS WRONG

That listening is important is hardly breaking news. We all know that we should listen. Yet the gap between theory and practice can be enormous. This is because, while we are often told that we *should* listen, we are rarely told exactly *why*. The case, however, is compelling. For instance, repeated studies link poor listening by doctors to medical negligence lawsuits. It turns out that doctors who get sued are not necessarily worse doctors than those who don't, but they are worse communicators. Patients are a lot more likely to sue a doctor they perceive to be unempathetic, with poor listening a crucial component of this.[15] The annual cost of medical negligence claims in the UK alone hovers around £2.5 billion, meaning that the risks of poor listening are stark.

Listening is one of those meta-skills that either enable or inhibit other skills we might have. In this example, those doctors may be amazingly knowledgeable about medicine, but without the corresponding soft skills their medical nous is blunted. Outside of the medical world, not listening well can lead to:

- Unengaged and apathetic team members.

- Poor customer service.

- Missed sales and upselling opportunities.

- Ineffective collaboration, including missing out on possible solutions to pressing problems.

- Energy squandered on conflict in difficult relationships.

That's just in the professional sphere. When you stop to consider the effects of poor listening on a marriage or on our friendships, working to excel at listening swiftly becomes a no brainer. The trouble is that, while we aren't told why we should listen, nor are we taught *how* to listen.

Research suggests that on average we spend 70 per cent of our time communicating with others. Forty-five per cent of that is spent listening, compared to 30 per cent spent speaking and 9 per cent writing.[16] Yet, while there are endless educational opportunities available for us to improve our speaking and writing, there are almost zero for developing our listening skills. Perhaps the closest you've got to learning how to listen was a short course on 'active listening' at work. But the trouble with 'active listening' is that, while it's better than nothing, it simplifies the complexities of both listening and being listened to.

Many of the behaviours taught with active listening – such as nodding, smiling and making encouraging noises while the other person speaks – are not essential for good listening. In fact, you could be doing all those behaviours while thinking about something else entirely. Becoming a good listener, therefore, isn't as straightforward as learning a few observable behaviours. As doctor and academic Ian McWhinney puts it: 'You can learn to be a better listener, but learning it is not like a skill that is added to what we know. It is a peeling away of things that interfere with listening.' The beauty of improvisation exercises is that they allow us to build awareness of these interfering elements, so that gradually our attention can become totally focused.

What does interfere with our listening? Fundamentally, it's the scripts we've got running in our heads. We'll explore the nature of these scripts in this chapter. And we'll see that great listening is not just about the moment of listening but the moments that follow it too. How do you know someone has listened to you? By what they do with what you have said. Improvisers define listening as *the willingness to be changed*. When you and I step out to do a scene together, your words land on me, affect me and change my response. I throw away my script of what I planned to say, in order to react and adapt to the real moment in front of me. Rather than talk *at* you, I relate *to* you.

THE RULES OF LISTENING

Becoming a good listener starts with making the decision to listen. This might seem strange, as listening is something that just seems to happen. We do it without thinking, don't we? Think about it: we can be in a pub surrounded by people talking and yet be in our own world, listening to none of it. This is the distinction between hearing and listening. Hearing is an involuntary and often unconscious process, whereas listening is an active behaviour which begins with a choice and is directed at a specific target. To illustrate the difference, let's do a quick exercise. I want you to shut your eyes and just sit in silence listening to everything in your environment. Try doing it for a minute. (Unless you're listening to this on audio book and you're driving, in which case, 45 seconds is fine!)

It's a simple but surprising experience. If you tried the exercise, you would have become aware of a huge variety of sounds that previously you'd unconsciously filtered out. By choosing to listen, you would have processed a lot more information. Will you use all of this information? Of course not. But now you have the option to. We can only use information we've heard. That much is obvious. But we often behave in conversations and meetings as if this were not the case. As if we can choose to only tune into the important stuff when it comes up and filter out the rest. As if we alone possess a radar that magically picks up only the salient facts. If only this were true!

So, good listening begins with making the choice to do so. To take it up a level, listen like an improviser, and connect with anyone, here are four simple rules you can apply right away.

Rule 1:
PAY ATTENTION AND STAY PRESENT

The next time you have a conversation, pay attention to what is going through your head as the other person is speaking. How much of what they are saying are you actually taking in? The chances are that you're not really listening but waiting to reply. You're formulating a rebuttal in your head. Or, if you're not forming an argument, you might be thinking about a similar experience you've had or projecting later into their story, predicting what they are going to say next. You might even be thinking about lunch or whether you left your hair straighteners on this morning. You might be wondering if your friend Dave is right, and people really do urinate in hotel kettles.

How often do we enter a conversation focused on listening? Imagine my right arm is stretched out horizontally from my shoulder. My arm represents a sentence someone is saying. My shoulder is the start of the sentence and my fingertips are the end. How far down my arm do you think most people listen? Elbow? Bicep? Armpit? Maybe you listen to the start of the sentence and then the end and guess the rest. Perhaps it's dependent on who is speaking. You might listen intently to your best friend but zone out your mother in law. Listening through to the end of the sentence, staying entirely present with that person as they speak, is a rare event.

If you've ever wondered why it's so hard to stay present and fully listen to another person, the answer lies in the 'Speech-thought differential': we think faster than other people can talk. We can comprehend around 400 words per minute as a listener, yet most people tend to talk at around 130 words per minute.[17] This leaves us a lot of spare brain capacity, which we almost inevitably use for thinking. The trouble is, if we get lost in thought, we stop listening. Indeed, the rate at which we can form thoughts is estimated to be between 1,000 and 3,000 words per minute. So, we listen faster than we talk, and we think faster than we listen. No wonder we drift off!

▶ Exercise

LAST WORD, FIRST WORD

We can see that staying present to the person we are listening to is difficult. This is why improvisers do a lot of exercises to practise listening right to the end of the sentence, such as this exercise. It's designed for two people, but if you can't find a partner then challenge yourself to do it in the next regular conversation you have and see if the other person notices!

1. **Have a conversation together for around 90 seconds.**

This conversation can be about anything at all, but if you struggle to get started, give yourself a topic: for example, the gym.

2. **You should each speak for roughly the same amount of time. The twist is that the first word in**

your response should be the same as the last word of your partner's response. For example:

A: 'I have a membership for the gym, but I haven't been for a long *time*.'

B: '*Time* is of the essence if I am going to lose this weight before my *holiday*.'

A: '*Holiday!* Chance would be a fine thing. I've already used up all my *leave*.'

B: '*Leave* carbs alone, that's what my personal trainer tells me.'

3. **Don't worry if some of your sentences are inelegant or some of your grammar is a bit dodgy. This exercise is about listening rather than speaking!**
   This is a great listening training game because, having no idea what word your partner will end on, you can't pre-plan what you are going to say.

▲ ▲ ▲

Rule 2:
BE OPEN TO (AND CURIOUS ABOUT) WHAT IS *REALLY* THERE

The most frequent thing I hear after an improv show is the conspiracy theory that it wasn't improvised at all. It was too good to have been truly off-the-cuff and so the whole thing must have been written in advance. But improvisers really do make it all up. In fact, one of the key tenets of improvisation training is to not to pre-plan anything. To some people, this seems like complete madness. After all, what if, when it comes to your turn to speak, you can't think of anything to say? That's awkward for everyone: the improviser, their scene partner and the audience. Surely then it's safer to pre-plan what you're going to say?

Pre-scripting the scene in your head before you perform it is a terrible idea for a number of reasons. First, and most obviously, the audience call the shots. If you pre-plan what you're going to say, you don't honour their suggestions. Second, it means that only you have the script; your scene partner has no idea what's going on. Not only is this a recipe for confusion, it also means you're bound to be unresponsive to their offers. Instead, you'll steamroller the scene with your ideas, forcing what you *want* to happen on to the scene instead on building on what is *actually* happening.

This forcing or 'directing' of the scene is not only not fair on your scene partner. It also closes you off to the brilliant opportunities that exist in the moment. No matter how brilliant you think your pre-conceived idea is, the discoveries you make onstage when you enter a scene with a spirit of genuine co-creation are always more interesting. In order to make these discoveries, you need to be open to them happening in the first place. You need to drop the script running in your head.

CASE STUDY: Courtney Williams, scientist

Doing improv has helped me to be more relaxed and think on my feet when attending scientific conferences, where I often have to speak to hundreds of people over several days about the work my organisation does. This is not something I'm naturally good at, but improv has helped me fake it to some extent. Because now I focus more on listening to people and what they are contributing, rather than freezing up or following a mental 'script'. It helps me to respond better to the moment but, more than that, these conversations are a lot more rewarding for me now too. And hopefully also for those I'm speaking to! ∎

Rule 3:
LISTEN WITH YOUR WHOLE BODY

Clearly we listen with our ears. We want to pay attention to another person's words and also their tone. But when it comes to decoding meaning, our ears are just one input of many that help us truly *understand* a piece of communication, to grasp the subtext. Eye contact makes a huge difference to the quality of our listening. Not only does looking someone in the eye keep us connected with them, it also allows us to take in the myriad non-verbal clues that are present in any spoken communication.

For example, if someone says they are really excited about their new job, but they're looking at the floor when they say it, that tells you an awful lot more about the truth of the situation than the words they used. The experts at this sort of listening are TJ and Dave, widely regarded as the best improvisers in the world. Hailing from Chicago, the spiritual home of the art form, TJ and Dave improvise 60-minute comedic plays inspired by … nothing. There is no audience suggestion. They go onstage. They promise the audience that the next hour is totally improvised. The lights go to black. When they come up again, seconds later, both TJ and Dave immediately seem to know exactly who their characters are, how they relate to one another, and what is going on. Which begs the question: how do they do it?

> [When] the lights come up, immediately we look
> at the information we have available right now.
> We ask ourselves, 'In this moment, what do I
> know?' The answers, of course, are in our stage
> partner. We notice the eyes, the proximity and
> body language. We notice the perceived sense of
> status. We notice if it feels like we're inside or out-
> side. It's a process of elimination.[18]

Their aim at the start of shows is to work out what they call the
'*heat and weight*' of the situation. Heat refers to the intimacy and
intensity of the relationship between the characters. Weight refers
to the context or tone of the situation they find themselves in. To
bring this to life, imagine we are in a pub on a Thursday night.
When we look at the couples occupying the other tables, we are
able to intuitively gauge the heat and weight of each conversation. We know one couple are having a break-up chat. We can
just tell that this conversation contains a lot of weight. Then we
look across a room and see a couple who clearly want to rip each
other's clothes off; there is a lot of heat here. And then there is
a blind date gone wrong. We can tell that both these people are
filling time until it's late enough to politely make an exit. There is
neither heat nor weight here.

The point is, we are incredibly adept at noticing the subtext
when we care to pay attention. But most of the time we don't.
To use a subtler example, looking closely for 'heat' and 'weight'
allows us to sense when someone is upset. People can be very
skilled at keeping their feelings well hidden. They know how to
avoid the classic body language clues of anger or hurt or fear.
They are too savvy to have their emotions to be betrayed by their
tone. However, if we pay close attention, we can pick up on subtle

hints about their true feelings in how they move through space, in how they respond to a request for a cup of tea or even in how they sit in a chair. These subtle signals may even only register on an intuitive level, but they do register – if we are attuned enough to notice them, that is.

Improvisers listen with not just their ears and eyes, but with their hearts and guts. By listening with our whole selves, we access one of our most profound sources of intelligence as human beings: that ineffable but often inescapable feeling, in the pit of our stomach, that *something is up*.

Rule 4:
SURRENDER CONTROL

Before we get into this next rule, I'd like you to try an exercise.

▶ Exercise

THE WORD AT A TIME STORY

This is a classic improvisation listening exercise which requires you to respond to the last thing your partner says. It keeps you present and in the moment, rather than stuck in your mental script. Here's how it works:

1. Find a mate to play with.

2. You are going to create a story together, using only one word at a time, taking it in turns to speak.

3. Your story starts with one person saying 'One' and the next person saying 'day'. You continue by each

saying one word at a time to create the story. For example:

A: 'One'

B: 'Day'

A: 'We'

B: 'Went'

A: 'To'

B: 'The'

A: 'Park'

B: 'When'

4. **Take the pressure off yourselves: don't try to tell a good story. Just listen and respond with whatever comes to you in the moment.**

▲ ▲ ▲

I run this exercise in every improvisation workshop I facilitate because it so purely demonstrates the art of improvisation. As the game is played, the room always fills with laughter, the participants giggling at the often bizarre associations thrown up by their unconscious mind. I'm glad they enjoy it, of course, but the real point of this exercise is what it reveals about listening. In the debrief, I ask everyone what they found difficult about the game. The responses are similar every time and fall into one of two categories. One: people tell me they found it hard to say only one word when they felt the urge to say lots. Two: people say that they thought the story was going one way, and then their partner pulled it in another, meaning they had to wrestle it back to 'keep it on track'.

Both of these responses speak to the same desire: we like to control conversations. If we lose control of conversations we feel like they've gone wrong. Wrestling it back into its original shape, or adding extra words, allows us to 'fix' the story and show leadership. But this thinking is absurd. If you're playing this game and you think the story is about a robot, and then your partner says the word 'lion', they haven't ruined the story at all! How could they have? It didn't exist yet. And who are you to decide what the story *should* be anyway?

As we explored earlier, to listen well is to allow yourself to be changed. This is an unusual treat in life. How often have you been in a conversation where the person you are talking to ignores your response, only to go on to say exactly what they were going to say anyway? It's not only dispiriting, it stops collaboration in its tracks. Be one of the good guys: if you are listening well, your colleague's ideas should change what you say next. Good listening means letting what is *actually* happening happen. Good listeners respond to the moment they are actually in, rather than the one they expected (or wanted) to be in.

RECAP: ARE YOU LISTENING LIKE AN IMPROVISER?

Here are the four rules of improv listening and some simple tests to see if you're meeting them:

1. Pay attention and be present

- Am I forming a response in my head, or am I listening through to the end of the other person's sentence?

- Am I multitasking (or on my phone), or am I fully focused on the person speaking to me? (This is especially important when in virtual meetings: turn off your email notifications and shut those other tabs!)

2. Be open and curious

- Am I open-minded about how the conversation is going to go, or have I assumed what the other person is going to say before they say it?

3. Listen with your whole body

- Am I making consistent eye contact with the other person?

- Am I listening for tone, body language and other contextual clues beyond their words?

4. Surrender control

- Am I responding to the last thing that's been said, willing to be changed, or am I ignoring what's been said to wrestle the conversation back to the territory I want?

Having unpacked how improvisers listen onstage, let's now take the skill offstage to see how to apply these principles in daily life. Clearly, listening is crucial to effective collaboration. We're going to look at that in depth in Chapter 5. In this chapter we'll focus on listening to:

- Persuade others.

- Help others.

- Network with others.

LISTENING TO PERSUADE OTHERS

We are all in the persuasion business, whether we realise it or not
– whether that be pitching your service to a potential client, coax-
ing your boss to adopt a new initiative or even convincing your
errant teenager not to get that horrible tattoo. To demonstrate how
improv techniques can make you more persuasive, I'm going to
work through an example of the first sort of persuasion: the pitch.
Later, we'll see that many of the concepts that come out of this
business example can be applied to other contexts too.

Sean is a personable young account executive at a fictional
cloud software company called Sphinx. He is a salesperson basically, but they don't like to use that word at Sphinx because it puts
potential clients off. Sean's job is to go and meet with 'prospects'
(possible future customers) and persuade them to buy Sphinx's
cloud storage software. For the pitch, Sean has a deck of slides
that he takes prospects through, including case studies and other
supporting evidence of credibility. Sean is very diligent in his
preparation, taking care to research each prospect before he
meets them, and he always makes sure that he knows his pitch
word-perfect.

Sean's pitch this morning is with Sandeep, the head of technology at a pharmaceutical company called Tamgem. They are
a major global company, so this is a big opportunity for Sean to
impress his boss and also earn some chunky commission along the
way. Tamgem are looking for a cloud computing solution and have

sent a brief in advance detailing what they are looking for. Sean arrives at reception where he is told that he is actually meeting the head of infrastructure, Steve, instead. This is because Sandeep was made redundant a couple of days previously. This knocks Sean off his stride as he knows nothing about this new person at all.

Steve tells Sean that, rather than the 40-minute appointment he thought he had, he actually has 25 minutes and Sean mustn't overrun as Steve's got back-to-back meetings. 'I should say,' says Steve as they walk to the meeting room, 'following Sandeep's departure, I am reviewing strategy at the moment. I anticipate some changes …' Sean nods along respectfully, but he isn't really listening. He's thinking about how he can cut fifteen minutes' worth of slides from his presentation. When they finally sit down to talk, Steve says he'd much rather Sean just chat to him like a normal conversation rather than go through a deck. After all, he's seen enough of those in his career. Sean tells Steve that there are some 'compelling customer case studies' on his deck that he'd like to show him and pushes on with the presentation regardless.

Barely two minutes later Steve stops him. 'Sorry, I don't care about any of this,' he says. 'You're talking about features that we don't need.' Sean is lost for words; his pitch is exactly as per the brief Sandeep had sent. 'How can your product make my life easier?' asks Steve. 'That's all I want to know.'

Sean skips past his next twelve slides and lands on one of his beloved case studies. 'Let me tell you about how we helped this customer. They're a lot like you …'

'No, they're not,' says Steve. 'How are they like us?' Uncomfortable being put on the spot, Sean is panicked now, and lets out a stream of garbled nonsense until he is finally interrupted by Steve. 'Thank you for your time today, Sean, but I don't think

Sphinx is for us.' As quickly as it began, the meeting comes to an end. Punch drunk, Sean walks back to the carpark wondering how it all could have gone so wrong.

Let's do a post-mortem on Sean's performance. Despite preparing well, Sean made a number of easily avoidable mistakes.

MISTAKE 1

Sean came into the meeting with what I call a 'champagne bottle' mentality. Sean has diligently prepared a lot of content and has gone in and sprayed it at Steve. This is a bad approach for a number of reasons. First, it's simply not very engaging to be talked at by someone for any length of time. Second, unless the material you present is bespoke to the individual you're talking to, you're bound to talk about things they don't care about. Sean's presentation was bespoke to Sandeep and his brief, but not to Steve, who has clearly not seen Sandeep's original document.

One of the reasons we spray our prepared script at people is that we are afraid we're not going to 'get through' all our great content if we go off course. But what's the benefit of getting through your 'stuff' if much of it misses the point? Sean's mistake wasn't that he prepared for the meeting but that he didn't improvise when the scene around him changed. In the introduction, we defined improv as the art of acting when your plan turns out to be incomplete or irrelevant. We improvise when our planned pitch meets the reality of the moment: both the unique person we encounter in the room and the changing context in which we present. By refusing to improvise, Sean alienated his audience.

So what could Sean have done differently? The most basic thing he could have changed is to have listened before he spoke. Rather than launching into his prepared pitch, he could have checked in with Steve to see if his existing assumptions about what Steve needed were right. After all, Sandeep had left his post. What did Steve see as Tamgem's needs in this area? If Sean had done this, he would have gathered a lot of useful intelligence. Steve did give Sean a big clue that the original brief might have changed: he even told him that he was reviewing strategy with a view to changing it.

Listening and exploring assumptions before you speak allows you to start where they start. This is really important in persuasion. Because so often when we are selling our ideas to another person, we're actually selling them to ourselves – based on what we care about or what we'd like to hear if we were in their shoes. The important question to ask is: *What do they care about?* Where was Steve starting here? Was he interested? Disinterested? Did he have any knowledge about Sphinx already? Or about cloud software full stop? What were his goals or pain points? If Sean had listened to Steve properly and explored who he was first, he could have told the story of Sphinx in a way that made Steve the hero of the story. If he had done that, then Steve would have cared.

MISTAKE 2

Despite not listening before he spoke, and despite not beginning the meeting with some basic questions to test his assumptions about Steve and Tamgem, all was not lost for Sean. Although he abruptly ended the meeting, Steve actually did his best to help Sean with his pitch. He gave him a lot of offers which Sean either ignored or blocked.

For example, Steve cut the meeting short by fifteen minutes. Implicitly this could mean that Steve didn't think the meeting was worth so much of his time; he may therefore have needed more convincing about the value of Sphinx than Sean anticipated. Or it might have meant that Steve is very busy at the moment, which is an offer in and of itself. Steve had said that he was back-to-back with meetings all day.

If Sean had paid attention here, he could have taken a 'yes, and' approach and made it a point of rapport. For example, he might have said: 'You must have a lot on your plate covering two roles at the moment?' At the very least he could have seen that Steve wanted an abbreviated version of his spiel. The meeting would have got off on much stronger footing if Sean had begun by saying something like: 'I know you are super-busy today, so I am going to give you the top line here, and I'm obviously happy to answer any questions to clarify. Is that OK?'

Another big offer Steve gave Sean was that he was 'reviewing strategy'. This was a green light for Sean to follow up with questions that explored what sort of changes Steve was contemplating, as this would have given a clear indication of what was important to him personally. Implicitly, Steve was saying: 'I am planning on making some changes around here.' This should have been catnip to Sean as he could have explained how Sphinx could be part of Steve's attempts to shake things up. After all, what better way to show you are sweeping out the old and bringing in the new than some sexy cutting-edge technology?

Sean's mistake here is getting stuck in the script in his own head rather than being in the room. Our job in conversations is to be Sherlock Holmes, picking up verbal and non-verbal clues. As the old saying goes, knowledge is power. The more offers you can pick up on, the more opportunities you have to make the person sat opposite you feel understood. *To persuade someone, you've got to understand them first.* Once you show me that you understand me, it totally changes our relationship. We move from salesperson and customer to colleague and colleague. There is suddenly *complicité*: it's like you are on my team. I drop my guard and give you permission to persuade me. It all begins with listening.

MISTAKE 3

Because Sean thinks persuasion is more about speaking than listening, he has a plan for what he's going to say but he doesn't have a plan for what he's going to listen out for. The most obvious thing we listen out for are the words the other person uses. To establish rapport and avoid misunderstanding, it helps to speak their language. In order to do this, we want to use words in the same way that they do. We want to *go to their island*, rather than forcing them to come to our own. For example, if you're discussing an event and they call it a 'party', then refer to the event as a party. A small concession, but one that helps show empathy.

Being present to the words people use can reveal much bigger aspects of their character and big needs or pain points. For example, when Steve asked Sean, 'How can your product make my life easier?', he revealed that whether or not Sphinx's product can reduce workplace stress would be a crucial factor in his decision to buy.

When we listen to words, we aren't just listening for their face value meaning but also for:

- **Currencies**: what does this person value?
  For example, if someone says, 'I really want this event to be a bit different,' they're really saying they value originality.

- **Beliefs**: what are the controlling beliefs for this person?
  For example, if someone says, 'You get what you pay for,' they are showing that they believe that price is a mark of quality.

- **Levers**: what has power over them?
  For example, if someone says, 'I'll need to present this to my manager,' they are showing that their goal might not just be to find the best solution to the problem at hand but the solution most likely to impress their boss (which is not necessarily the same thing).

- **Pain points**: where does it hurt?
  For example, if someone says, 'There've been a lot of changes here,' they might be hinting at a lack of trust and general low morale.

- **Idiosyncrasies and interests:** what are their quirks? What are they personally into?
  For example, it might be as simple as discovering that they do yoga every morning.

- **Ideas**: what possible solutions have they already considered?
  For example, if they say, 'I've had a few thoughts,' then you're likely to find out which approaches didn't work (and they are unlikely to try again) or the sort of things they are considering, which might shed light on their priorities.

- **Commonalities**: what do you have in common
  with them?

  For example, perhaps you grew up in the same area
  or support the same football team. Our aim should
  always be to connect on an emotional and human
  level with the people we're trying to persuade.

  We tend to be influenced by people who we like
  and who are like us. These subjective judgements
  are important, often even more so than objective
  criteria, such as quality.

There are many more things we can be listening out for, of course.
The key takeaway is that when we go in with a plan for listening
and not just a plan for speaking, it helps us quickly latch on to
things that allow us to understand (and to *show* that we understand)
the person in front of us. Remember, it is people who buy things,
not abstract businesses or job titles.

Sean needed to reflect this in his pitch by tailoring it to
the man opposite him. This doesn't mean pretending that
the product can do things that it can't but instead means explaining the product through the filters that Steve had so clearly
presented.

MISTAKE 4

At the start of the meeting, Steve said that he'd rather have a
conversation than have Sean walk him through a pitch deck. This
was a clear indication he didn't want this to be a one-way affair; he
wanted it to be a dialogue. Sean responded to this offer with 'Yes,
but …'. In fact, he didn't involve Steve at all. Stuck in his script,

Sean did all the talking. Consequently, there was no space for Sean to check for understanding or emotional engagement from Steve. Because of this, his pitch was bombing and he had no idea until it was too late.

The fix for Sean here is not to throw away all his preparation. Instead, it is to leave spaces *within* his prepared structure for improvisation. What does this look like in practice?

If we are trying to fully understand the person we're attempting to persuade, it's vital not just to listen to what they say but to *bring to the surface what they don't say*. Simply put, there are some things that people won't express unless you really push them to. People are, in general, pleasant and polite. They would rather be indirect, dishonest or say nothing at all than say something that's hard for another person to hear. As we will discover in Chapter 6, this is why people find giving feedback so difficult.

But just because someone hasn't articulated a difficult message, it doesn't mean they aren't thinking it. As improvisers we deal with the reality of the present moment. We have to face facts, even when they are unpalatable. Because they aren't going to go away if we don't address them. The person won't magically stop thinking about them. All that happens is they'll leave the room with their objection unresolved. That isn't going to help you change their mind. So we need to bring to the surface these unspoken objections (and confusions) while we have the chance.

Remember, improvisers treat everything as an offer. An objection is a signal that someone has either misunderstood what you've said or isn't clear on the value your idea holds for them. You should be grateful for objections: they give you a second chance to communicate, but this time with more accuracy and potency. An unspoken objection may require a degree of detective work. It might be audible in a reticent tone of voice or visible in a confused facial expression or glazed eyes. Improvisers have three techniques we can use in these situations:

1. Labelling the emotion

2. Inviting questions

3. Asking questions.

LABEL THE EMOTION

Improvisers are taught to call out emotions in scenes. It's a simple technique. Say you and I are doing a scene together. I look at you and say, 'You seem …' or 'You look …' and fill in the blank. It has the effect of cutting to the chase in the scene, of bringing us straight into the heart of the drama. I label the emotion, you accept it, and we are off. For example:

> **A:** 'I suppose what I'm trying to say … what I want to say is … you could have put the milk away. It's been left out all day …'
>
> **B:** 'You seem sad.'
>
> **A:** 'Yes I am sad, Geoffrey. I always said I'd never turn into my mother and now here I am. Clearing up after you!'

You can use a similar technique in your conversations. Of course, it doesn't need to be as dramatic. It might be as simple as saying: 'You seem unsure of this.' It encourages the person you are speaking to either to confirm your suspicion or to disavow it. Either way, things are moving forwards.

INVITE QUESTIONS

The second technique you can use is to invite the other person to ask you questions. This is a great way to bring the unsaid to the surface. When someone asks you a question, it shows you the gaps you need to fill in for them, and, more than in any other sort of speech, it shows you what is important to them. How might you go about this in a conversation or pitch? You could simply say: 'Do you have any questions at this stage? I am very happy to answer any question at all.'

Of course, people can sometimes be reluctant to ask questions. If this happens, it's often helpful to direct them to a certain part of what you said. For example, Sean might have said: 'Sometimes clients find some of the features a little hard to get their head around. Did you have any questions in this area?' Often people have questions, they just need permission and encouragement to ask them.

ASK QUESTIONS

A third technique you can use is to ask questions yourself. Open questions are useful in keeping the other person talking. And the more that person talks, the more they reveal. For example, a useful question you might ask is:

'What would "good" look like for you in this area?'

You do have to be careful with questions. As well as opening up the conversation, questions can actually close it down too. This is because every time you ask someone a question, you are, in some way, changing the subject. A question switches the conversation from their agenda to your agenda. As soon as we interrupt someone with a question, we distract them from saying what they wanted to say and prevent them from revealing information that might help us to understand, and therefore persuade, them.

THINKING ON YOUR FEET

Why are we uncomfortable going off-script in these sorts of situations? Why do we dread difficult questions, objections or unexpected moments when we make a presentation? Simply put, we fear that we won't know what to say or do in response. That, under pressure, our normal ability to think and speak coherently will desert us.

The solution lies in preparation. Not in memorising scripts, like Sean, but in working out our method. Before we even enter the room, we must expect the unforeseen to occur and have a strategy to fall back on when it does so that, rather than panicking, we can react – to borrow an improv term – at *the top of our intelligence*, responding with coherence, clarity and intention, rather than waffle.

What can you do before you enter the room? First, visualise what these curveballs might be and how you will respond in the moment. This gives you an air of 'been there, done that' when they actually happen. Just jot down the top five questions you dread from an audience. How might you respond? Second, be aware of the things we often stop doing when put under pressure, such as breathing (slowing and deepening your breathing will calm you down) and smiling (smiling helps you look in control and gives you a more positive mental attitude). Third, make sure you come with the right mental approach: remember, it's not about you!

This is the big one. Often when we get nervous it is because of the direction of our energy. We direct it inwards, going into our heads, with catastrophic self-talk and negative mental movies that take us out of the moment and, crucially, away from our audience. It is much more empowering and impactful to turn this energy outwards: to transform it into enthusiastic body language, vocal tone and intensity of focus. We need to get over ourselves and instead focus on the person or people in front of us in that moment. Remember, our most important job is to be a good scene partner – onstage or off.

We get nervous when we present because we believe that the subject of our presentation is us, that we and our performance are being judged. But the audience don't care about you! The audience are interested in themselves, in what they can get out of what you are presenting. They are focused on how they can use your product, experience or knowledge to achieve their own objectives. When we realise that questions and objections are simply another chance to be of service to our audience, to add more value and be more generous, we become less self-absorbed and the butterflies disappear. Or at least they begin to fly in formation.

Another common fear that can inhibit us going off-script is the idea that we don't know what we're talking about. The first thing to say here is that *no one* thinks they know what they're talking about! We all have imposter syndrome to an extent. I've delivered thousands of hours of workshops and speeches in my life and I still get butterflies before each and every one, along with the accompanying self-doubt: *I wonder if today is the day I get found out?* The point is that it's normal to think and feel like this, and you can learn to act despite it.

What I focus on when I notice this sort of unhelpful rumination is that *fear is a story we tell ourselves, and this story is often false.* (We'll get into how to deal with this in depth in Chapter 4.) Generally, I'll reframe this negative self-talk by saying to myself: *I have never known more about this subject. There is no reason why this won't go the best that it's ever gone.* Another thing you can remind yourself of is that it's OK not to know everything about a subject. Not knowing an answer to a question doesn't mean you are stupid or not credible. It just means you are human.

It really is OK to say to someone: 'I'm sorry. I don't know the answer here.' Or, 'I don't know. That's a good question though. I am happy to look into this and follow up with you after the meeting.' Sometimes, I even turn it to the group and say: 'I'm not sure what I think here. What does everyone else think?' This gives me the time to rack my brains, allows me to keep control of the situation, and turns the challenge into an opportunity for group reflection and collaborative learning. In short, I turn the difficult question into an offer. Remember, everything is an offer if you let it be.

Let's look now at what you can do when you're actually in the room. It's important that you react to a difficult question or objection with positive, confident body language. If you are standing, literally 'step into' the question to show you aren't backing away from it. When you 'own' these difficult moments, with a confident posture and vocal tone, it puts the other person at ease. If you look flustered or embarrassed by the fact that you can't answer a question, this is when the audience gets uncomfortable and you lose authority in the room.

You'll find that adopting the body language of certainty helps you find fluency too. One of the best bits of advice I was given early in my improv career is that if you get stuck, unable to think of anything to say, make a deliberate move towards the front of the stage. It provides you with a certainty and vigour that can help you find your voice. So, move forwards (or sideways if more appropriate) before you answer a question to buy yourself time and confidence.

Another thing worth considering here is our relationship with silence. Again, silence is only awkward if we are not in control of it. If you are in control of silence while you think about your response to a question, this actually increases your status in the room as people are waiting for you to speak. But if you look at your feet and mumble 'err' and 'umm' to fill the silence, it has the opposite effect. Pause before you answer and understand that this looks totally normal to everyone else in the room. (Silences always feel twice as long to the speaker as they do to the listener.) The key thing in these difficult moments is to not panic. If you take a breath and stay calm, then you are more likely to respond with grace rather than blather. Other tactics you might find useful include:

- **Actually listen to the question!** Sometimes in the midst of panic we forget to actually take in the whole question, making it impossible to answer coherently.

- **Do you understand the question?** A great response to a question is: 'Can you tell me a little bit more about that …?' This not only buys you time, but it also gives you a clue as to *why* the person might be asking the question, which can often inspire your response.

- **Repeat the question.** This ensures you have correctly heard and understood it in the first place, while also buying you a few more seconds of thinking time before you respond.

'Yes, and' thinking is also useful here. Our aim is to treat objections as offers. Rather than ignore the objections as they come up or simply deny them, we want to build on them. Remember that 'yes' doesn't mean you're agreeing with the objection but instead that you're accepting the reality the other person has presented. The 'and' is then a bridge to our answer as we attempt to show that the stated objection need not be a reason not to buy what we are selling after all. We might not build on the specific detail in the offer but on what lies behind it. For example, the classic objection 'You are too expensive' is hard to overcome. But what thought lies behind it? *You haven't shown me why what you do is so valuable yet.* This is an opportunity if framed right, as the case study below shows.

CASE STUDY: Zara Swanton-Fallowell, account executive

I find 'yes, and' is particularly helpful when clients raise concerns. For example, in a presentation I gave to a major potential client recently, they mentioned we were more expensive than our competitors. So I responded: 'Yes, we are at the top end of the market when it comes to pricing, and this is because, unlike many of our competitors, we bespoke our service to every client. We offer a huge amount of flexibility, according to what suits the individual client. This is why many of our clients have been with us for over twenty years.' ■

Notice here how Zara repeated the objection. This is another really good hack to improve your listening. Incorporating a word or phrase that your conversational partner has just used into your response helps to show you have listened to them; more than that, it keeps you connected and present. It forces you to start where they start. A good way to practise this is a pair exercise called Anecdotes.

▶ Exercise

ANECDOTES

In this exercise you and a partner are going to be remembering a fictional shared experience. Imagine there is a stopwatch in front of you. By the end of the exercise you both should have spoken for roughly the same amount of time.

1. One person starts by saying, 'Remember when ...?' and then filling the blank. For example:

   A: 'Remember when we got lost in the woods?'

2. The other person responds, 'Yes [include something they just said] and ...' For example:

   B: 'Yes, we got lost in the woods! And then night fell and it was really spooky.'

3. And so on, for 90 seconds or so as you build on each other's ideas, using 'yes, and' to flesh out the reality of this memory. For example:

   A: 'Remember when we got lost in the woods?'

   B: 'Yes, we got lost in the woods! And then night fell and it was really spooky.'

   A: 'Yes, it was *really* spooky. And the wolves began to howl and suddenly we heard footsteps.'

   B: 'Yes, we heard footsteps, and then I felt a hand on my back.'

A: 'Yes, you felt a hand on your back. And you turned
round, and standing there was a witch!'

▲ ▲ ▲

LISTENING TO HELP OTHERS

Some of the trickiest conversations we have are with people who
need reassurance or advice. These conversations are difficult
because the other person is often upset or unsure in some way.
They look to us to help them get back to some sort of equilib-
rium or to move towards a difficult decision. We can feel a heavy
responsibility in these conversations, and it's easy to feel we don't
have the skills to be as helpful as we might like. The anxiety here
comes from the belief that someone who is 'good' in these situations would be a fountain of wisdom, a veritable warehouse of
prescient anecdotes. When we can't think of anything useful to say,
we feel like we're letting the other person down.

I certainly felt like this when I started dating my now partner.
She suffers from anxiety. Some days are good and you would have
no idea. But some days are bad and she finds it hard to leave the
flat. I love her very much and, at the start of our relationship, my
inability to help her in her worst moments made me feel both guilty
and useless. The mistake I made was to try to 'fix' her, either by
offering glib reassurance – outlining all the positives in her life – or
by asking questions to try to 'get to the bottom' of things. I meant
well, of course. But I was a blunt and often irritating instrument.

The main mistake I made was in assuming that it's what we *say*
that helps people, rather than how we listen. I slowly realised that
she didn't want me to fix her anxiety at all. She wanted me to be
a witness to it. She wanted to have someone who would listen to

her without judgement, so that she could be truly seen and heard. The irony was that the better I learned how to deeply listen to her, the more helpful I became. I have begun to apply this principle to other spheres of my life too: to the people I manage, to my role as big brother to two siblings, and to my other friendships. It is always improvisational. Because how you need to listen to someone is different every time.

How do you feel when someone offers you help or tries to give you advice? If, like me, you bristle and go on the defensive, then the answer lies in the 'status interaction' involved. As I mentioned in the previous chapter, status is central to so many of the communication challenges we face at home and at work. In his book *Helping*, organisational psychologist Edgar Schein offers an acute analysis of the social dynamics of offering and receiving help.[19] Schein points out that at the outset every helping relationship is in a state of imbalance. Why? Because the person being helped is 'one down' and therefore vulnerable, whereas the person doing the helping is 'one up' and therefore powerful.

The takeaway here is that when you receive help or advice it feels like a loss of status. On the other side, when you give advice it raises your status. This is one reason why giving advice feels good and why we sometimes seek to give it when it's not wanted (even if this desire is subconscious). So, what can we do about this? We need to communicate with other people in a way that doesn't diminish their status: we need to use listening as our main tool for helping others rather than speaking, to see silence not as passive, but as an active choice.

The aim is to enable the person to follow their own train of thought without interruptions – that is, without us jumping straight into solution mode or chiming in with our own experiences. (Clue, if you use the pronoun 'I' a lot in these conversations, rather than 'you' or 'we', you are probably doing it wrong.) Through listening, we're allowing people to find their own clarity and insight. People often have the answer to their problem; they just need someone to listen to them talk for long enough about it so that they can find it. Or they only realise they knew the answer all along when they say it out loud.

This doesn't come naturally to us. Not speaking is often harder than speaking because on the whole we're nice people. We want to help. We also have egos. We think, *When is it my turn to speak?* And we get easily bored. We must avoid taking the most direct route to our outcome, which is always to force things by what we say. We need to be more patient. Our aim here is not to talk ourselves, but to keep the other person talking as much as possible. Of course, the convention in conversation is that we take it in turns to speak. So, how do we pass our turn to speak – without sounding weird? Try this, inspired by the former FBI Chief Hostage Negotiator Chris Voss:[20]

- **Take your conversational turn as briefly as possible, by using connecting words**, such as:
  'Go on …'
  'Tell me more about that.'

- **Ask questions, but keep them as short and as open as possible.** For example, don't ask: 'Does that make you feel good or bad?' This is a closed question. Instead ask: 'How does that make you feel?'

But be careful. Every question we ask triggers some sort of emotional response. For example, the question 'Why?' often causes people to get defensive. Instead, Voss encourages you to focus on 'how' or 'what' questions to tease out information. For example: 'What do you have in mind?'

One of the key things a great listener does is help a speaker feel in control. You can do this by using open questions to slow them down and help them explore their options, so that they feel more empowered and less trapped by a situation. A good question here is, 'What else could you do?'[21]

- **Use minimal encouragers.** For example:
  'OK.'
  'I see.'

Non-verbally this also includes nodding, perhaps smiling, and generally looking interested.

- **Paraphrase.** This is where we reflect back what someone has said by summarising the main points. For example: 'So, you feel like you want a new challenge at work. But, on the other hand, you worry about what a reduction in salary might mean for your family.'

Again, be careful not to editorialise here. It's easy to put words in people's mouths and accidentally impose your own agenda.

- **Use 'mirroring'.** Mirroring is a much shorter alternative to paraphrasing. With mirroring, you simply repeat the last few words that person said in order to encourage them to continue. By encouraging people to expand on what they've just said, they often say more than they planned to originally. For example:

A: '… and that made me really upset!'
B: 'It made you upset?'

You can see from all these tools that, far from just happening, listening well is exhausting. Which is why improvisers only try to do it for an hour at a time. We can't listen amazingly all the time. Don't beat yourself up if you fall off the listening wagon. A good analogy for mindful listening is meditation. The point of meditation is not to have no thoughts at all. The point is to bring yourself back to breath when thoughts do occur. Similarly, with listening our aim is to cultivate self-awareness so that when we realise our attention has drifted away, we can bring our focus back to our conversational partner.

Another practice that is useful here is to schedule your most valuable conversations at high energy times like the beginning of the day when you are more likely to be able to bring your best focus. I've learned through bitter experience to never have hard conversations late at night! But what about conversations that are lower-stakes, the sorts of chats that we have at work every day? It is to this final category that we turn next.

LISTENING TO NETWORK

They say your network is your net worth. Making connections and building relationships with new people is always going to be part of career progression. Yet the idea of 'networking' makes a lot of people cringe. We associate it with forcing small talk at dull conferences, yawn-fest after-work drinks and awkward hobnobbing.

People rarely look forward to it. I hope in this final section of the chapter to give you a few tips and tricks for making these events more enjoyable and less anxiety inducing.

The big thing that comes up when I talk to workshop attendees about the perils of networking is: 'I don't know what to say.' I think we've all been in the position where our conversation has run dry or we don't have anything to chime in with in a larger group chat. The main thing that helps here is to remember that your job isn't to be the life and soul of the party; your job is to make the other person look good. In improv parlance, your job is to be a good scene partner, and that all begins with listening. If you want to be interesting, be interested.

Something I find useful when meeting new people is to bear in mind the sort of questions they're likely to be running in their head when they're talking to me. These will most likely be the same questions that we're all wondering about, like:

> *Is this person similar to me?*
> *Does this person think I'm interesting?*
> *Am I important?*

Your job is just to answer these questions in the affirmative for the other person. So, listen out for commonalities. Where are your chances to say: 'I do that too!'? Also, look out for notable aspects about the other person that you can engage with. For example, if they mention their children, you might ask: 'How do you balance being a dad with your job?' Finally, listen for places where you can be impressed by the other person. For example, if they say they are training for a marathon, you could say: 'Wow. I really admire your discipline. That training is really tough.'

By putting the focus on them, you get them doing a lot of the talking (newsflash: people love the sound of their own voice), but it also takes the pressure off you to be clever or funny. As always, it all comes down to listening and responding to offers. That's all you have to do: listen and link. Listen and then either: (a) ask a related follow-up question; or (b) 'yes, and' the other person to show you have listened to their point, then build on it with your own, connected perspective or anecdote. (We'll be looking at storytelling in Chapter 6.)

One of the challenges of networking is that sometimes we come up against unhelpful characters. One example is 'The Interrupter', the guy who can't stop interrupting you. He might apologise afterwards, but it's too late: he's already spoilt your flow. There are a number of reasons why someone might interrupt. Perhaps they imagine that by listening and not talking, other people will think they don't know about the subject at hand. So they get involved to show everyone they know their onions. Or perhaps they worry that if they don't jump in and speak they won't get their chance to put forward their own point of view.

There is normally narcissism or competitiveness at play with The Interrupter. So what can you do? Remember: you can't control how others communicate, only how you respond. You could call them on it. Sometimes people genuinely interrupt you not out of malice but from a lack of self-awareness. If you say, 'I haven't finished my point actually,' that might do the trick. There isn't a magic bullet here, I'm afraid.

Another challenging sort you may come across is 'The Over-talker'. Cousin of The Interrupter, The Over-talker doesn't so much butt into what you are saying as simply talk over the top of it. The Over-talker is especially prevalent in video calls. Then there is The Egotist. They dominate the conversation and somehow make everything about them. With all of these difficult people the best strategy is to go talk to somebody else! The second best is to Gandhi it: be the change you want to see. If you model great listening, it might set the tone for the conversation. At the very least, you'll be doing the right thing.

CASE STUDY: Amy Hoffbrand, account director

Taking creative briefs from clients can feel like a process of mind-reading. In reality, the insight into what they really want can come through in a turn of phrase or a really small nugget they say over the phone or face-to-face in a meeting. Since doing improv, I now listen a lot more for what they say off the top of their head, their tone and their phrasing, rather than what they might have included in the formal brief. These phrases often reflect conversations they've been having internally with other stakeholders and are therefore a better reflection of their world. I find that great listening is not just shown up in conversations but in written communications too, such as writing up summaries of a call in an email or putting the client's words into a proposal. Clients always appreciate it, simply because good listening is sadly so rare. ∎

CONCLUSION

We've reached the end of our exploration of the art of listening. Listening may not be as cinematic as speaking, but I'd argue that it's more important – and increasingly so. We live in a world dominated by technology, in a time of permanent distraction, whether it be from laptops or phones, smart watches or TV screens. In the era of the notification, genuine attention is in short supply. Yet it is attention which creates our world. And it is a lack of attention which can destroy our relationships.

The prevalence of social media has changed the way we communicate with one another. As the philosopher Marshall McLuhan put it, the medium becomes the message. Is it any surprise, then, that for many people self-expression trumps self-reflection these days? There are many benefits to technology and social media, of course. But when everyone else is on transmit, if you can learn to be a great listener, you'll gain a competitive advantage – at work and beyond.

Great listening requires so many character traits that allow you to be both a good improviser and a good person. You need humility because to listen effectively you must quieten your own ego. You need curiosity too – especially if the person speaking appears a little dull. (To quote Mary Lou Kownacki's much shared adage: 'Frankly, there isn't anyone you couldn't learn to love once you've heard their story.')

Then you need patience because a great listener lets a conversation find its natural form, rather than hurrying the speaker to some easier, preordained destination. Related to this is the need for flexibility because, as we explored earlier, listening is the willingness to be changed. But fundamentally, being a great listener is about caring: caring for the person you are listening to and for the craft of listening itself. Listening can be a transformative act. Or not. By listening poorly, we can make another person feel invisible. Conversely, by listening well we can make that person feel seen. And, when it comes down to it, isn't that all most of us want?

Chapter 3

SPONTANEITY AND PLAY

*'Every child is an artist. The problem is
to remain an artist once we grow up.'*
—Pablo Picasso

As we discovered in Chapter 1, we are all born creative geniuses, but then for many of us things go badly wrong. Our
aim here is to get to the bottom of what happens to those genius
five year olds. We'll discover that we can all be extraordinarily
creative if we get out of our own way. So often we inhibit ourselves
without even being aware that we are doing it. Improvisers have
learned how to stop the rot. In this chapter, I'll share their secrets
with you. By the end of the chapter, you'll have learned practical
techniques to:

- Come up with lots of ideas, fast, and have fun while
  you do it.

- Find your flow in conversations and stop being
  self-conscious.

- Inject more spontaneity into your everyday life.

To begin, I'd like you to try a quick exercise. This involves some
simple word association. I'd like you to go down the list of words

below, one by one, as quick as you can, simply saying whatever word you associate with it out loud. OK, here it goes.

DUCK
FOG
GOLD
BIG
LETTUCE
SKIN

How did you get on? This is an interesting exercise because, when you do it, you experience your *imagination*. You experience thoughts naturally 'popping up' on the canvas of your mind. When you act on these ideas, in this instance by saying them out loud, you are being *spontaneous*. Spontaneity is the natural state of children – for good and for ill! It's what makes them so naughty and messy, but it's also what helps them be so wonderfully creative. Spontaneity is also a foundational skill of improvisation. Consequently, most improvisation training is based around helping adults play more like children. But what is it that stops adults from being spontaneous? It's what happens in 'the gap'.

IMAGINATION — — — — — — THE GAP — — — — — — SPONTANEITY
· Thoughts   · Speech
· Feelings   · Action
· Hunches and Instincts

We all have an imagination. But we aren't all spontaneous. The reason for this is what happens in the gap between thought and action. The question is, what mediates this relationship? What affects whether we act on the sparks of our imagination or not? There are a number of factors, which we'll explore in this chapter. Fundamentally, though, it is the presence of other people. How do you think you would have got on with the word association exercise if you had to do it in front of your colleagues? In my experience in workshops, people tend to self-edit a lot more in this situation. Rather than expressing their genuine spontaneous associations, they censor their choice of words in order to present a certain persona to their workmates. Only certain ideas that pop up on the canvas of their mind are allowed out to play in the big wide world.

You might be thinking, *So what? Isn't censorship a good thing?* After all, filtering our thoughts and feelings before we express them is crucial if we are to maintain any decent professional or personal relationships. For example, you can't blurt out that your boss has put on weight, nor can you make sarcastic asides to clients. And that's absolutely right. In some contexts and for some sorts of thoughts, censorship is really useful. We all need a bouncer in our head, letting certain words and ideas past and not others. But in situations where we want to generate innovative ideas, either alone or with other people, we need the bouncer to get lost.

THE SCIENCE OF IMPROV

While improvisers have known for years about the benefits of improvisation training in their own lives, robust scientific evidence to back up their beliefs has been hard to come by. However, over the past ten years or so, scientific studies have been published that suggest how improvisation affects our brain and, more specifically, how it can make us more creative. Much of this research comes out of Dr Charles Limb's lab at the University of California in San Francisco. It all started a decade ago as a labour of love.

A surgeon and neurotologist, as well as a lifetime jazz music obsessive and dedicated amateur musician, Limb was working as a hearing specialist at the National Institute of Health in the United States when he wondered whether the fMRI scanner he used at work every day could tell him something about the brains of those musicians he was so fascinated by. Particularly, he was interested to study their creative brains in action to see what was going on at a neurological level. In 2008, Limb and neurologist Allen Braun conducted a study where they scanned the brains of jazz musicians while they played memorised scales and then improvised riffs on a specially commissioned plastic piano – all while lying flat on their backs![22]

An fMRI scanner (functional magnetic resonance imaging) is a metal tube that looks much like one end of a Christmas cracker. It measures blood flow in the brain. The more blood that flows to a certain brain region, the more brain activity in that area. Limb and Braun discovered that during the improvised riffs, the jazz musicians' medial prefrontal cortex (the area of the brain associated with language and creativity) significantly increased in activity, whereas their dorsolateral prefrontal cortex (the conscious-control part, where you judge and correct your behaviour) became dormant.

Fascinated by these results, Limb has gone on to carry out similar studies with freestyle rappers and, most recently, with improvisational comedians, with very similar results. These studies suggest that, in moments of high creativity, the improvisers were able to switch off the self-censoring areas of their brain.[23] Can we all learn to do the same and put ourselves in a similar state of higher creativity? The answer is yes. We'll turn to the specific techniques improvisers use to get themselves there. But before we do, I'd like you to try a quick exercise.

▶ Exercise

INFINITE BOX

This simple game only takes a minute or so. It might look like nonsense at first glance, but trust me on this. Here's how it works.

1. **Imagine there is a box in front of you. This box contains anything you can conceive of in the entire world.** It includes objects, celebrities, concepts and so on. For example, this box might include a spaceship, a lemon, regret, water skiing and Cher. All very different things, yet all included in this box.

2. **Your task is to spend 60 seconds pulling out as many items as you can from the infinite box.** Ideally, say them out loud. But, if you're on a bus, you can just keep it to yourself! This is also a good game to play with a partner, so get a friend involved if you like. There are only two rules: first, *there are no wrong answers.* Everything you pull out of the box is correct. And second, try to do the exercise for a whole minute. You'll probably pull out about ten different items.

▲ ▲ ▲

How did you get on? I often use this exercise in workshops because it illustrates what can get in the way of spontaneity. Non-improvisers struggle with this game because they try to be too clever. Rather than pulling *any* idea out of the box, they try to pull *interesting* ideas out of the box. They hesitate. They 'ummm' and 'errr'. Then they tell me they can't think of anything. They say they're blocked. Actually, what they mean is not that they can't think of any ideas, but that they can't think of any *good ideas* – or what they perceive to be good ideas.

Sometimes though, they start the exercise fluently. They shout, 'Banana! Apple! Pear!' And then all of a sudden they clog up. 'Why did you become blocked?' I ask. 'Because I didn't want to say another fruit,' they reply, 'because that's boring.' But I never told them: 'Do not say more than one thing in the same category.' They imposed this false stipulation on themselves. Similar to the problem of coming up with interesting ideas, this stems from the thought: *I must say something original.* Yet this isn't the instruction of the game. It is the snarky voice of your inner critic, the imaginary person who patrols your imagination–spontaneity gap!

We all have an inner critic. I find it useful to anthropomorphise mine. It helps me to separate myself from it. My inner critic is a sarcastic fifteen-year-old boy, sat on the back seat of the bus, sniggering. What exactly is our inner critic? Let's return to the person above who became blocked because their inner critic told them: *Say something original!* Tied to that sentiment is the thought: *Because people will think I am stupid if I do not.* Your inner critic is not concerned about you at all but about how you look to others. Like my spotty teenager on the bus, your inner critic just wants to look cool. Or if not cool then at least 'normal'.

Fundamentally it's this fear of other people's opinions that blocks us creatively. In our past, we needed to behave in a way that didn't get us thrown out of the tribe upon which we depended. Shame, in this sense, was useful for our survival. Research by psychologist Sara Valencia Botto suggests that human beings start caring about the opinions of others at just 24 months old.[24] By the age of four or five years old we have learned to almost entirely conform to the norms of the groups we are part of. Censorship, unfortunately, is innately human.

Viola Spolin, one of the great early pioneers of improvisation, called this 'Approval/Disapproval Syndrome'. Everyone suffers from this syndrome, but some more than others. According to Spolin, we all aim for the approval of other people. And conversely, we aim to avoid their disproval. Our inner critic is, in fact, the voice of others (or what we *imagine* they are thinking). This is why, when people play a game as simple as Infinite Box, they think:

> *That's a silly idea.*
> *That's stupid.*
> *That's weird.*
> *That's offensive.*
> *That's boring.*

By listening to this voice, they are taken out of the moment, and can no longer directly experience their imagination.

There are long-term and short-term costs to having our inner critic win the day like this. The short-term costs are temporary and fairly harmless. We might not contribute to a brainstorm at work, not turn up to the art class we booked, or not send our boss an email with that idea we had over the weekend. World-renowned creativity expert Dr Ronald A. Beghetto calls these little acts of sabotage 'creative suppression'. However, Beghetto also identifies a more serious iteration of this sabotage: 'creative mortification', where we withdraw from creative work *forever*.[25] This is sadly prevalent in grown-ups.

If a five year old said to you, 'The thing is with me, I'm a numbers guy. I don't do ideas; I leave that to the other kids,' you'd think that kid was insane. And yet adults say things like this to

111

each other all the time. When adults self-identify as 'not creative', they aren't being falsely modest, they genuinely believe it. They have become so used to shutting down their imagination through a million tiny instances of creative suppression that eventually they become totally alienated from it. After all, why pay attention to something you aren't going to use?

It doesn't have to be like this. The trick is to treat your imagination in a much kinder way. There are two tools from improv that can help you do exactly that.

LET YOURSELF BE AVERAGE

We've explored how, if you want to be more spontaneous, you need to put your inner critic back in its box. While we can never get rid of our inner critic entirely, the good news is that we can quieten it down. Improvisers have a principle that allows them to do this onstage: *Let yourself be average.* Like many concepts from improvisation, its origins can be traced back to Keith Johnstone. This counterintuitive instruction was based on Johnstone's observation that every time his students tried their best, their improvisation got worse.[26]

They spent so long trying to think of something intelligent or original to say that they stopped listening to their scene partner. And not only that, when they finally did say something they thought was 'original', it was often just a version of something they thought an intelligent person might say. The thing is, when we try to be original, we're often nothing of the sort. When we try to be clever or funny, we're often simply derivative and corny.

For example, imagine an improv scene where a character says: 'I've got you a present. How about you unwrap it?' This is a straightforward offer. A beginner improviser, desperate to be interesting, will invariably try to invent a response to this line that they think is clever and funny. When they unwrap the present, they'll say something like, 'Oh my God! You got me the leg of a giraffe!' But this isn't interesting at all. It's contrived.

If you want to be original, it is far better to simply say the *obvious thing* – the thing that's obvious to you in this moment. Again, this is counterintuitive. After all, who on earth wants to be obvious? Obvious isn't interesting, right? But beginner improvisers soon discover that what is obvious to them is not obvious to anyone else. In fact, it's often inspiring to another person. This is because your obvious association to something will be different to my obvious association. Your obvious offer, therefore, takes on the illusion of originality. What's more, as *your* obvious also won't be the *audience's* obvious, it will surprise them. And, therefore, it has a good chance of making them laugh.

We can apply these two principles offstage too. In your next conversation, let yourself be average. Rather than feeling the pressure to be witty, or to use pre-prepared lines, just say what is obvious to you in the moment. Let's see what that this might look like in the context of an awkward wedding reception. I'll set the scene. The MC announces it is time for everyone to take their seats for dinner. You wander into the marquee and check the seating plan. To your horror, it turns out that you don't know anyone on your table. You are sat with a random assortment of other single people, as if you've been quarantined.

You wander over to the table to sit with the rest of the lonely human shrapnel. The only person already sat down is a woman in the chair immediately to your right. You take your seat. You know you should say something, but what? You play with your hand-written name card for a moment. *I. MUST. SAY. SOMETHING*, you think. Eventually, you turn and look at her. You smile. *What is obvious?* you ask yourself, subtly scanning her (in a non-creepy way). *She's wearing some nice jewellery!* And you're off.

> **YOU:** 'That's an unusual locket you're wearing.'
>
> **HER:** 'Yes.'
>
> **YOU:** 'It looks old.'
>
> **HER:** 'Yes. It's my grandmother's.'
>
> **YOU:** 'Your grandmother's?'
>
> **HER:** 'Yes. She passed it down to me.'
>
> **YOU:** 'It's beautiful.'
>
> **HER:** 'Thank you.'
>
> **YOU:** 'There must be a story behind it?'
>
> **HER:** 'Yes, actually. In the Second World War …'

And so on. Look at how simple and obvious every line of dialogue is, from both sides of this conversation. And yet look how quickly it became interesting. Conversational fluency is the graceful side effect of not trying too hard. It turns out that smooth people are just being obvious. If only someone had told me that at school.

EXPANDING YOUR ADJACENT POSSIBLE

Of course, spontaneity is about much more than being witty at parties. Fundamentally, it's about being able to express your innate creativity and come up with new ideas. You can use these two tools, 'be average' and 'be obvious', in everything from contributing to brainstorms at work, to writing a marketing newsletter, or planning your best friend's hen-do. When trying to solve a problem, start a mind-map and let yourself begin by brainstorming the most obvious ideas.

Starting with obvious ideas gets your creative juices flowing. It takes the pressure off and frees you up. You'll also find that from these initial obvious ideas, new associations quickly start to form in your mind, spreading outwards in a conceptual web. Avalanches can start as snowballs. As the tiny snowball cascades down the mountain it picks up other snow, soon building unstoppable momentum. This is what creativity feels like when it's going well. This momentum moves you, unthinkingly, towards more original solutions. You get it all started by allowing yourself to be obvious.

Keep in mind not to judge your ideas as they emerge. Coming up with ideas only becomes painful when we insist on labelling them as 'good' or 'bad', 'right' or 'wrong'. As Keith Johnstone says, if we can learn not to judge our ideas, imagination becomes as effortless as perception.[27] We explored in the Introduction how as an improviser I don't really come up with ideas but *offers*. An offer is just an invitation to explore. When we can see ideas as beginnings, not ends in themselves, we allow them to be a means to get somewhere else. Each idea simply asks: 'What if … *this*?' It may lead somewhere, it may not, but that's OK. By treating my ideas like this, it frees me up to pitch them. It's suddenly not so intimidating anymore.

It really doesn't matter if you come up with 'bad' ideas anyway. Steven Johnson, in his book *Where Good Ideas Come From*, talks about the 'adjacent possible': every time you share an idea with me, regardless of its quality, there is suddenly a whole new network of connections for me to make.[28] Even impossible and highly impractical ideas are worth considering because of where they shift our thinking.

To recap, there are three main ways to quieten your inner critic, the bouncer who patrols the gap between your imagination and your spontaneous response. First, delay judgement of your ideas and say 'Yes, and …'. Second, feel free to say the obvious thing. Finally, let yourself be average.

THE GENIUS OF GAMES

There is one final technique that improvisers use to overcome their inner critic. Rather than sitting down to consciously 'think up' new ideas, improvisers let themselves discover them through *play*. The ideas then emerge as a happy consequence. This is why games are the basis for all improvisation training. This approach can be traced back to the pioneering work of Viola Spolin. Spolin's logic was simple. Our mind is a censoring device. It is also a device of habitual thinking. Both inhibit true self-expression. The beauty of games is that they preoccupy the mind by giving it some simple rules to focus on. When the mind is kept busy, our constant self-judgement quietens, and the doorway to our imagination opens up.

In Spolin's words, games allow the improviser to 'evoke the genie'. Isn't that a wonderful phrase? It speaks to me of rediscovering our innate imagination: a source of creativity lying dormant deep within us, waiting to be awoken, if only we'd drop our guard and let ourselves play.

There are two obvious objections here. First, the word 'play' has a branding problem. In many people's minds play equals 'messing around'. It's childish, unprofessional and uncommitted, the very opposite of work. But this misunderstands the role of play in the workplace. I'm not suggesting we play just because it's fun. We should play because it helps us come up with more creative solutions. Rather than being unprofessional, the act of play is another tool we can use to be better at our jobs.

The second objection I often hear when I talk about play in the workplace is that play is no substitute for logical, methodological thinking. And I agree! Clearly, play is not suitable in every part of your job. (We probably don't want a playful attitude to fire evacuation procedure, for example.) Play is not intended as a substitute for structured thought, but as a complement to it. We need both. In fact, even when we want to be creative – where we benefit from the looser, more open approach of play – this freedom is supported and informed by structure and planning. It all comes down to what creativity is *for*.

According to the pioneering educational reformer Sir Ken Robinson, creativity is 'the process of having original ideas that have value'.[29] We can see from this definition that it's not enough for us to just playfully generate ideas. These ideas have to be valuable. How do we know if an idea is valuable? First, we've got to look in the right place for it: are we solving a problem that anyone cares about? Second, when we come up with ideas, we need to be able to evaluate whether they are genuinely novel (and whether they are any good). This takes a lot of knowledge and experience in our chosen field. For example, it takes a great chef to recognise a breakthrough recipe. We can see that play is necessary but not sufficient for creativity by itself. As we are about to explore, creativity is a much bigger process.

In his seminal 1953 book *Applied Imagination*, Alex Osborn, a founding partner in the now globally renowned advertising agency BBDO, showed how outstandingly creative people come up with ideas using a process he termed *creative problem-solving*. Osborn's work on creative problem-solving has been tested and developed by various academics over the years, most notably Sid Parnes, who went on to set up the International Centre for Studies in Creativity at Buffalo State College in New York. The Osborn-Parnes Creative Problem-Solving Process comprises four stages. The latest iteration looks like this:

Stage	Step	Purpose
CLARIFY	Explore the vision	Identify the goal, wish or challenge.
	Gather data	Describe and generate data to enable a clear understanding of the challenge. *i.e. Research the problem/issue; talk to other people who might have worked on it.*
	Formulate challenges	Sharpen awareness of the challenge and create challenge questions that invite solutions. *e.g. 'How might we ... increase the rate of customer referrals?'*
IDEATE	Explore ideas	Generate ideas that answer the challenge questions.
DEVELOP	Formulate solutions	To move from ideas to solutions, evaluate, strengthen and select solutions for best 'fit'. *i.e. Which idea wins based on our set criteria?*
IMPLEMENT	Formulate a plan	Explore acceptance (sell the idea to the key stakeholders) and identify resources and actions that will support implementation of the selected solution(s). *i.e. Make the idea happen.*

Adapted from the Creative Education Foundation's Learner's Model, based on work of G.J. Puccio, M. Mance, M.C. Murdock, B. Miller, J. Vehar, R. Firestien, S. Thurber, & D. Nielsen (2011). http://www.creativeeducationfoundation.org/creative-problem-solving/the-cps-process.

You can see that bringing an idea into the world is a multifaceted, complex process that requires many different sorts of thinking. Where improv can really help you is in the Ideate stage of the process. Taking a playful approach to creativity will not just help you to have a lot of fun coming up with ideas, it will also help you come up with more *original* ideas. As Tim Brown, chairman of the design firm IDEO, says in his TED talk on play, adults have the tendency to categorise things as quickly as they can. We rush to conclusions about a solution before exploring other options. In short, we struggle to look beyond our habits, in ways that children don't.

For example, if an adult looks at a colander, they see a tool to drain vegetables. If a child looks at a colander, they might also see a soldier's helmet, a dream-reading device, a camel's hump, and on and on. When we become more open to exploring different possibilities, we increase the likelihood of stumbling across more novel ideas. Taking the playful approach of children, we can learn to see like them. As Keith Johnstone puts it: 'Many teachers think of children as immature adults. It might lead to better and more "respectful" teaching if we thought of adults as atrophied children.' We adults need to relearn the art of play. We'll turn our attention now to doing exactly that.

LET YOURSELF BE WRONG

Imagine you are in a sand pit and you're told that you will be judged on the quality of your first sandcastle. How does that make you feel? How would you approach the task? Does it feel like a very playful situation?

Now imagine you are in the sandpit and you're told that, rather than being judged on the quality of your first sandcastle, you will be judged on the total number of different sandcastles you can produce in a given period of time. How would that change your approach?

Bring a sand pit mindset to your creativity. How? Suspend judgement, try stuff out and let yourself make lots of mistakes. Rather than trying to prove you are clever or creative by searching for the one 'right' solution, focus on coming up with lots of ideas instead. If you come across an idea that looks promising, don't explore it in too much depth at this stage. Jot it down and try another approach. You can always come back to it. Don't worry if this next idea isn't as good, keep generating new solutions. Embrace the mess.

▶ Exercise

TURBOCHARGED BRAINSTORM

Try to 'gamify' your humble brainstorm by imposing ambitious targets around volume and time. For example, tell everyone they have to come up with 50 ideas in five minutes. You'll find this constraint frees people up from the need to have 'good' ideas which, ironically, helps them to have them.

WHAT'S THE WRONG ANSWER?

In this game you invite the group to design what is definitely not the right answer to the problem at hand. This puts them in a fun, playful space as the need to be 'good' is totally lifted. Often when we define what we don't want, what we actually do want becomes a lot clearer.

▲ ▲ ▲

DON'T PLAN. EXPLORE

When you play, you don't have a plan for how you want things to turn out. You take it one small step at a time and let what's happening happen. In short, you surrender control. A good example of this is an improv exercise commonly called 'Lord of the Machine'. In this exercise the coach will give a group of five or so people an object or machine to build using just their bodies. For example, they might have to build a car. In the first round of the exercise, the group always descend into a debate about who should do what and what sort of car (say) they might create. Eventually, one person usually self-nominates to be the 'director' and takes control of the situation, telling everyone else what to do. It isn't pretty to watch.

But in the second round of the exercise the instructions change. The participants are told that, in this version, they are not allowed to speak at all and they have only five seconds to build their object. This tends to be met with a mixture of fear and irritation. *How on earth do you expect us to do that?* However, when it comes down to it, every group miraculously builds an object far more interesting than in their first round attempt, and in a fraction of the time. Why? Because they drop their preconceptions about what the result should be and therefore become more open to other options that emerge in the moment.

▶ Exercise

IDENTITY THEFT

In this game, developed by Claire Bridges of creativity consultancy Now Go Create, you identify some famous creatives you admire, and brainstorm around how they would tackle the problem you are considering. It immediately gives you a new perspective, which opens up new possibilities and forces you to break out of any preconceptions you may have. Some of the ideas will be crazy, of course, but don't worry about that. Remember: these impossible ideas can be stepping stones to ideas that are possible. This game also works well with brands rather than celebrities.

For example, if David Bowie had to develop a solution here, how would he approach it? Or, if Apple were dealing with this problem, what sort of ideas might they explore?

▲ ▲ ▲

MAKE THINGS

When children play, rather than thinking about what their painting might look like at the end, they simply start painting. As they paint, more and more ideas occur to them about what they could do next. Choices create choices. Similarly in an improv scene, the story is never pre-written, it is something we discover incrementally. The reality of the moment we are in makes what we should do next obvious and easy. We act ourselves into the future, we don't think our way there.

By acting rather than thinking, creativity is not just easier, we also stumble onto different sorts of thoughts. We have both a conscious and a subconscious mind. Play helps us find and express these subconscious thoughts that we can't get to with a more linear thinking style. Play, then, helps us access a different part of ourselves and, through doing so, helps us break habitual patterns of thinking that can stop us seeing new possibilities.

▶ Exercise

TALK IT OUT

If you are creatively stuck, then find a sounding board for your idea. Conversation can be a (generally) pain-free way of realising what you actually think and feel about something. You simply talk until your stumble across the answer.

WRITE IT OUT

Essayist Joan Didion once said: 'I don't know what I think till I write it down.' To work out how you think or feel about something, grab a notebook and write a stream of conscious: whatever comes to you related to the problem. With the previous method you are in dialogue with someone else, whereas with this method you are in dialogue with yourself. This 'free-writing' methodology has been popularised by Julia Cameron in her book *The Artist's Way*, with her 'morning pages' ritual since becoming legendary in arty circles.

DRAW IT OUT

Art psychotherapists get patients to draw pictures in order to express thoughts and feelings that may be subconscious. The beauty of drawing is that it bypasses the logical mind and allows you to access other parts of yourself. It also allows you to express what you may not have words for. It's not about being good at drawing – stick men and women will do – it's about opening yourself up. If you don't want to draw, then can you make your brainstorm process visual in some other way? Maybe by mind-mapping, using flipcharts or even the ubiquitous Post-it Notes.

BUILD IT OUT

Like the previous method, this is all about using your hands to quickly build a prototype of an idea, which can often shed new insight and stimulate new ideas. So, write a first draft of that article quickly. Design a rudimentary poster for that marketing campaign. Do a collage of that webpage you're about to code. As IDEO co-founder David Kelley puts it: 'Think with your hands.'

▲ ▲ ▲

INHABIT A NEW ROLE

When we play we are allowed to be something we are not and exist in a different reality for a while. As a child I might delve into my dressing-up box and become Robin Hood for an hour. As an adult, I might go to a murder mystery party and be a detective for the evening. We probably wouldn't want to do something as absurd as dressing up at work. But here are three things you might want to try:

1. Live in the customer's reality for a while

When we create a character onstage we talk about the 'who', the 'what' and the 'where' of their life: Who are they? What do they do? Where do they do it? We also talk about the 'objective' – What do they want? – and the 'conflict' – Where are their pain points? We talk too about the key specifics of this character: What are they really into and what do they hate? If this fact is true of them, what else might be true? All of this builds a three-dimensional picture that goes beyond the often anodyne personas we can fall back on (for example, 'Susan, mum of three, urban dwelling'). Empathising in this more playful way can throw up lots of insights.

▶ Exercise

STORYBOARDING

This is a technique borrowed from design thinking.[30] Pick a specific aspect of customer experience to map out, for example, the journey from landing on your website to completing a purchase and receiving an email confirmation. On blank record cards, Post-its or small bits of paper, sketch out the activity in that specific step or scene, along with a caption to describe it. Don't spend too long – it doesn't have to be a work of great art. At the end, write a list of questions that emerge. You'll often see an aspect of the experience which could be improved that you'd previously walked past.

▲ ▲ ▲

2. Ask, 'What if?'

Asking 'What if …?' is a wonderfully divergent type of question that helps us explore our often self-imposed limits when it comes to problem-solving. Here's an improv exercise that does exactly that, but the technique can easily be translated into an offstage context.

▶ Exercise

WHAT IF?

1. **Try this one with a friend or colleague. Get them to start by improvising a story about anything at all.**
   In workshops we give people a location to inspire them, such as 'in the mountains'. Coming up with a story from scratch sounds like a lot of pressure for the person starting, but this is where 'What if …?' comes in.

2. As the other person tells their story, your job is to pitch 'What if ...?' suggestions. They are then tasked with accepting and incorporating these into the story.

For example:

A: 'I was making my way up the mountain trail, with a big rucksack on my back ...'

B: 'What if you heard some strange music?'

A: 'When I heard some strange music. It was coming from above me, where I could see an opening in the rock face ...'

B: 'What if inside that rock face lived a Buddhist monk?'

And so on.

▲ ▲ ▲

Applying this strategy offstage in our working lives, we might ask useful 'What if ... ?' questions, like: 'What if we did the opposite?' 'What if we had an infinite budget?' And, 'What if this were easy?' We'll explore other ways to use empowering questions later in the chapter.

3. Break the rules

When we play, we simply live in a reality until it stops being useful or fun. We pretend in a particular way in order to produce a particular result. So, in this light, how can we play in a new reality for a while to see if it broadens our thinking? What if we broke all our normal rules and assumptions about the problem at hand? What ideas could that throw up? It might throw up no useful ideas, of course. But this is all about stimulating ourselves to approach finding ideas from a totally different angle.

▶ Exercise

CHANGE THE RULES

In this game you draw a line down the middle of a piece of paper. In one half, you list all the rules and assumptions you are bringing to a problem you are trying to solve. In the other, you go through these rules and assumptions one by one and break them.

For example, the marketing team at Red Bull used to operate on the rule that they advertised at sports events by sponsoring teams. One day they posed themselves the question: What if we broke this rule? What if, rather than sponsoring sports teams, we actually owned them? This transformed how they went about promoting the brand. Red Bull now own teams all over the world, including Red Bull Racing, which won three consecutive Formula One World Championships between 2010 and 2012.

▲ ▲ ▲

BUILD TRUST IN THE GROUP

In his book, *How I Escaped My Certain Fate*, stand-up comedian Stewart Lee recounts a story of a summer holiday to rural France. One day, in an unnamed ancient French village, he followed a group of drama students who were staging an annual performance of a medieval tradition in which the village clowns, or *bouffons*, were given the run of the place. Normally the lowest status people in the village, on this date they were able to do or say whatever they pleased. When the performers reached the church in the town square, they drew a rough circle in chalk on the cobblestones outside. When the *bouffons* entered this circle, they were free to say whatever they wanted about the Church, God, the Virgin Mary and so on, without fear of censure. As Lee writes:

> The *bouffons* were in a charmed circle […] a sacred and clearly delineated space where they were free to work their magic without interference. The director of *The Aristocrats*, Paul Provenza, once told me that he saw the stage of a stand-up club as a great pair of inverted commas, framing the performer, saying 'What is being said here is only being said, not actually being done, so judge it accordingly.' Could there be any clearer image for the special privileges of the comedian than this moment, where the clowns marked out their own unassailable territory in the very shadow of the church, the great forbidder that binds with briars our joys and desires?

What I take away here is that for play to happen we often have to create a special place for it. A space with its own rules where we are able, perhaps, to give voice to the impermissible. It is a space that gives people permission to take risks they would not take outside of the space, to be versions of themselves and to discuss ideas that they would not be or discuss beyond the boundaries of this place of play. How do we delineate this space? Companies like the trendy marketing agency from Chapter 1 do it through naming the space a certain way. (We're not meeting in 'meeting room 5', we are meeting in 'Alfred Hitchcock'.) Other organisations do it through decoration and design.

The most effective thing to do is to draw the metaphorical chalk circle before the meeting where you want people to play. It is a symbolic moment, where you cross into a world with a different set of expectations. IDEO do it through having their brainstorming 'rules' written on the walls of their meeting areas.[31] After all, play is not anarchy. Play needs rules too, especially group play. Think about it: board games aren't fun if we aren't all playing within the same limits. We also can't trust each other if there isn't a baseline of common rules, and trust is what enables groups to let themselves be vulnerable enough to take creative risks.

▶ Exercise

IDEO BRAINSTORM RULES

At the top of your next meeting, read out these rules or pin them up on the walls so that everyone knows what behaviours are expected of them in this playful space.

- Defer judgement.

- Encourage wild ideas.

- Build on the ideas of others.

- Stay focused on the topic.

- One conversation at a time.

- Be visual.

- Go for quantity.

▲ ▲ ▲

SHIFT YOUR ENVIRONMENT

We've just looked at how it's important to clearly delineate and differentiate any space you want people to play in. But sometimes it's fun to shift your environment entirely. (After all, many of us work in environments that simply aren't that inspiring.) Just as children don't only play in the playground or playroom but in the street, in the park and even in the supermarket, how can we change our scenery to put ourselves in a more imaginative head space?

▶ Exercise

CREATIVE FIELD TRIP

Go to an art gallery. Go to a museum. Go to a library. Go see a play. Go to a restaurant you don't normally eat at. When you're there, actually be there. Look at the art, for example, and treat it as a stimulus. Does it bring up any associations for you that could help you solve the problem? If you can't get out of the office, bring the stimulus indoors. Just as children have toys to inspire their play, what materials could you use? The newspaper? A bunch of images on a mood board? A playlist of songs? We want to try anything to give our minds a holiday from the everyday for an while.

INCUBATE AWAY FROM YOUR DESK

All the research shows that incubating ideas is a huge part of the creative process. Give yourself time off from a problem and do something else for a while, such as going for a walk. Your subconscious carries on working on the problem in the meantime. This is why we often have bolt from the blue insights when we're in the shower or doing something unconnected but repetitive like preparing dinner.

SEARCH FOR USEFUL CONSTRAINTS

As Spolin said, games help us quieten the inner critic and be creative because they give us rules to follow. These game rules distract us enough to overcome the judgemental voice that prevents us from being spontaneous. They also force us to think more laterally than we might have to if we have more space. Constraints are a gift, not a curse. Just as the formal constraints of rhyme and metre force the poet to reach for a fresher image or word choice, you can impose artificial constraints on your problem-solving process to find more original solutions.

▶ **Exercise**

DEFINE A TIGHT PROBLEM STATEMENT

It's very hard to play a game when we aren't clear about what winning it might look like. Imagine playing a board game without knowing what it would take for the game to end. It wouldn't be fun and you would swiftly lose motivation. Yet this how we often approach brainstorms. To unleash your and other people's creativity, boil down the brief to a clearly defined 'How might we ...?' style question that focuses minds and, crucially, applies constraints. For example, the Department of Health might pose the question: 'How might we use a public health campaign to safeguard teenagers against unhealthy mobile phone use?'

BREAK INTO CHUNKS

Often when we try to solve a problem we approach it as one big beast, which can become overwhelming as there are so many aspects we could focus on. A solution here is to break the problem down into smaller pieces and play with each in turn, before looking at the problem as a whole. For example, if we were solving the government's problem above, you could focus on:

- How do people use mobile phones at the moment?

- What are the different media forms a 'campaign' might take?

- What does public health really mean?

FALSE DEADLINES

Apply false deadlines to force people not to be precious about their ideas. For example, even if you have three months to get a pitch together, set a deadline for one month. In meetings, use a timer to put time limits on brainstorms.

▲ ▲ ▲

A MORE CREATIVE FUTURE

All these techniques are playful, indirect and open-ended. Central to all of them is moving at speed, rather than plodding slowly and logically from problem to solution. I recently watched a documentary about the legendary painter Francis Bacon. He was interviewed in his flat, chaotic with the residue of his process: brushes, easels and paint everywhere. He attempted to explain how he creates his extraordinary works of art. The truth, he said, is that he simply picks up a brush and then, 'chance and accident take over. Consciously I don't know what I'm doing [...] By making these marks – which I don't know how they will behave – suddenly there comes something which your instinct seizes on as being a moment from which it can begin to develop.'

This is how improvisers create. The subconscious mind, forced by the necessity of reaction, makes seemingly random suggestions. Your conscious mind witnesses this and then, seeing a pattern or an opportunity emerge, takes over to wrestle these associations into something coherent and beautiful. It is the inter-action of these two minds: conscious and subconscious, rational and intuitive, that produces the product. Bacon continued: 'I want a very ordered image [...] but I want it to come about by chance.' This is creativity: instinct harnessed by craft. The serendipitous manipulated by the strategic. The rational mind at the reigns, the subconscious providing the horsepower – but only if you let it.

To reiterate a point I made earlier, spontaneity and play are no panacea. They are not a substitute for method, logic and planning. In fact, they thrive *within* it. The creative process is impossible without them. We need to be able to transition in and out of play. We are back again to those two modes from Chapter 1, divergent and convergent thinking. Sometimes we need to be divergent, where we are generating lots of ideas, exploring various possibilities. And sometimes we need to be convergent, where we are explicitly identifying the solution from the choices available and looking to develop it. We need playfulness in the divergent mode. In the convergent mode we need to be more serious. But it's not a binary choice, you're not either playful or you're serious. You need to be both, depending on the context.

FIND YOUR SPARK

I'd like to explore one final aspect of creativity here. You might be thinking that your problem with creativity is not to do with lacking courage to *express* your ideas, nor with lacking a *process* to pull them out of you, but instead to do with having the ideas in the first place. Why is it that when you stare at the blank page, or at the blinking cursor on your Word document, that you can't think of anything at all? If spontaneity is about acting on the sparks of the imagination, how do we generate more sparks? It is to this question that we turn next.

Earlier we saw that Sir Ken Robinson defines creativity as a process. This process doesn't exist in isolation from the rest of our life. If we want to be creative, we need a lifestyle that supports it. To conclude this chapter we're going to explore the simple habits you can adopt to help you generate more creative sparks. Steve Jobs once famously said that creativity is just connecting things. But, in order to connect things, we need to collect them first. Improvisers have three main ways of doing this.

My job as an improviser is to be the most interesting person I can be onstage because it helps me serve you as my scene partner. To be interesting onstage, I need to be interesting offstage too. Living an interesting life isn't about travelling the world or having an extraordinary job; it is about being *interested*. There are many ways of doing this and they are all enjoyable. Read, watch and listen widely. Develop a diverse network of friends and talk to people. Get a hobby or two. Curiosity will give you a richer imagination. We put a great focus in life on our intelligence quotient (IQ). We've seen in applications of 'yes, and' how important emotional intelligence (EQ) is too, in our ability to listen to, collaborate with and make space for others. But if you want to boost your creativity, you need to look out for your curiosity quotient (CQ) as well.

Why does being curious boost our creativity? Simply because, if you give your brain lots of dots, it will connect them for you eventually. And sparks will fly. Decades of research into creativity confirm that every so called 'new' idea is a remix of something that has come before it – a new connection between familiar dots, if you will. The most obvious place this occurs is in music. Sampling, covers and remixes are part of the culture of the artform. As Kirby Ferguson shows in his award-winning film about the practice, *Everything Is A Remix*, musicians routinely copy the work of others and transform it into something new, often by combining it with something else.[32]

Take the song 'Gold Digger' by Kanye West. That song is heavily indebted to 'I Got A Woman' by Ray Charles, which in turn nicked the melody from 'It Must Be Jesus' by Southern Tones. Or take 'Bittersweet Symphony' by the Verve, regarded by critics as one of the best songs of all time. It samples an orchestral cover of 'The Last Time' by the Rolling Stones, which is itself a remix of a song by the Staple Sisters! This practice of copying, combining and transforming is visible throughout culture. The printing press was one the most transformative technologies of all time when it was invented by Johannes Gutenberg. It relied on the ancient technology of the wine press.

We even borrow from nature. The science of biomimetics is about exactly this: imitating nature in order to solve human problems. For example, Velcro was conceived by Swiss engineer George de Mestral in 1941 when he decided to look more closely at the burdock burrs he found clinging to his clothes after a hunting trip. De Mestral inspected the burrs under his microscope and discovered that they were covered with thousands of tiny hooks.

These hooks had attached to the looped fibres in the fabric of his clothing. De Mestral realised that, if he could create a synthetic version of this fabric, he would have a new way to fasten things together – one with huge market potential.[33]

Creativity researchers call this process *conceptual transfer*, otherwise known as analogical thinking. Analogies help us solve problems. To be creative, it helps to be aware of as many analogies as possible to the problem we are trying to solve; being interested in the world really helps, as our next example of biomimetics will show. Japanese 'bullet trains' are super-fast trains, among the quickest in the world. This speed brought with it a problem: noise pollution. Every time one of these bullet trains entered a tunnel, it forced air out of the other end of the tunnel, resulting in a loud boom and disruptive vibrations that would shake the homes of nearby residents.

Lead engineer Eiji Nakatsu was a keen birdwatcher and realised that the kingfisher had an analogous problem. The bird had to dive at high speed from air into water with barely a splash. What made it cut so cleanly into the water? The shape of its beak. Which begged the question, what if Nakatsu designed the nose of the bullet trains to replicate the shape of the kingfisher's beak? His team built a prototype and tested the new design, to huge success. It not only reduced the boom effect, it also increased speeds and reduced energy expenditure. All thanks to birdwatching.

The second technique you can borrow from improvisers to have more creative sparks in your life is collaboration with others. We're going to look at collaboration in depth in Chapter 5, but it's worth exploring here too. If we think about creating new ideas as connecting the dots (existing ideas and stimuli), then we need to come into contact with as many dots as possible. This is the reason improvisational troupes are so extraordinarily creative. Each member brings their own vast store of ideas, influences and experiences. An improv show is a hadron collider of minds, designed to maximise the number of creative collisions between all the different players – which more often than not leads to serendipitous connections and discoveries.

In increasing the number of collisions between us, collaboration increases our exposure to different analogies. This is crucial when we're trying to solve problems, as it helps us avoid fixation. Fixation is when our thinking becomes whorled in on itself, compacted and circular, like tinned tuna. When we get stuck in a rut of looking at problem from one angle, a new analogy completely opens up our mind and allows sparks to fly again. Want to be more creative? Then surround yourself with a diverse network of other minds and jam with them.

How can you do this in your day-to-day life?

- Ask yourself: *Can I team up with someone else for this project?* What you lose in control, you gain in creative potential.

- If it's not possible to team up, then don't wait too late in the process to share your work with others. Pitch your rough idea or show an early draft to other people and see what their thoughts are. The earlier you do this the more likely you are to be open to changing your approach, as you'll have less energy, time and ego invested in the process.

- Aim to get the input of a broad church of people – so, not just people who are like you. This way you'll get a more diverse set of perspectives which will open your mind to other ways of seeing what you are, and could be, doing. (It's especially important to involve the potential audience for your idea.)

- Beware that most people are nice and will lie to your face without necessarily meaning to! For example, you pitch them your new product idea, and they'll say: 'Oh yeah, I would definitely buy that!' Therefore, you need to ask good questions. What is a good question? One that makes it easy for colleagues and friends to point out flaws. For example, 'Imagine this [presentation/product/etc.] failed. Why did it fail?' When author Tim Ferriss asks friends for feedback on his book manuscripts, he asks them: 'If you had a gun to your head, and you had to tell me what 10 per cent of this chapter to cut out, what would it be?' According to Rob Fitzpatrick in his book *The Mom Test*: 'You should be terrified of at least one of the questions you are asking in every conversation.'[34] That's pretty good advice.

BREAK YOUR HABITS

If you want to generate more creative sparks, be interested and collaborate with others. There's one final thing that can help you too: *break out of your usual habits*. Too often in life and at work, we drift through on autopilot, doing the same things, in the same places, with the same people. If we always stick to what we know, we will never be creative. Instead, we need to break out of our old scripts, to play in spaces where we don't yet have the answers. If you want to jump-start your spontaneity, you need to try something different. You need to change your habits of action and your habits of thought. Here are three ways you can do exactly that.

1. Try something different

Stuck in a rut? Then change something. The change might be extreme, like switching job, but it doesn't need to be. Read something you'd never normally read. Dabble in a hobby you'd never normally try. Listen to a different podcast. Take a new route to work. You get the point. The fundamental principle is that it is much easier to act yourself into a new way of thinking than it is to think yourself into a new way of acting. Thinking differently starts with doing different things.

2. Set new goals

Your brain is amazing at solving problems. When you give it a goal, it immediately starts coming up with ways for you to achieve it. But sometimes goals get stale and your brain switches to auto-pilot. The solution is to set yourself new goals. More than that, set yourself *big* goals. Business thinkers Lisa Goldman and Kate Purmal call this the 'Moonshot Effect'. When President Kennedy announced in 1961 that the United States would put a man on the moon by the end of the decade, many experts considered it impossible. And yet in 1969 it happened. This extraordinary goal inspired the creativity of thousands of people at NASA simply because this new, outrageously ambitious target forced everyone to think differently. It posed the question: 'If we were to go to the moon, what would we have to do to make it happen?'

What are your goals like? If you've set specific goals, they are likely to be incremental. Incremental goals are ones where you'd be happy with 10 per cent improvements. Perhaps you want to increase your salary, or your Twitter followers, by 10 per cent.

These are worthy ambitions and, as we'll see in the next chapter, incremental goals certainly are important. But do they challenge your thinking? If you want to incite the incredible power of your creative brain, try to think exponentially, rather than incrementally. Exponential thinking is all about how you can get 10× change. *What would have to happen for you to 10× your salary?* What ideas might your brain throw up then?

These exponential goals don't have to be obviously achievable in order to be valuable. As Edward De Bono – who coined the term 'lateral thinking' – puts it, these goals represent an 'intermediate impossible', valuable not because they are immediately practical in themselves but because of how they stretch our thinking. Want more and better ideas? Give your brain a bigger and more inspiring problem to solve. Stop hunting mice and start hunting antelope. It takes the same amount of effort. The trouble is, human beings aren't good at challenging their goals. We are obsessed with climbing the next rung on the ladder – so much so that we don't pause to think: *Is this even the right ladder?* This brings us on to the next technique.

3. Ask different questions

If you want to be more creative, ask yourself better questions. The questions we ask ourselves are not neutral but are filled with assumptions about our goal, the problem we're looking to solve and the world. Questions, then, can either empower us or limit us because they define which boxes we look inside to find the answer. Good questions, however, are climbing frames for the mind. They put us in a very generative space.

A good alternative to brainstorming is a technique known as 'question storming'. Where brainstorming is all about finding solutions, question storming is all about identifying problems (or at least finding a new frame for an existing problem). It works like this:

▶ Exercise

QUESTION STORMING

- Identify the aspiration, project or challenge that you are trying to address.

  For example: 'Get more Twitter followers.'

- Set a goal for the number of questions you (or your team) are going to come up with in response. Remember to go for volume and set a deadline. For instance, 30 questions in twenty minutes.

  Examples might include: 'How could we piggyback off people with more followers?' 'What sort of content would our audience want to read?' 'Who are the role models in this area?'

- When you've generated lots of questions on a topic, identify the top five you are going to focus on answering. Pick the questions most likely to deliver impact.

  You'll find that by expanding the range of questions you ask yourself, you'll expand the range of ideas you can come up with. Your muse loves a challenge! Build it and they will come.

▲ ▲ ▲

CONCLUSION

The sparks of our imagination do so much more than telling us what to create; they also show us who we are. This is crucial in a world that so often forces us to be something we are not. We fall into roles perhaps we never envisaged for ourselves and then get stuck. We tell ourselves that one day we'll do what we *really* want to do. The trouble is, we censor who we are for so long that eventually we forget who we are at all. Spontaneity, therefore, is not just about discovery – it is about *rediscovery*. It is about remembering parts of ourselves we've ignored for too long.

This rediscovery of our 'authentic' selves is not always about remembering our past selves. It can also be about catching up with who we are now too, about realising that we've changed and that we want and need different things. Spontaneity allows us to throw off old habits of seeing and doing so we can be who we are today, not the person we were yesterday. Spontaneity, then, is also about *reinvention*. It is about re-connecting to impulse and giving ourselves permission to follow it. When we do that, previously impossible things become possible.

To return to a familiar theme of the chapter: spontaneity is not enough. Some of the most rewarding parts of our lives are the most consistent and the most planned. One only needs to think of our families, our friendships and (if we're lucky) our careers to see this. The need for balance is an age-old challenge. Scholars call it the Apollonian–Dionysian conflict.

Apollo and Dionysius are figures from ancient Greek mythology. Both sons of Zeus, they represent forces that are in constant tension in our lives: Apollo appeals to rational thinking, order and prudence; Dionysius appeals instead to emotion, instinct and chaos. They were not thought by the ancients to be opposites or rivals but entwined: each necessary in our lives, but not sufficient without the other. Chinese philosophers have a similar concept in Yin and Yang, which says that seeming opposites like light and dark are interdependent and complementary.

In a similar way, spontaneity is harnessed by reason, but this reason is meaningless without spontaneity. The improviser's premise is that too often in life we over-balance towards Apollo and lose the illuminating force of Dionysius in our lives. To be more fulfilled, sometimes we need to stop thinking so much and start *playing*. Doesn't that sound much more fun?

Chapter 4

FAILURE

'Courage is resistance to fear, mastery of
fear – not absence of fear.'[35]
—Mark Twain

A diamond ring, a zippo lighter, a crumpled love letter. All exhibits in the Museum of Broken Relationships in Zagreb. Conceived by two Ukrainian artists when their relationship fell apart, the museum is a collection of items and stories donated by people who have suffered similar disintegrations. It's a melancholic reminder of the impermanence of love, of the inevitability of heartbreak and the ashes passion leaves when it burns out. Where once that love letter was a symbol of glorious hope, now, sat on a plinth encased in glass, it seems a monument to naivety. Nowhere is failure more present and more painful than in love.

But failure's sting is omnipresent. We fail at work; we fail in the gym; we fail in the kitchen. We fail everywhere and every day. It is essential, therefore, to learn how to fail well. In this chapter, I hope to show you how to do exactly that. We will learn that failure isn't simple. Much like the end of a romantic relationship, failure is rarely black and white. Instead, we will get to know failure in all its nuance, to avoid the human habit of exaggerating failure until it looms over us, a monster of our own creation. It is the stories we tell about failure that give it power.

We'll look at having a strategic relationship with failure: to treat failure as a tool we can use deliberately, rather than simply as an unfortunate event we suffer from. We don't want to fight failure. Fighting failure makes it seem as if defeat is permanent, as if failure is the opposite of success. Failure is not our enemy, nor is it our friend; it's like a sibling. We don't get to choose it. It will always be there. And our attitude to it will define whether it irritates us or not.

Let's not sugarcoat it. Despite trite aphorisms like, 'Everything happens for a reason,' the fact is that failure changes us. But the nature of that change is down to the story we tell ourselves about it. Is it an empowering or a disempowering story?

Martin Seligman's work on positive psychology shows that people who are depressed tend to exhibit 'learned helplessness', interpreting their failures as personal ('It's my fault'), pervasive ('I'm a total failure') and permanent ('I can't change'). By doing so, they give away control to their environment. Positive psychology offers the depressed person a way of reframing their experiences in a kinder (and more accurate) way, so that they can regain agency. In the same way, having a healthy relationship with failure is not about lying to yourself. It is about telling yourself the truth. The nature of that truth is the subject of this chapter. We'll discover that failure really is nothing to fear.

Our lives seem more filled with failure than ever before. There are two culprits, I think. First, the sheer speed of change requires us to surrender old, comfortable skills and learn new, unfamiliar ones constantly. Inevitably this is a rocky road. Second, the ubiquity of feedback these days means that there is always something for us to work on. In the modern world we need to be failure fit. With that in mind, let's head to the gym.

ERROR IS THE BEDFELLOW OF INVENTION

Improvisers talk a lot about how to deal with mistakes and failure because, given the difficulty of the art form, they're bound to encounter a lot of both. However, rather than merely 'deal' with mistakes when they occur, improvisers actively celebrate them. What's important isn't whether or not we make mistakes but our attitude towards them.

To show you what I mean, I want to tell you about two mistakes from the same improv show I performed in recently.

The first error went like this. A performer came out onstage alone to begin a scene. He bellowed his initiating line: 'I hereby call a meeting of the Famous Five!'

Hearing his offer, five of us fellow players joined him onstage. The consequence being that this meeting of the so-called Famous Five now had six people in it. We'd made a cock-up.

Not skipping a beat, the player who began the scene looked at one of our assembled group and said: 'Look, man, this interning thing isn't working out. We're going to have to let you go.'

Being an experienced improviser, this player responded with a strong emotional point of view. 'What do you mean?!' he said. 'The Famous Five is MY LIFE!'

Quickly the scene became a sketch about how hard it is to dump a friend that just won't take the hint. A crisis was averted, and the audience loved it.

The second mistake came later in the same show. I was in a scene with one other player. We were in an office kitchen, making tea, and it was a struggle. I felt like I was wading through treacle and the audience were not on-board. Then, a couple of minutes into the scene, I accidentally called this other character by the wrong name. I had no idea I had done so, but the audience were certainly aware of it. The audience notice *everything*.

So, rather than ignore my mistake, my colleague said to me: 'How do you know my *real* name?' It brought the house down. Our sketch suddenly stopped being a humdrum scene about office small talk and became a gripping Cold War-flavoured epic. My mistake had revealed that this 'office worker' was actually an undercover spy. Entirely by accident, I had made an original move.

The lesson here is that mistakes can become offers if we treat them as opportunities rather than problems. An improviser's default reaction to a mistake is not, 'Oh no!' but instead, 'How can we use this?' As jazz legend Miles Davis once said: 'It's not the note you play that's the wrong note – it's the note you play afterwards that makes it right or wrong.' Improvisers treat mistakes as gifts because they expand our range of possible creative connections in a very lateral way. For example, in the scene above about the undercover spy, we couldn't possibly have got there without my error. The greatest strength of that scene, the aspect that made it original, was the mistake. The stumble didn't just become part of the dance. It became the whole dance.

Mistakes can also lead to chance discoveries offstage too. It is often simply a matter of reframing; what is not functional for one purpose may be functional for another. Some of the most valuable products in the world have arisen in this way. Everything from penicillin to Instagram to the humble Post-it Note arose out of what was initially considered to be error. Post-its evolved from 3M research scientist Spencer Silver's attempt to create an ultra-strong glue for use in aircraft construction. The adhesive he ended up creating turned out to be the opposite. Weak and easy to peel away, it was not fit for purpose. But Silver didn't give up on it. He was sure it could be used for something.

For more than five years he searched in vain for a way to use his new glue in a product. Then one day he met a 3M colleague called Art Fry. Fry had heard Silver mention his mysterious glue in an internal seminar and a couple of days later he had a brainwave. A keen chorister at his local church, Fry had grown frustrated at how his bookmark kept falling out of his hymn book at inopportune moments. Could Silver's new weedy glue solve the problem? The rest is history. 3M now make more than $1 billion from Post-it Note sales every year.

PRODUCTIVE FAILURE

What makes improvisation unique as an art form is that mistakes are – paradoxically – part of a successful show. Beyond the discoveries mistakes make possible, improvisers soon learn that the audience actively enjoy seeing mistakes made onstage. Audiences want to see the performers walking a tightrope. They want to see them wobble and recover. And sometimes they want to see performers fall off the tightrope entirely, just to know it's dangerous. Without mistakes an improv show wouldn't be the same. Because, just as when you have a BBQ you want to taste the burn on the food a little, in improv you want to taste the failure.

This is all very well, you might be thinking. But in the environments in which you live and work, mistakes don't make the product better at all. It's true that most mistakes don't fall into the serendipitous or entertaining categories. A lot of mistakes are simply a pain in the arse: for example, embarrassing typos in an email, missing a meeting because you forgot to put it in your diary or snapping at a colleague when you're tired. In the interests of clarity, it's useful to have a taxonomy of failures here. Amy Edmondson, a professor in leadership and management at Harvard Business School, has produced exactly that. She outlines three different kinds of failure we might encounter in life: *preventable failures*, *complex failures* and *intelligent failures*.[36]

Snapping at colleagues, missing meetings and typos are all examples of preventable failures. They are easily avoidable with a little more care, and it's hard to see if anything positive can come from them. If we were being generous, we might identify the small learning that may arise from each mistake (for example, double checking the copy of your next email before you send it). In lieu of much of a silver lining, you just apologise for preventable failures and try to do better next time. We all make these sorts of mistakes and so, with a bit of contrition, most reasonable people will forgive you and move on.

While we want to avoid preventable failures, complex and intelligent failures are much more useful. First, let's see what Edmondson means by a complex failure. A complex failure occurs when, despite our best attempts, despite following best practice processes and protocols, things still go wrong. In short, in a very complex and volatile world, sometimes shit happens and there isn't much we can do about it. This is because it is not possible to understand every aspect of a complex system and so outcomes are hard to predict. A good example of where complex failures might occur is in the aviation industry, as explored in depth by Matthew Syed in his book *Black Box Thinking*.[37]

Airlines follow endless procedures and checklists to ensure every flight goes smoothly, yet problems do occur. Still, airlines these days have incredible safety records. The accident rate hovers around 0.25 per 1 million flights. This is because of the focus the aviation industry has historically put on gathering and sharing data on mistakes and faults. Ironically, the safety of the industry now is based on a litany of previous failures. The takeaways here are that failures in complex environments are inevitable, no one is necessarily to blame for them, and they can be useful if we report and learn from them.

Finally, there's intelligent failure. This occurs when we're working in areas in which we don't have expertise or experience, areas that are unknown to us personally or uncharted in a broader sense, such as when we're trying to innovate a new product or service, solve a problem we've not encountered before or learn a new skill. In these cases failure is an essential part of the process. We don't just fail, as is the case with preventable failures, instead we fail forward. For example, according to chef Heston Blumenthal, The Fat Duck's famous bacon and egg ice cream was in development for over three years before it reached a fit state to be on the menu. It has since undergone more than 50 iterations. The learning from these accumulated failures led to the innovation. Why? It taught Heston what *not to do*.

Thomas Edison once famously said, of his efforts trying to produce a new battery: 'I have not failed. I have found 10,000 ways that won't work.' Edison did not consider this a failure because he was trying to bring something new into the world. To make the unknown known. To do this, there is no instruction manual. You can only do it through trial and error. In this context, failure is intelligent. If you don't know what to do (and there is no best practice example to follow), then you should keep trying stuff until you find the answer. But it's important to emphasise that the goal is not to fail, the goal is to succeed. We don't want to simply fail *more*. We want to move from failure to success as quickly as possible. In order to do that we have to fail faster.

ACCELERATE YOUR RATE OF FAILURE

In his groundbreaking workshops, improvisation teacher Keith Johnstone would tell his students that if you want to get skilful at something you should *accelerate your rate of failure*. This stemmed from his struggles in learning how to draw, in particular learning how to draw human faces. In his book *The Natural Way to Draw*, the artist and teacher Kimon Nicolaides writes that an aspiring draughtsman must make 5,000 mistakes before he or she is adept enough to correct them. Johnstone took his advice and, over the next year, completed his 5,000 attempts at drawing faces, acting on the logic that if it's going to take 5,000 mistakes to get good then you might as well cycle through them as quickly as possible. Despite frequently feeling he was making no progress at all, Johnstone eventually went from inept to excellent.[38]

A significant aspect of learning a new skill is experience. We can't just pick up the skill from reading about it in a book. We have to do it and get it wrong in order to learn how to do it right. The trouble is, if we don't understand this, we're liable to give up trying entirely. And that really will condemn us to failure. Swathes of research shows that high performance takes a great deal of time to achieve in any field. In the arts this has been characterised as the 'ten year rule,' as identified originally by psychologist John Hayes in 1989.

Hayes found that it takes years and years of effort for a creative person to acquire the knowledge and skills to produce work of a noteworthy calibre.[39] The ten year rule is a crude estimate, with different lengths of preparation time seemingly needed in different domains. He found that composers, for example, didn't create any of their significant works in the first ten years of their career. Painters took on average six years. Poets five. Research on expertise beyond the world of creativity by Anders Ericsson – immortalised by author Malcom Gladwell as the '10,000 hours rule' in his book *Outliers* – suggests that being world class at anything takes a huge amount of 'deliberate practice'.

Clearly, staying the course will require us to be resilient in the face of failure. This fact is relevant not just to those on the path to excellence themselves but to anymore who manages a team, too. As Amazon founder Jeff Bezos pointed out in his annual letter to investors in 2018, communicating realistic expectations around scope is crucial if we are to help people reach high performance:

> A close friend recently decided to learn to do a perfect free-standing handstand. No leaning against a wall. Not for just a few seconds. Instagram good. She decided to start her journey by taking a handstand workshop at her yoga studio. She then practised for a while but wasn't getting the results she wanted. So, she hired a handstand coach. Yes, I know what you're thinking, but evidently this is an actual thing that exists. In the very first lesson, the coach gave her some wonderful advice.
>
> 'Most people,' he said, 'think that if they work hard, they should be able to master a handstand in about two weeks. The reality is that it takes about six months of daily practice. If you think you should be able to do it in two weeks, you're just going to end up quitting.' Unrealistic beliefs on scope – often hidden and undiscussed – kill high standards. To achieve high standards yourself or as part of a team, you need to form and

proactively communicate realistic beliefs about
how hard something is going to be – something
this coach understood well.

One of the most important things we emphasise with students in
our improv classes is to expect failure as par for the course and
that getting good will take time. Rather than depressing people,
we find it relaxes and emboldens them. All they want to know
is that their *failure is normal*. We constantly reassure them that
their progress won't be a straight line but a game of snakes and
ladders. Some days they'll feel great, some days they'll feel useless. It's important neither to get too pleased with yourself when
it goes well nor to punish yourself when it goes badly. The key
thing, regardless of whether you are coming back off a success or
a failure, is to keep on moving forward through your repetitions.
This relentless focus on the journey, or the process, rather than
the on outcome, allows you to learn most effectively. And the way
you think and talk about failure is the most essential element in
staying on that journey.

HOW WE TALK ABOUT FAILURE

The reason we need to be careful in how we talk about failure
is that losing optimism can be the biggest barrier to us meeting
our learning objectives. Learning anything worth knowing is hard,
both mentally and emotionally, and maintaining a long-term perspective is crucial if you are to reach mastery in the end. This
long-term perspective is what psychology professor and bestselling author Angela Duckworth calls 'grit'. She studied children
and adults in a variety of challenging settings, such as West Point
Military Academy, the US National Spelling Bee competition and

the toughest schools in America, trying to answer the question: 'Who is successful here and why?'

Her research showed that it wasn't those with the highest IQ or emotional intelligence or the best physical attributes. It was those people with the most grit. As Duckworth describes it:

> Grit is passion and perseverance for very long-term goals. Grit is having stamina. Grit is sticking with your future, day in day out. Not just for the week, not just for the month, but for years.

The challenge, then, is how to keep up this sort of enthusiasm for the long term when you encounter the painful setbacks that we so often suffer when going after our most desired goals. According to Duckworth, you need to develop a 'growth mindset', a phenomena first identified by psychologist Carol Dweck. Dweck's theory arose out of her desire to solve the puzzle that, while some students in school are able to overcome challenges, other students are flattened by them. After studying the behaviour of thousands of children, Dweck coined the terms 'fixed mindset' and 'growth mindset' to explain what happens. Her studies showed that students who thought talent was given at birth and was unchangeable (a fixed mindset) saw failures as a judgement of their innate ability. However, students who saw their talent as changeable with hard work (a growth mindset) viewed their failures simply as a judgement of where they were *now*.[40]

What's more, whereas students with a fixed mindset were likely to avoid situations where their lack of talent might 'be exposed', students with a growth mindset were likely to seek learning opportunities outside of their comfort zone. After all, they had nothing to hide. Failure didn't mean that *they* were a failure, it just meant they were 'not yet' a success. This final point is crucial because we improve our skills most when we practise them in 'the ugly zone' – a phrase coined by acclaimed sports coach Dave Alred MBE to refer to when we are operating just beyond our current level of ability at a particular task. To get in the ugly zone we need to stretch ourselves, and that means being comfortable making mistakes.

According to former chess Internationl Master and tai chi world champion Josh Waitzkin in his book *The Art of Learning*, if you want to master anything in life you need what he calls 'an investment in loss'. This means that you have to accept performing worse for a little while as you try out new skills and approaches. Beginners are more likely to give themselves to the learning process in this way because, unlike those with more experience, they have less to lose. For those who aren't beginners in a particular skill, the key takeaway can be put in more prosaic terms: if you want to get better at it, *give yourself permission to be shit.*

Beyond having a growth mindset and making an investment in loss, here are six practical tips and exercises to help you think and talk about failure in a kinder, more useful way.

1. FOAM PIT THINKING

When snowboarders want to work on new tricks, they don't do them out on the snow. Instead, they first try them out in a foam pit. That way, any mistakes they make are lower cost. When they've perfected the trick in the safer confines of a training centre, they are ready to go out and do it for real in the snow. Stand-up comedians do a similar thing when they are working on new material – polishing their nascent jokes at smaller gigs in front of crowds who, lubricated by cheaper tickets, are more tolerant of their experimentation.

▶ Exercise

Is there a foam pit equivalent for a skill you want to be better at? For example, if you wanted to be better at public speaking, you might join a local Toastmasters club. If you wanted to write a book, you might start a blog.

▲ ▲ ▲

2. THE MILK BOTTLE ILLUSION

In the documentary *Becoming Warren Buffet*, Buffet's right-hand man, Charlie Munger, tries to explain how Warren Buffet managed to grow his investment company Berkshire Hathaway from nothing to being worth over $60 billion dollars. He says it's simpler than it looks. Imagine, he says, a juggler juggling 25 milk bottles. You look at this juggler and think: *How on earth does he do something so extraordinary?* But what you didn't see is that this juggler started by juggling one milk bottle. Then he added another. And another. And so on. Each incremental milk bottle was only a small jump in skill and yet, when all added up, the progress becomes extraordinary.

This is what Matthew Syed refers to in his book *Bounce* as 'The Iceberg Illusion'. When we see a successful performer, we only see the tip of the iceberg: their excellent performance. We don't see what lies beneath the water level: the struggle that went into producing it. Once you understand the whole picture you see that, while talent is obviously not irrelevant, it's not enough by itself. Star performers have had to push through innumerable failures, just like you.

▶ **Exercise**

Knowing that the greats are not so different from you and me helps us maintain optimism when things get tough. So, pick up some biographies or watch some documentaries about star performers in your chosen field. Often what is most inspiring is not their extraordinary successes, but their very ordinary failures.

▲ ▲ ▲

3. SET THE RIGHT SORT OF GOALS

There are endless books dedicated to the virtues of goal setting and the best way to set them in your personal and professional lives. While goals are important in structuring the direction of our time and energies, what's more important if we are to keep perspective with failure is to set the right sort of goals. What are the right sort of goals? In addition to 'be good' goals, such as 'Get a book deal', you should also set incremental 'get better' goals that focus on the process rather than the outcome. For instance, 'get better' goals for the writer might be:

- Write 500 words every day.

- Read two novels a month.

- Contact five literary agents over the next six months.

The good thing about setting 'get better' goals is that you are less likely to fall victim to comparing yourself with others. After all, another person getting a book deal does not stop you from becoming a better writer. Rather than trying to win a race, you are simply trying to set a personal best. And clearly, if you get a lot better at your chosen skill through meeting your 'get better' goals, becoming successful in terms of the outcome goal is more likely anyway.

▶ Exercise

Take your most important 'be good' goal and make sure it is supported by a list of 'get better' goals that you can meet without achieving the main overall outcome.

▲ ▲ ▲

4. DON'T OVERCORRECT

One of the biggest obstacles to a healthy relationship with failure is that the language we use to talk about it is binary. We view things either as a 'success' or a 'failure', devoid of any nuance. This leads to either overly generous evaluations or overly catastrophic critiques, both of which focus on the outcome instead of the process which created it.

For example, I've clocked up thousands of hours of stage time. I've been everything on a spectrum from hilarious to awful. I've died onstage lots and lots of times. Were those bombs failures? Well, I certainly didn't achieve the outcome I wanted. My aim was to make the audience laugh, and they didn't laugh; so in those terms I failed. But there were lots of things I did do well in those shows. For example: I listened well; I always supported my fellow players onstage even as it became apparent the ship was sinking; there were many moments of creativity; and I had the courage to enter the arena in the first place. In many ways, therefore, I succeeded in those shows.

Improvisers learn to debrief their failures with this sort of texture: to include more elements on their scorecard than simply 'pass' or 'fail'. They see not just the outcome of the show but also the technical side of the performance that helped create it, and the context in which the show happened. With a comedy show, sometimes it genuinely is the audience's fault! Sometimes the room is swelteringly hot and so they're bad-humoured. Sometimes the room isn't dark enough and so they feel weird laughing (strange but true). Sometimes the whole audience turns out to be a load of non-English-speaking Dutch adolescents (genuinely happened to me once). Failure is different in this context, and so an appropriate analysis should take this into consideration.

▶ Exercise

I find daily journaling on my performance to be one of the most import-ant rituals in my life. If you want to try it out yourself, try writing in a notebook just before you go to sleep each night, for five minutes or so. My reflection is structured into three segments. First, what went well; then, things I could have done better; and finally, the one big thing I am going to focus on tomorrow.

▲ ▲ ▲

5. BUT DON'T UNDER-CORRECT EITHER!

Deliberately reflecting on what went well in a performance, as in the journaling exercise above, takes much of the sting out of a failure. You realise that things are often not as catastrophic as they seem. But while you don't want to overcorrect your behaviours after a failure, you don't want to under-correct them either. Failure can be inspiring if it leads to insights that help you towards your long-term target. But you've got to harvest these insights first. It's amazing how much learning can be squeezed out of each performance with a transparent and structured review. Try the exercise below to see how you can facilitate this sort of reflection with your own team.

▶ Exercise

It helps to schedule a regular time or place for your debrief. As an improv group, we'll do it at the beginning of the next rehearsal for twenty minutes or so. To get the most out of a group debrief, structure it around these four key questions:

- **Did we hit or miss our objectives?**

- **What caused our results?**

Try to get to root causes rather than the easy, surface level conclusions. The '5 Whys' test is useful here. This is an exercise borrowed from management consultants where you ask 'Why?' five times in a row to get to the true cause of a success or failure. For example:

> 'The audience didn't laugh.'
> 'Why?'
> 'Because the show was confusing.'
> 'Why?'
> 'Because we didn't listen.'
> 'Why?'
> 'Because the cast arrived late and we were flustered.'

And so on.

- **What should we start, stop or continue doing?**

- **What do we specifically need to do next?**

For insights to stick, they need to be captured and turned into tasks. *What has to happen next? What is the first step? Who is going to do that and when?*

▲ ▲ ▲

6. PRAISE AND CELEBRATE THE RIGHT THINGS

A final and important point here is that we can't control how others perceive our work or whether they will consider what we've done a 'success' or 'failure'. I know from bitter experience that in any gig, even in a sea of laughing faces, there will be always be people who look like they've sat on a spike. This has consequences for what we praise and celebrate, for ourselves but also for our colleagues, friends and children. Rather than praising the successful achievement of an outcome, it's more important to praise the *effort* and *character* that went into the process. After all, effort and character are within our locus on control, whereas success, as perceived and defined by others, often is not. In fact, Carol Dweck counts this sort of praise as one of the most important aspects of developing a growth mindset in both ourselves and others.

So, if we prepare a brilliant presentation for a job interview, but are pipped at the post by another candidate, we need to learn to celebrate the work and creativity we put into it, rather than writing the whole thing off as a failure because we didn't achieve the desired outcome.

I came across a good example of this principle in action at an advertising agency I worked with recently. This agency not only displayed the creative work that clients bought, but also the work they prepared for pitches that they didn't win. The title of the exhibition was 'Work the World Wasn't Ready For'. What a great balm for those people who worked so hard on making it. And what a great way to encourage them to bounce into their next pitch with the same enthusiasm with which they tackled their last.

▶ **Exercise**

How often do we let success go unrecognised because we assume that the other person knows they have done a good job? As 'yes, and' sorts of people, we can do better than that. Think about a colleague, a client, a friend or a family member who did something recently that you thought was great. This thing can be as simple as cooking you dinner, doing you a favour or giving a presentation at work. Next, compose a short text message or email to them saying 'thank you', followed by a specific thing you appreciated about what they did. Specific is really important here. People say thank you all the time, but the thank you that makes our day is for something we thought no one had noticed.

▲ ▲ ▲

SUCH A SHAME

As we explored earlier, when you consider failure a learning event rather than a judgement of yourself, then it becomes easier to move on from. But for this to be the case, you do actually have to learn from the failure. The ideal response to failure is not simple persistence. Otherwise you are doomed to repeat the same mistake, with no benefit to your long-term growth. The ideal response to failure is, first, to own it by admitting that it's happened; second, to conduct a transparent, thorough and thoughtful analysis; and finally, to adjust your approach in an appropriate way.

We'll be looking at that final aspect in Chapter 6. Here we will focus on talking about errors in the first place. The trouble is, we often *don't* talk about them. We gloss over our own failures because we don't want to dwell on them. We gloss over other people's failures because we're nice! (We'll look at this more in our exploration of feedback in the final chapter.) And because we don't want to open that Pandora's Box: as soon as we get honest with others, they'll get honest with us. That's the last thing we want. So everyone muddles on in this conspiracy of silence, not learning as much as they could. The question is, why are we so terrified of failure?

Studies suggest that shame is at the core of our fear of failure.[41] This is the general feeling that, because we have failed, other people will love us less, and that we are less worthy of this love anyway. Clearly, we were not born ashamed. According to Dutch sociologist Johan Goudsblom, shame is *social pain*. It is inflicted on us by others. We associate failing with shame because others have shamed us for failing in our past. But who are these others? The poet Philip Larkin once wrote, 'They fuck you up, your mum and dad,' and the research on shame seems to bear this out.

Maybe your dad put pressure on you to be successful at his favourite sport and you fell short, disappointing him. Or maybe your mum once asked you: 'Why can't you be smart like your sister?' But it's clearly more complicated than that. Many of us have good relationships with our parents. I would argue that shaming people for failure is embedded much more deeply into the fabric of our culture. For example, we turn on the TV and see adverts that imply: 'Buy this thing and you too can be like this successful/gorgeous/rich person. *(Unlike now, you poor, ugly failure.)*' We log into our social media and see our friends sharing the highlights reel of their lives, and their humble brags to boot: 'If only I spent less time volunteering for charity I'd finally have time to drive this new Mercedes of mine!'

We're brought up in schools where day after day, week after week, year after year, we have our work tested and graded. Then we compete with our classmates to go to the best universities. Then we enter the job market and compete for promotions, salary and perks – inside companies that compete for clients, market share and profit. I don't lay this all out to make a political point; this sort of culture is not necessarily good or bad. I do so to show you that, in our relentlessly competitive culture, the incentives reward winning. And the stories we are surrounded with all feature the same implicit message: you are valuable if you succeed and you are less valuable if you fail. All this considered, is it any real wonder that we fear failure?

The trouble is, for people who really fear failure, all events where failure is possible are potentially shameful events. These people will therefore do almost anything to avoid them. But this means taking themselves out of situations where they are likely to build new skills or make interesting creative breakthroughs, the situations which carry the greatest risk of failure. Businesses are slowly waking up to this fact. They make all the right noises about wanting their employees to 'embrace failure' and its learning potential. But it's often empty rhetoric.

They like the idea of embracing failure (from what they've read in business books) without wanting the actual risks – practical and emotional – it entails. I was once commissioned to work with a marketing agency that specialised in the pharmaceutical industry. I was worried it was going to be a little dry. At the initial briefing, an executive proudly told me that the first of their two company values was 'Don't be afraid to make a mistake.' This was music to my ears! Maybe this wasn't going to be as hard as I thought. 'What's your second value?' I asked. 'Get it right the first time,' she said. I laughed out loud. But she wasn't joking.

The businesses that do get it right understand that it's not just the literal act of shaming that makes us feel shame. It is the idea that one *might* be shamed at some point in the future. Sociologist Charles Cooley coined the term 'looking glass self' to describe this phenomenon. It refers to the way we judge and feel about ourselves according to how we *think* others judge and feel about us. Shame is rooted in the imagination. This leads to another quite startling conclusion, put forward by the sociologist Erving Goffman: the mere anticipation of shame is enough to change human behaviour. To foster group creativity, we need to keep this front of mind.

SHARE YOUR FLOPS

A temptation when it comes to the fear of failure is to drown it in platitudes. 'You're brilliant!' we might say. 'You are so talented!' The trouble with this approach is that shame is such a powerful emotion that, when we receive these lovely messages, we can't quite bring ourselves to believe them and so they change nothing. The solution is to come at our fear from a counterintuitive angle; rather than saying we're good, talented and wonderful, we should focus on the opposite. We should admit that, yes, we can be imperfect and messy sometimes. But so is everyone else. When we drop the aspiration of perfection and embrace our rough edges, the shame and fear associated with failure drops away. Surprisingly, the biggest thing we can all do to overcome our fear of failure is to talk more about our failures.

CASE STUDY: Sabrina Luisi, charity fundraiser

One of the biggest things I've taken out of improv is how I talk about failure. During my improv training I started managing a team for the first time, and I instigated this little ritual where every week at the team meeting we'd have a 'Chumbawamba moment' where we'd all share an example of where we'd got knocked down and then got back up again! I have done this in every organisation I've been in since. I think it's important that we all get used to talking about failure so no one feels embarrassed to admit when it's happened. ■

The Italian design company Alessi has a private museum in which they display their flop products. In fact, they hold their weekly team meetings in there to emphasise that if they aren't failing then they aren't trying hard enough. Similarly, innovation researcher Dr Samuel West has curated the Museum of Failure in Sweden, showcasing over 100 failed products and services from some of the world's best companies, including toothpaste manufacturer Colgate's brief and disastrous foray into the heady world of frozen lasagne. Venture capital firm Bessemer makes a list of all the successful companies it refused to invest in publicly available, as their so-called 'Anti-Portfolio'. It includes such companies as Apple, eBay and PayPal.

Other huge, global organisations use awards to signal an appetite for failure. Tata has an annual 'Best Failed Idea' prize; Proctor and Gamble has a 'Heroic Failure Award'; and Astro Teller, Captain of Moonshots (really) at (Google) X, has instigated a reward every three months for the team who can boast the biggest failure. Not content with that, some companies also host their own Fuckup Nights, a global movement that originated in Mexico and now sees events all over the world where attendees present tales of their most inglorious balls-ups.

The simplest way we can destigmatise failure in groups is to sincerely share stories of how we personally have failed in the past. The word 'sincere' comes from the Latin 'sin', meaning without, and 'cere', meaning wax. It derives from a Roman practice in which goldsmiths making jewellery and other ornaments would use wax to smooth over the imperfections, blemishes or cracks in the metal to make them easier to sell. Sincere then is 'without wax': it is presenting yourself with all your imperfections to the world.

There is a strong culture of this in comedy. Comedians never tell stories about good gigs. It's the horror shows that are always the best! But it can be hard to model failure. It requires vulnerability – to drop the façade of Mr Strong or Ms Superhero and admit to the times when things went really wrong. But the good news is that, according to vulnerability researcher and bestselling author Brené Brown, vulnerability creates trust. Far from making you look weak in front of your colleagues, talking about your failures helps you establish rapport with others – all the while giving them tacit permission to fail too. The key takeaway is that the antidote to shame is not sympathy or pity – 'Poor you'; it is empathy – 'Me too'. Try the following exercise to see how you might apply a similar approach in your own daily life.

▶ Exercise

CREATE A FAILURE RÉSUMÉ

Your task here is to create an 'anti-CV'. It is inspired by an article in the science journal *Nature* by Melanie Stefan, a researcher at the University of Edinburgh. As Melanie writes:

'My CV does not reflect the bulk of my academic efforts – it does not mention the exams I failed, my unsuccessful PhD or fellowship applications, or the papers never accepted for publication. At conferences, I talk about the one project that worked, not about the many that failed.'[42]

So she created a failure résumé and published it to inspire her students. Here's how you can do the same.

1. **Create a chronology of your career from when you left education to now, and for each year try to remember specific failures from that time.**

2. **Put in as much detail as you can bear!**

3. **You don't have to release it to the public, but keep it as a living document.**

Update this by adding new failures to your anti-CV. You'll notice how most failures have no effect in the long run. But it will also change your relationship to failure as the process allows you to completely own them, with no obfuscation. And it allows you view them as milestones on the way towards successes. As Stefan writes: 'Sometimes I look back [at my failure résumé] and see how much I've actually struggled to be where I am. That's a powerful reminder that I deserve to be here.'

A related exercise that I am fond of is Collect No's. Collecting rejections is better than collecting successes, because if you only aim to collect yeses you're likely to not take enough risks. To start collecting more no's in your life, brainstorm some answers to this question:

4. **Where in your life would you benefit from getting more rejections?**

▲ ▲ ▲

YOU DON'T HAVE TO BE PERFECT

We feel such a pressure in life, especially in our professional lives, to be perfect. To present a front of infallibility, confidence and control. But, while we shouldn't deliberately aim to make mistakes, unchecked perfectionism can make us deeply unhappy. Claude Monet, for example, regularly took a knife to his own work, destroying almost 500 paintings throughout his career. Towards the end of his life, already an acclaimed artist, he said: 'My life has been nothing but a failure, and all that's left for me to do is to destroy my paintings before I disappear.' How sad that a man so brilliant could torture himself in this way.

Of course, you might argue that, regardless of how unhappy it made him, it was Monet's perfectionism that drove him to such creative heights in the first place. But we need a balance between striving and self-flagellation. We need to aspire without being paralysed. In my life, improvisation has been a great way to find this balance. Onstage, while I aim for excellence, I've learned to be kind to myself when I miss the mark. In improv training, there is a little ritual that emphasises this. It's called the *failure bow*. Rather than being an exercise in itself, the failure bow is an embellishment of other improv games, a simple add-on where participants are required to bow vainly whenever they make a mistake.

They are then applauded for it by the rest of the group as if the error were the performance we had all come to witness. The aim of this –admittedly cheesy – gesture is to help the students rewire their learned shame response to failure, that in-the-moment physical repulsion at their own mistake. We've all been there and felt what that's like. The chest tightens, the heart pulses, the stomach ties itself in knots. From the outside it looks just as uncomfortable: the eyes squeeze shut, the face grimaces, the head drops, the shoulders collapse downwards. This shame response is what improvisers battle against from their first improv class until their last performance. Learning to respond to shame rationally, rather than react to it emotionally, is a central part of the training.

In every class, in every rehearsal and before every show improvisers will play games that are designed to make them fail and celebrate it when they do – from tongue twister exercises they are guaranteed to mess up to exercises like Hot Spot, where they circle up and take it in turns to stand in the middle and sing short excerpts from famous pop songs. In games like Hot Spot, the focus is never put on your performance but on your *commitment* to the performance. You might not know the words, you might have a terrible voice, but when you are in the middle of the game, your job is to sing with everything you've got. It's your commitment that your coach will reinforce, not your success or failure. They'll say: 'Congratulations! Yes, you were scared. But you got up there and gave it heaps.'

Commitment is something beginner improvisers struggle with. It's a classic fear response. They don't want to take something so silly so seriously in case they get judged for it. Or, subconsciously, they think that if they don't properly commit to something, it will make them feel less bad if they fail. After all, they didn't really try. When I first began improvising, I too dreaded these silly warm-up exercises. To me it just seemed like we were being silly for silly's sake. But eventually the penny dropped. The point of these embarrassing exercises was that they made me feel embarrassed! They forced me to constantly dance with discomfort. To feel that shame response in the pit of my stomach when I failed. To listen to what my inner critic was saying to me in those moments. To get used to his voice so that when I finally made it out onstage I realised that's all it was: my inner critic, mouthing off, trying to ruin my night.

YOU ARE NOT YOUR CHIMP

When you are stuck in the midst of Hot Spot, singing 'Simply the Best' by Tina Turner, your self-talk is fairly unambiguous:

> *You look like an idiot.*
> *You can't sing.*
> *You only know the chorus.*
> *Everyone here thinks you're embarrassing.*

Remember that your thoughts are not facts and, even more importantly, your self-talk is *not you*. The trouble is that so often we identify with these negative voices and assume we are just an unconfident, fearful person. We assume that other, braver people don't have these doubts. But confident people hear exactly the same voices as you do. They just recognise them for what they are and act anyway. Confidence is not an innate attribute you either have or you don't. Confidence is a thinking strategy that can be learned. So let's learn it.

This negative inner voice has been personified in various ways. Bestselling author Seth Godin calls it the 'lizard brain'; the novelist Steven Pressfield calls it 'the resistance'. Some refer to it as their 'inner critic', others 'imposter syndrome', and others prefer to call it their 'evil DJ'. The metaphor I prefer comes from clinical psychiatrist Dr Steve Peters. Peters made his name working with world-conquering British Cycling between 2005 and 2014, a period of unprecedented success for the team. Peters writes about his psychological model in his brilliant book, *The Chimp Paradox*.[43]

According to Peters, it's helpful to think of your brain as a machine. Like a machine, it's made up of different parts and each part does a different job. Peters breaks the brain down into six areas, but there are only three you need to focus on for our purposes here. First, there's your frontal lobe, the rational part of your brain which Peters refers to as your 'human'. Then there's your parietal cortex, or your 'computer'. This deals with skills you execute automatically, like driving. And then there's your limbic system, the emotional centre of your brain, which is your 'chimp'.

While the job of your human is to help you thrive, to go and do the things you really want to do, the job of your chimp is to help you survive. Often those two jobs come into conflict. Our brains are built for a different context than the one we now inhabit. As primitive man and woman, we lived in an environment full of physical threats. Therefore, we evolved a brain that could sense threat and stop us getting attacked. Fear was a very a useful emotion. If a lion was prowling around our camp, our chimp would panic and tell us to get out of there ASAP. However, we obviously live in a very different environment now. These physical threats have largely gone and yet we are still left with basically the same primitive brain.

What all this means is that our 'chimp' reacts to perceived social threats as it would do to a physical threat, that is, with a fight or flight response. This is manifested in you feeling nervous and also in the catastrophic self-talk that goes through your head in these moments. Very baldly, your chimp is saying, 'I don't like it here, we've gotta go,' even if that will undermine the projects that are important to you. Your chimp isn't just loud though, it's smart too. And your chimp can spin all sorts of convincing stories to make you leave the performance arena.

According to Peters, the crucial thing to bear in mind is that you are not your chimp. You and your chimp have very different values. Your chimp wants safety. You want growth. And you cannot grow without leaving your comfort zone. Therefore, your chimp is always going to be getting uppity. The thing to remember is that the thoughts it throws into your head are just suggestions. They are invitations to act a certain way. But you have a choice, and this is the inspiring thing. Because, while your chimp is not under your control, you can learn how to manage your chimp so as to thrive despite its often unhelpful nature.

Peters offers two basic strategies. The first is to *distract your chimp with a task*. In improv the task we focus on is listening. The key thing here is to get away from thinking about the outcome (as in, making the audience laugh) and instead to focus on executing the minutiae of the process (making the other person look good and so on). This strategy can be applied offstage too. For example, when you are giving a presentation at work, that 'performance' can be broken down into a series of process points which you can focus on executing one by one, rather than thinking about the overwhelming question of whether your audience likes you or not. For example:

- Making eye contact.

- Pausing after each of your main points.

- Communicating your three key messages.

The second strategy Peters offers is to *put your chimp in a box*. This involves observing, non-judgementally, what the chimp is saying and then feeding the chimp with facts and truths to counter its emotional arguments. Essentially, you are reframing the flight or fight arguments with more rational points of view. For example, when your chimp says: 'You're not funny. Why are you bothering?' You say: 'It's not about being funny, it's about being a good scene partner.' Or you say: 'I've done lots of successful gigs in the past; there is no reason why this shouldn't be successful now.' This next exercise will help you apply this offstage, too.

▶ Exercise

MEET YOUR CHIMP

This is an exercise that I've found effective in helping people who want to lose their fear of public speaking. But it can be easily applied to whatever area of your life where you experience a fear of failure. Get some paper and a pen and answer the following questions.

1. **Make a list of the phrases which come up in your recurring negative self-talk.**

   The aim here is to build your self-awareness so that when these thoughts come up you recognise them for what they are: the irrational mewling of your chimp. For example, with public speaking the recurring self-talk might be:

   People think I'm stupid.

   If I mess this up this is going to screw up my career.

   People are going to realise I don't know what I'm talking about.

2. **What is another way of seeing these negative statements that is more positive but true?**

   Go down the list of the negative self-talk phrases and rewrite them so that they are kinder, while also being believable. For example:

People think I'm stupid.
People want me to do well. After all, when I watch a
presentation, I don't judge the person giving it.

If I mess this up this is going to screw up my career.
If this goes badly then it will be disappointing,
but it's not important in the grand scheme of
things. Plus I'll learn lessons for next time.

People are going to realise I don't
know what I'm talking about.
I am expert in what I do and I've
prepared well for this presentation.

▲ ▲ ▲

I appreciate that this might all seem quite exhausting. But this is where the parietal cortex comes in. Once you consciously execute this reframing of your negative self-talk a number of times, you start to do it automatically. And performing (or whatever it is you are doing) suddenly gets easier. When you begin your improv career, it is impossible to imagine not being terribly nervous about a show. But as you get a lot of gigs under your belt, you earn the right to feel confident. Confidence is something that appears in the rear-view mirror. It comes from repeating our skills under pressure and delivering the goods.

The beauty of the Chimp approach is that you can learn to manage your nerves sufficiently well to throw yourself into the arena in the first place.

NOTICE SUCCESSES

We are coming to the end of our exploration of failure in all its nuance. Like a mackerel, iridescent as it swims past, failure looks different depending on the angle. The key thing is for us to maintain perspective – always seeking to keep the improviser's mindset of *treat everything as an offer*, in order that we can see mistakes as gifts and not as showstopping disasters. But before we finish this chapter, there is one final and big caveat: while improvisers think a lot about how to use failure, they also think an awful lot about how to use success too. After all, failure might tell us what not to do, but our successes, when noticed and understood, contain the recipes that allow us to repeat them.

There is a concept in comedic improvisation called the 'game of the scene'. The game of a particular scene is the element that is unusual or fun or that simply makes the audience laugh. An example of 'game of the scene' in a sketch is the classic *Two Ronnies* Mastermind sketch. In this scene, the game that makes the audience laugh is that Ronnie Corbett's character answers the question that came before, rather than answering the question that's just been asked. For example:

> **Q:** 'Who is the archbishop of Canterbury?'
>
> **A:** 'He is a fat man who tells blue jokes.'
>
> **Q:** 'Correct. What do people kneel on in church?'
>
> **A:** 'The Most Reverend Robert Runcie.'

The sketch lasts for two minutes and 45 seconds, and this simple game is played again and again and again. The audience know what is coming next, but they don't mind, because they are having so much fun. The scene is carefully scripted, whereas obviously an improvised scene is not. In an improvised scene, therefore, the 'game' emerges in the moment as the scene unfolds, which means improvisers have to be extra vigilant. When the audience laugh, this is a signal that we might have stumbled onto the 'game' of that scene. What's important, then, is for us as performers to notice the laughter and then to make a very quick analysis of why the audience is laughing. *What exactly is the 'game' they are enjoying? And why is it funny to them?*

When we've worked out what they are laughing at and why, we can then do a lot more of that funny thing. Sounds pretty easy when put like that, doesn't it? But if as performers we are stuck in a preconceived script about what we think the audience will find funny or interesting, it's easy to miss these success signals. Instead we just get on with our plan. Beginner improvisers struggle with this. They might get a laugh but not even register it. If they do notice the laugh, they lack the experience to understand what caused it. Or, if they do realise what the 'game' of the scene is, they refuse to let themselves play it again – much to the audience's frustration.

Imagine being in the studio audience for the Mastermind sketch, only for the performers to surrender the 'answer the question that came before' game after 30 seconds. You'd want to tear your hair out. Yet how often in life do we do exactly this sort of thing offstage? How often in life do we stumble into a success, no sooner to stumble out of it to try something else instead? As we've seen already, trying something else is a great strategy if you've failed. But it's a crappy one if you've succeeded.

I often wonder why people are so reluctant to build on their successes. The main reason, I think, is a familiar one for readers of this book. We are reluctant to let go of the plan for how we think our life, our business or our project should go, in order to address the feedback we are getting in the moment.

Perhaps another reason is that we are fearful. We worry on some level that this success is not enough, that either we must do something else to be worthy of the success (a form of imposter syndrome) or because we are worried about the consequences of being successful. Success is exposing. Suddenly the stakes are higher. *Don't mess it up!* we think, and the fear of failure grows. So, we leave the goldmine we've just discovered to begin the thankless task of finding another. We're back to the improv principle from Chapter 1: *Everything you need is already there.* All we have to do is be present to it and say 'Yes, and ...' to the offers inherent in our own successes.

Let me give you an example of some people who notice and build on successes extremely well: the pintxos bar owners of the Basque city of San Sebastian. San Sebastian is regarded by many as one of the gastronomic capitals of the world. But while it boasts some amazing restaurants, it is best known for the hundreds of little pintxos bars that densely populate the rat runs of the Old Town. Pintxos are the Basque equivalent of tapas. Hordes of tourists come every day to tour these bars and taste the best of what San Sebastian has to offer. The market is competitive, to put it mildly. So how on earth does one of these bars stand out?

Simply by noticing which of their particular pintxos is most popular and then doubling down on it, making that one dish the best version of it in the whole city. Take Bar Nestor, for example – one of the most successful pintxos bars in town. Their calling card is the humble tortilla. They serve it twice a day – at 1pm and then again at 8pm – and it is so popular that in peak season you have to get there hours beforehand to put your name down for even a chance of a slice. Bar Nestor have built a thriving business from basically selling one thing. They've realised that you don't have to be good at everything to stand out, just to build on a strength until it becomes a point of difference. There is huge confidence in having this sort of focus. So, what's your equivalent of Bar Nestor's tortilla?

▶ Exercise

LEARN FROM WHAT'S WORKING

In this exercise I am going to challenge you to get out of the 'fix it' mentality that so often dominates our thinking in life, where we focus on correcting the things that aren't going well or working on the things we can't do. Instead I'd like you to try the opposite attitude of doubling down on the good stuff. You can apply this exercise to yourself as an individual, to your company, or even to a project you are currently involved in. Here it goes.

1. Make a list of your super-strengths

What are the capabilities that you have in unique abundance compared to other people? It may be a broad skill or character trait, such as communication skills or warmth. Or perhaps you have a relative strength within your specific context. For example, a chef might be brilliant at sauces whereas a marketer might be brilliant at pitching to clients. Try to come up with a big list and then prioritise your top two or three. If you are struggling to come up with this list of strengths yourself, ask for feedback from colleagues, friends and family. Other people are often best placed to spot our successes.

If you want to apply this to your business, side-hustle or work project, rather than to yourself, you can still make a list of its super-strengths. For example, for a business, you might write 'large and engaged social media following' as a super-strength. And so on. The key thing is to always ask yourself the question: 'What's going well here?'

2. Double down

What else can you do with these strengths to maximise the returns on them? For example, if your company had a large and engaged social media following, you might choose to focus marketing investment here and aim to be 'famous' for this in the same way that Bar Nestor became famous for its tortilla. If your super-strength was your written communication, you might start an industry-focused blog. Try these questions below for starters:

- Does my current plan make the best use of my unique strengths or the strengths of my business/project?

- How can I use my strength more often?

- How can I dedicate more of my time and other resources to developing this strength?

- In what other contexts might I apply this strength?

3. Apply the same thinking to others

We often get into conflict with others because we become blind to their strengths and obsessed with their weaknesses. If you find yourself butting heads with someone, whether it be a colleague or even a family member, take some time to think about what they do well rather than just what they don't. This change of perspective can help you engage with them in a more positive way.

▲ ▲ ▲

THE ART OF THE SWEEP

There is one final, important point here. To follow our successes we need to create some room for them in the first place. This means that sometimes there are things we need to quit. 'Never give up' is bad advice. Instead we need to learn the art of the sweep.

'Sweeping the scene' is how improvisers end a particular sketch. One person jogs across the front of the stage to signal to the audience – and the other players – that this scene has finished and another one is about to begin. A scene is swept when the performers get the sense that it is no longer enjoyable or useful. For example, perhaps the comedic idea has worn thin for the audience. Or maybe the scene has begun to repeat itself.

But sometimes we sweep a scene because it just isn't very good! We draw a line under it and try something else. A sweep in this sense is a creative act. It is the first part of our next attempt to be successful. Sweeping a scene can be scary because it leaves a vacuum to be filled. Beginner improvisers will often let a terrible scene go on forever because they know that ending it presents a scarier situation than a bad scene: an empty stage.

How often do we do the same thing offstage, sitting in hopeless situations which make us miserable because we fear change more than we fear unhappiness? If a scene isn't working, we need to end it! By ending something that isn't working, we create time and space for something that might. Improvisers soon learn that, rather than being scary, sweeping a scene is empowering.

It shows us that we aren't stuck in any reality we've created. If we aren't enjoying it or if we aren't being successful, we can simply start over and create something new in its place. Improvisers know that there is always another opportunity, another scene, another show to come. No failure is permanent. We only fail when we don't try again.

CASE STUDY: Mike Indian, political journalist

I struggle with self-confidence. I am very shy and I tend to withdraw from people. In my line of work, that's difficult! I've also struggled with mental health problems in the past, particularly anxiety. With anxiety you are very much stuck in the future, catastrophising. It's a very self-centred condition. With improv, however, you are taught to live in the moment and put the focus outside of yourself. It wires you to pay attention first and foremost to other people, and this can help stop the loops of rumination.

Improv has also helped me be comfortable with failure because improv teaches you it's OK to make mistakes. I used to dwell on my mistakes, but improv has taught me to brush it off and get on with it. It's the equivalent of when you were a kid and you wanted to breathe on glass and draw something. It fades quickly. And you make something else. I've learned when to say, 'OK this has gone on long enough,' and to draw a line under the scene. Fundamentally, improv teaches you a way of looking at the world that stops you taking yourself too seriously. Because you learn that failure really isn't the end of the world. ∎

CONCLUSION

I began this chapter talking about love, and so maybe it's fitting that I return to love at the of end it. My favourite quote about failure comes from what you may consider a rather unlikely source: the Oscar-winning film, *Call Me by Your Name*. Based on the novel by

André Aciman, it tells the story of Elio Perlman who falls in love, accidentally, reluctantly, but deeply, with Oliver, an assistant to his father, Michael, an archaeology professor in rural Italy.

Oliver has come to stay for the summer from the United States, and their nascent relationship is cut off months later when he is forced to return home. Elio grieves for his lost lover, until his father, who he'd previously understood to be an uptight man and who he thought knew nothing of the relationship, offers some succour. Sat on the sofa next to his tearful son, Michael says:

> We rip out so much of ourselves to be cured of things faster that we go bankrupt by the age of 30 and have less to offer each time we start with someone new. But to make yourself feel nothing so as to not feel anything – what a waste.

Heartbreak is a very particular sort of failure – perhaps like no other. But Michael's sentiment is instructive in what we must avoid in the ruins of our worst disappointments. It is easy when we are foiled by disaster, broken by life, to stop desiring things, to narrow our horizons and flatten our emotional landscape. To do so might make us feel safe. After all, if we don't try, we cannot fail, and if we don't fail, we cannot hurt. Yet if we don't feel sorrow and pain, to turn to Elio's father once more, we cannot feel joy either. And without joy, what's left?

Chapter 5

COLLABORATION

'Ubuntu: I am because we are.'
—Ancient African proverb

Collaboration is central to our lives. We spend most of our time on this planet with other people building things, whether that be bringing up children, growing a business, raising money for charitable causes or almost anything else we do to find meaning in the world. In fact, the historian Yuval Noah Harari argues in his book *Sapiens* that it is humans' ability to co-operate that explains our pre-eminence on Earth over other species. Teamwork really does make the dream work, and it seems it always has done.

In our professional lives, our ability to collaborate is more important than ever before because, as we began to explore in the introduction to this book, our world is changing fast. I have run improvisation training programmes with companies all over the globe, including with huge businesses such as PWC, Unilever and Proctor & Gamble. They all come to me with a similar challenge, and many of them use the same metaphor to describe it. The world of work used to be like scripted theatre, they say. There was a director calling the shots. All the actors knew their roles in advance and were told where to stand, what to say and when. Their task was to learn their lines and deliver the same performance night after night. The goal of the organisation was to do the same as before, only better. But then the world changed.

The workplace is now organised much more like an improvised theatre troupe. While the director may still exist, they are less relevant than before. Instead, the team rules. The cast of performers on the front line see the problems and opportunities emerging from the audience first and so are best placed to respond to them the quickest. Collaboration reigns, ideas rise up from the bottom, and hierarchy is more fluid. Instead of the leader calling the shots, the cast take it in turns to lead according to whatever the situation demands. The goal of the new organisation is no longer to do the same but better. The goal of the organisation is to innovate, and faster, too.

To put it another way, the companies we work for are being organised radically differently in order to become more agile in an increasingly complex world. You might have noticed this already where you work. Research shows that we now spend 50 per cent more of our time in meetings compared to a decade ago. Some studies suggest that 85 per cent of managers' time at work is now spent collaborating.[44] And the nature of this collaboration is more complex than ever before. For example, we are seeing:

- A huge rise in remote working, especially in response to the COVID-19 pandemic.

- An increase in job specialisation.

- More diversity of all kinds, including of race, gender and age.

- The rise of cross-functional teams in which workers are increasingly required to focus on achieving a series of short-term goals, forming and disbanding rapidly as the business needs change.

- The rise of a 'network of teams' where we are part of several teams simultaneously.

- A rise in peer-to-peer knowledge sharing and feedback.

We all need to learn new skills to thrive in this new context – such as being able to co-create solutions to complex problems alongside a diverse range of people and personality types, to communicate with clarity and influence under pressure, to form trusting relationships quickly, and to step forward and lead rather than simply to follow. In this chapter, we'll borrow skills and approaches from improvisers to show you how you can be better at them all. Much has been written about 'collaboration fatigue', but, whether we like it or not, collaboration is a fact of life.[45] We might as well get good at it.

THE BENEFITS OF COLLABORATION

Improvisation is a good place to look for collaboration tips because improvisers have no choice but to collaborate effectively with one another. Their task is to go onstage with nothing and create a funny, coherent and often moving show entirely in the moment, solely by accepting and building on each other's offers. But improvisers don't just collaborate because they have to. Improvisers believe that the collective intelligence of the group working together is far bigger than the intelligence of any one individual acting alone. This collective intelligence is also greater than the aggregate of all the individuals that make it up. Improvisers call this concept 'group mind'; it is an example of a more general phenomenon known as 'emergence'.

Emergence occurs when something has a property that its constituent parts do not and could not have on their own. For example, one neuron is not conscious. But 1 million neurons interacting in the brain produces consciousness. You can see that when emergence occurs, more of the thing is not just more of the same, more is *different*. An example of emergence is a flock of starlings swarming. Starlings behave very differently when they fly together compared to when they fly alone. This swarming behaviour looks acrobatic and extraordinary to the human eye. Just as in an improv scene, it is hard to imagine that this incredibly ornate and seemingly choreographed display has emerged spontaneously. Yet that is exactly what is going on.

For years scientists struggled to understand how starlings managed to do something so complex. The mystery was eventually solved in 1986 in a computer simulation designed by an artificial life expert named Craig Reynolds. In this simulation, Reynolds managed to recreate this swarming behaviour by programming each artificial bird with three simple rules. First, separation: don't fly into another bird. Second, alignment: fly at roughly the same speed as the other birds. And third, cohesion: fly in roughly the same direction as the other birds. Those three simple rules of the road were all it took to create the swarm.

What's interesting about this example is how a few simple rules, followed by everyone in a system, can produce an amazingly complex effect. This is how improvisation works onstage. As we've explored already, complex and funny improvised performances emerge as long as each performer abides by the simple rules of:

- Say 'Yes, and …'

- Listen with the willingness to be changed.

- Treat mistakes as gifts.

In this chapter we'll add a couple more rules to the mix:

- Give and take focus.

- Follow the follower.

As we go, we'll discover that these five basic rules underlie effective collaboration offstage too.

GIVE AND TAKE FOCUS

A fundamental principle of improvisation is that an improviser must learn to both take focus in a show and also give it to their fellow players. In a show, the entire cast share equal responsibility for the creation of the performance. They sublimate themselves to the needs of the show. The question is not: 'What is fun or comfortable for me here?' The only question is: 'What does the show need?' Sometimes it needs you to come in and light a spark. Other times what the show needs is for you to shut up and give space to others to take the limelight for a while. This applies offstage too.

There are natural givers of focus and natural takers of focus in life. Both can have good or bad motives. Often we give focus because we want to give other people the opportunity to shine. Or perhaps we genuinely think that they have a great idea and we want to give them a chance to forward it. Trouble arises when we give focus as a means of passing the buck because we want to avoid taking a risk ourselves, to avoid scrutiny and accountability. This not only denies the group the gift of your perspective, it's also unfair on your colleagues because it puts pressure on everyone else to pick up the slack.

Similarly, those who routinely take focus for themselves can do so for good reasons. Perhaps they want to show leadership. They want to inject their energy, expertise and experience, so they take focus for themselves in order to help others. This habit can be useful in a crisis but, when stepping to the front is your permanent mode of being, it can become dysfunctional. Always being the leader means dominating the conversation and drowning out quieter voices. In a similar vein, always taking focus causes other people to disengage. *What's the point in speaking?* they think. *No one is going to listen to me anyway.*

If people don't become disillusioned by serial focus-takers, then they become complacent. After all, if someone else will always take responsibility and initiative, there is no need for you to do the same. We can see how managers can accidentally create a team of dependents unable to think or act for themselves. Once people fall into these complacent habits, it can be hard to get them out. It's a vicious circle. Micromanaging people turns them into people who need to be micromanaged, and so we micromanage them even more. But we forget it was our management style that made them this way in the first place.

FOLLOW THE FOLLOWER

Closely related to the principle of *give and take focus* is the improv tenet known as *follow the follower*. Coined by Viola Spolin back in the salad days of the art form, the best way to understand it is by looking at the exercise of the same name. Follow the follower begins with an assembled group of five or so people stood facing one another in a circle. They begin totally neutral, a blank slate. When the exercise begins, the aim is for every facial expression and action made by one person in the circle to be mirrored by everyone else. You are trying to notice and reflect as specifically and as fully as possible what every other person is doing, from their head to their toes. For example, if one person smiles awkwardly, everyone else smiles awkwardly. If one person taps their toes, so does everyone else.

The important thing is that there is no designated leader of the exercise. When there is a change in the group action, it happens by accident, when trying to mirror another movement. The point of this exercise is not to initiate and make things happen yourself, but to follow others. No one should control or direct the action. But the amazing thing is that the exercise soon becomes so organic that it is impossible to know who has started any given movement. It's like watching those starlings swarm. Everyone is following the follower. And what emerges is so extraordinary that it would have been impossible to choreograph or pre-plan.

If we translate this slightly esoteric exercise into an impro-vised scene, a similar principle applies. No one performer leads an improvised scene. But that doesn't mean to say that there is no leadership. It means that leadership oscillates between the various members of the group as and when the scene needs them to show leadership. Offstage, the principle of follow the follower means that as a leader, or as someone who likes to grab the bull by the horns, you don't have to initiate every idea. There are times when it's best to give focus to other people on the team and put your energy into supporting them instead, knowing that soon it will be their turn to return the favour to you.

Improvisers don't do this because it's polite; they do this so that they can be as adaptive to the moment as possible. You can't do that if only one person in the group gets to call to the shots: it's too bureaucratic and it's too slow. But more than that, it also prevents us from achieving 'group mind', where we all express and build on each other's ideas. At this point you might be thinking: *Max, this is all very well. But my company is not like an improv troupe!* I hear you and, to be clear, I do believe that organisations need leaders. I'm not arguing that we get rid of leaders altogether but that we get more inclusive, distributed leadership. How do we do that? It begins with understanding status.

STATUS BATTLES

The next time you have a meeting with your team at work, look at where people sit in the room. Notice who places themselves at the head of the table. Notice how people hold themselves and who takes up the most space. Notice who speaks first and who controls the agenda. Notice who interrupts the most and who is allowed to make a joke. Notice, too, who laughs at the joke. There is an invisible dynamic to any room and to all relationships: the often subconscious dance of status. When you become aware of it you'll begin to see it everywhere.

Our old friend Keith Johnstone describes the ubiquity of status exchanges in human relationships as the 'see-saw principle'. This principle holds that everything a person says and does is an attempt to either raise or lower her status relative to someone else. As the see-saw imagery suggests, if one person goes up in status, then the other person must come down. These status moves may be quite deliberate and aggressive. One only has to think of the infamous 'manspread' or the infuriating 'arm rest grab' we so often fall victim to on flights, to see that status demonstrations can be bold. But most status moves are subtler than that and many aren't even conscious.

There is one classic example that we see almost every day. Two people walk towards one another on the pavement. They look at each other: they're on a collision course. At some point one of them will have to give way to let the other pass. How is that decision made? They scan each other for status, and the lower status one moves out of the way, often without even thinking. As Johnstone says, 'Status is basically territorial,' and how we use space is a significant aspect of our status. To see this in action, go and watch a West End show. Where does the star stand for their big solo number? At the front of the stage, in the middle. Conversely, when you see someone very nervous at a party, where do they stand? In the corner, next to the wall, hugging their drink like it's a lifebelt. High-status people take up space, whereas low-status people do the opposite.

But we don't just take up space physically; we take up space verbally too. Status in this respect is denoted by how much, how loudly and when we talk. (The flipside is that status is also denoted by how much, how intensely and when we listen.) According to Johnstone, while our status can shift according to context, and during the jive of conversation, we all mainly inhabit a preferred status in life. We play a learned role that we are comfortable with. As Johnstone puts it: 'A person who plays high status is saying, "Don't come near me, I bite." Someone who plays low status is saying, "Don't bite me, I'm not worth the trouble."'

We can never entirely break the shackles of our learned status. But those who are most successful in life can play either role in order to pursue an outcome they want. Note that we're talking about 'playing' a status role. This is where Johnstone came to a profound conclusion. He realised that status is not just about who you are and your position in a given hierarchy (such as 'the boss'). Instead, status is something *you do*; it is a behaviour. You can act low or high status, irrelevant of your hierarchical position. In this respect, you might have a very high-status toilet attendant and a very low-status Pope. Because status is something we play, it is therefore something we can decide to temporarily *give* to another person – or indeed to take away from them by either raising or lowering our own status behaviour.

To many leaders I have worked with this seems counter-intuitive. Why on earth would you want to give away status to someone else? But this misunderstands the concept. By playing low status you are not losing status in the hierarchical sense. You still remain 'the boss'. All you are doing is loaning status to someone else for a while in order to bring them into the collaboration as a more equal partner. Of course, you might think that it isn't your responsibility to bring people into the conversation in this way. After all, why is it your problem that they are playing low-status? You might argue that this is their look-out. Surely it's their job to speak up if they've got something to add?

We're going to explore this idea in more depth a bit later on. But the point is that if the goal of collaboration is to unlock the collective intelligence of the group, then temporarily sharing status is a very good idea indeed. When we give people status it encourages them to contribute. The best way to equalise the status between you and another person (or team of people) is not to lower your own status but to raise theirs instead. Here are some specific tactics you can use to do exactly that.

HOW TO RAISE ANOTHER PERSON'S STATUS IN A MEETING

- **Watch where you sit in the room.**
  For example, make sure the seating doesn't reflect hierarchy. Do you need to sit at the head of the table? What if you sat next to the most junior member of the team instead?

- **Allow other people to come up with the first idea.**
  Rather than speaking first, why don't you speak last?

- **Proactively seek people's opinions and bring quiet people into the conversation.**
  For example, ask: 'Jane, what do you think about this?'

- **Ask for advice or help.**
  For example: 'I'm a bit stuck here, guys. What would you do in this situation?'

- **Express gratitude and appreciation for something that person did.**
  For example: 'Tommy, I just wanted to say thank you for working late on the pitch. I really appreciate it. You did a great job.'

- **Check in with your body language.**
  This is an easy one to get wrong. You want to avoid any overly dominant behaviours such as stretching out or leaning back in your chair. Make sure your

body language is open enough that it isn't closing you off from anyone else in the room. (If you don't look at me then I feel invisible.) And finally, if you are interested in what your colleagues have to say, then remember to tell your face! A smile goes a long way.

- **React to and engage specifically with what the other person has just said.**
  We covered this in depth in the 'yes, and' chapter. To recap quickly here, the 'yes' affirms that you have heard and understood what they said and the 'and' offers a bridge into your perspective.

Things to avoid

For improvisers, silence is a gift. We give it to others so they might literally and figuratively find their voice. It's obvious to say that other people cannot speak without the space to do so, and yet how often do we honour this truth? I've worked with hundreds of business leaders all over the world. Many come to me to solve the same problem: the team they manage just won't speak up in meetings! 'How strange,' I say. 'Let's talk about it some more.' We have a conference call; it lasts close to an hour; I barely say a word. I don't get the chance. That is at the extreme end of most people's behaviour, of course. But to avoid this sort of thing happening to you, if you'd like to encourage everyone to contribute, here are a few status behaviours to watch out for.

- **Saying 'Yes, but …'**
  As we explored earlier, shooting down their idea lowers their status and shuts down the conversation.

- **Speaking over someone or interrupting them.**

  If you do it by mistake then apologise and hand the focus back to them.

- **Dominating the conversation.**

  Leaders instinctively go first, in order to lead by example or because they think that it's in the job description to 'inspire'. But if you want to be more inclusive as a leader, you need to learn to go second sometimes. Or third. Or fourth. Focus on listening instead of talking. And remember that more junior people are unlikely to want to contradict you, so by speaking first you encourage homogeneous 'group think'.

- **Mistaking silence for agreement.**

  Silence is not the same as agreement. Just because someone doesn't voice an objection doesn't mean that they agree. It might just mean that they haven't been asked yet. Be aware that many more junior people will defer to seniority; you will have to explicitly give them permission to speak up.

RAISING YOUR OWN STATUS

Of course, many people often aren't aware of their own behaviour. We can't assume that those high-status individuals we have to collaborate with will be open-minded enough to bring us into the conversation and give us the focus we deserve. Sometimes we have to take it for ourselves. You might be someone who is temperamentally shy or introverted. And there's absolutely nothing wrong with that, despite the frequent cultural pushback against it. As psychologist Susan Cain has explored in her powerful book *Quiet*, the 'extrovert ideal' reigns strong, and introversion often feels like a 'pathology' we try to eradicate.[46]

But while people who play low-status are not worse than those who play high-status, the opposite is also true. Some people worry about raising their own status because they associate high-status behaviours with being arrogant or unsympathetic. However, you can still play high-status while having a humble and empathetic mindset. Just think of leaders like Nelson Mandela or Desmond Tutu. Being high-status is not about aggression or dominance. Nor do you have to achieve it by competitively lowering the status of other people. It is about presenting yourself so that you get your fair share of the airwaves, in order that you can put your point across in the most credible way possible.

Consider too that you don't have to *feel* the status you want to play. You don't have to walk into a room feeling totally confident; if required you can fake the behaviours of confidence. Soon enough you'll find that the feedback loop that exists between physiology and psychology will make you feel more certain of yourself. Here are some practical steps you can take to raise your status and achieve a greater personal impact.

- **Be aware of your physicality.**
  In 1988, psychologists Fritz Strack, Leonard Martin and Sabine Stepper carried out a fascinating experiment to test whether a person's facial expressions directly affected their emotional state.[47] They gathered two groups of people together. The first group were asked to hold a pencil between their teeth, thus simulating a smile. The second group

were asked to hold the pencil between their lips, thus simulating a frown. Both sets of participants were then asked to watch funny cartoons. Those participants who had a smile induced reported finding the cartoons more amusing than the frowners. It seems that changing your physiology really can change your psychology.

The feedback loop between our bodies and how we think and feel is studied in the growing field of embodied cognition. Some of the most famous, and widely debated, research in this field has been carried out by Harvard professor Amy Cuddy. Cuddy has identified five specific ways of holding your body, or 'power poses', that can make you feel more confident. (You can find out exactly what the poses are in her enormously popular TED talk, 'Your Body Language May Shape Who You Are'.) But before you run off to your laptop, let's take a look at what a confident physiology looks like.

The basics of it are that we want to take up space. We do that by sticking our chest out, shoulders back, head level as if it were being held up by a bit of string, with our feet roughly shoulders-width apart, toes pointed open. Dave Alred, in his book *The Pressure Principle*, calls this the 'command posture'. An easy shortcut to getting the pose yourself is to make sure that when you stand up your head is over your bum. This will pull your back in, which will push your chest out and get those shoulders back too, all the while maximising your height. (As a man who comes in at five foot eight with a head wind, I'll take all the help I can get!)

This technique also works well to help you sit up straight and draw focus here too. Again, this is not about dominating others or invading their personal space. All we are looking for is to avoid the submissive behaviours that undermine our credibility in the room and our confidence in ourselves. Remember, you don't need to make yourself smaller in order to give space to others. You have just as much right to it as they do.

- **Make and hold eye contact.**
  High-status people are comfortable making and holding eye contact.

- **Be calm and still.**
  Linked to the way we hold our bodies and maintain eye contact is the quality of our energy. Lower status people tend to have more of an anxious, frantic energy. They rush around, they fidget a lot, and their heart seems to be going like the clappers. To raise your status, concentrate on slowing down your breathing by putting focus on your diaphragm and taking deep breaths. When you speak, try not to rush – use pauses – and avoid fidgeting, such as touching your hair, face or clothes. If you have a problem with self-soothing behaviours like fidgeting, then try putting one hand in your pocket and using the other to gesture (or hold a glass). You can also

lightly clasp your hands together in front of your waist.

- **Try going first.**
  Taking focus immediately raises your status in a meeting, and getting your contribution in early is a great way to relax yourself into it. So try making the first suggestion in a meeting. Or, if meeting new people, then take the lead in introducing yourself and initiate the handshake.

- **Speak up.**
  High-status people share what they know, think and feel, even if it's in opposition to what other people think or feel. They also ask questions, make requests when appropriate, and speak directly and to the point. Not only do they do all of this, they do it at a volume that everyone can hear. So, be loud and proud!

- **Push back against interruptions.**
  Higher-status people are likely to interrupt you when you are speaking with comments or questions. You don't have to give in to them, certainly not immediately. Respond to an interruption with, 'Thank you, but I'm not finished yet. I'll address that in a moment.' This way you won't get side-tracked. Or simply continue as if it hadn't happened! Now that is really high status.

Things to avoid

We encountered these errors in Chapter 1 when talking about committing to speaking up, but they're so commonplace that it's worth reminding ourselves.

- **Asking for permission to speak or to ask a question.**
  For example: 'Do you mind if I say something?'

- **Self-deprecation.**
  For example: 'I appreciate I'm new here.'

- **Asking for reassurance.**
  For example: 'Was that OK?', 'Did that make sense?', 'Did I speak too much there?'

- **Apologising for speaking.**
  For example: 'Sorry, this won't take long …'

- **Self-censoring language.**
  Obviously some censorship is important to avoid being gratuitously offensive. But many self-censoring behaviours lower your credibility in the room, such as: dancing around saying the thing that you want to say; editing your sentences by trailing off; or using modifying words like 'quite' or 'maybe'.

- **Leaving decisions to others when you could just as easily take them yourself.**
  You'd be amazed how much people appreciate someone taking a decision.

CASE STUDY: Naomi Bowman, IT director in investment banking

I work in a heavily male-dominated industry, and it's still an old boys' club. I work mostly with men who are very high-status, including traders and salespeople. After doing improv training I notice speed of speech, volume, posture, eye contact and overall physicality a lot more clearly. Especially when meeting people for the first time, if I adapt my own physicality and speech to match theirs, it puts me closer to the same level of status and stops me feeling intimidated.

I spent the first six years of my career fighting to be recognised as someone who actually works there, rather than just 'a female'. I had to fight to be taken seriously before I could get on with my job. Subtly matching status has helped to limit the amount of time I have to waste convincing people I can do my job and means I can actually get on with it.

True high status also means being very relaxed about where you stand, so when one man refused to acknowledge me and only shook hands with and spoke to the man standing next to me, I walked away. In the past I'd have stood there and let his dismissive attitude affect my confidence. ■

UNLOCKING THE POWER OF DIVERSITY

The team needs everyone to speak up, and for everyone to be brought into the conversation, because ideas must come from everywhere in order to express the collective intelligence of the group. This rarely happens in practice. Historian Oswald Spengler once said: 'It only takes 2 per cent of the population to create the basic ideas and everybody else applies them.' If this is true at a societal level then it is also true at an organisational level. The term 'innovation inbreeding' has been coined to describe this phenomena. Most of the ideas in teams come from the same people all the time. What a waste of resources! Most businesses' biggest costs are their people and their rent. Imagine renting a huge office and only using 2 per cent of its capacity. It would be absurd. And yet we do this with our people all the time.

The opportunity available to be unlocked is unbelievable. As I briefly mentioned above, our teams are populated with more diversity than ever before. There are people of different races, genders and sexualities. There's the spectrum of neurodiversity. There are introverts and extroverts. Multiple generations are now represented, with older workers who are retiring later rubbing shoulders with hordes of millennials. There are a lot more mums. And that doesn't even touch the sides of the great diversity within individuals, when we consider that all of us are polymaths. After all, we are not just our jobs. As well as being a 'project manager', we might also be a fluent French speaker, a marathon runner, and hold a master's degree in sociology. This diversity is a huge creative asset. The research is unambiguous: innovation is most likely to occur when people from diverse backgrounds, thinking styles and perspectives collide.[48]

But all this hard-won diversity is wasted if we don't behave in a way that unlocks its power. As well as being diverse we need to be *inclusive*. This requires us to pay attention to the conversations we have every day. Because, while most people would agree that inclusivity is a positive thing, we don't always walk the talk. It's easy to think you are being inclusive *if you personally are included*. Thanks to unconscious bias, it's easy to miss those people who are not included. The historically lucky ones – the straight, white, middle-class men – need to bring into the conversation, deliberately and without condescension, those who have been worse represented, who are likely to bring less status into the room with them.

Something we can all do, regardless of our habitual status, is to be an ally to those people who are routinely drowned out in meetings. A technique popularised by the Obama administration in the United States was *amplification*. When a woman made an important point in a meeting, other women would repeat the idea (with credit) to make sure it wasn't spoken over, interrupted or ignored. This is a form of 'yes, and' behaviour. Gender is an important part of this issue, but it's not the only one. Amplification is about all of us making sure everyone has an equal opportunity to participate. Isn't that what we all deserve?

THE IMPROVISATIONAL LEADER

Unleashing the collective intelligence of a group of people is about more than just inclusive meetings and conversations. If you're a manager or a leader, there are various steps you can take to encourage ideas and initiatives from everywhere in the team. Improvisation is based on a profoundly positive view of human nature and human potential: a view that everyone has the potential for amazing creativity, leadership and generosity if given the freedom to express it.[49] Not only that, improvisers believe that it is the opportunity to be creative, show initiative and be generous that motivates people to do their best work in the first place – far more than external rewards or threats.

The challenge for the leader of a team is to find ways to give people the sort of freedom that allows ideas to bubble from the bottom up. How do you achieve this without letting people do whatever they want at work and things descending into chaos? There is definitely a happy medium here. The secret is to be in charge but not in control – or at least, not in control *all of the time*. Spread decision-making across the group as much as possible, while maintaining just enough oversight to ensure things don't go off the rails.

To see why it's common sense to do this, let's draw an analogy with an improvised scene. Imagine if, before an improv show, the cast of eight people were told: 'Tonight, guys, Andy will be making all the decisions. He'll decide what the show will be about. He'll start every scene, and he'll decide when every scene should end.' It would be absurd. First, this set-up would require Andy to see all the opportunities and threats that come up during the performance, to have strengths in every area, and to have oversight of both the here and now and the overall direction of the show. That is an overwhelming challenge under such complex conditions. The rest of the cast would have ideas that would never get heard, hunches and instincts that would never be followed, and strengths that would never be utilised. What a waste! And worst of all, they would be bored to tears. Yet this is how many managers manage their teams.

So what can we do instead? According to management scholar and jazz pianist Frank J. Barrett, teams need what he calls 'guided autonomy'.[50] This is a balance between clarity and flexibility: people need to be clear about what the group is trying to achieve; at the same time they need some freedom to take decisions and make things happen themselves, away from constant management oversight.

As Barrett puts it, leaders should try to establish 'minimal structures and maximal autonomy'. Notice that we don't get rid of structure all together. Structure is still really important. Barrett quotes jazz bassist Charles Mingus who said: 'You can't improvise on nothing. You gotta improvise on something.' And just as jazz musicians need a song or a motif on which to riff, so too improvised comedians rely on structure to create. In an improv show, it isn't 'anything goes' at all. As we've seen, there is a set of rules everybody is expected to play by, including 'yes, and'. Then there's the basic format of the show and the expectations it creates: if you tell the audience you are going to tell them a story, then you better tell them story! And that's before you think of the structure that emerges within the performance itself. For instance, if the story is set in an air-raid shelter during World War Two, then that is the reality within which the players must create.

But while some structure is useful, too much structure stultifies. We want to ensure that people are free to experiment, follow hunches and do all the other things that make them creative. The pushback here is that this looser structure will lead to waste, errors and exposure to risks. But Barrett says that if you want to maximise your capacity for this improvisatory innovation you must say 'yes to the mess'. In this spirit, here are some practical ways you can unlock the power of improvisational innovation in the team you manage.

DON'T RUN EVERY MEETING

As a leader you don't have to run every meeting. Let other people take the reins, and participate as a team member instead. If it won't work to have a different person running the meeting, can you hand over to other people to facilitate certain sections of the meeting, for example, around certain projects or subjects?

An important thing to consider here is to let go of the script in your head for what you think should be discussed in these meetings. As Barrett puts it, you want to avoid the trap of 'too much consensus' and encourage different things to emerge than you had planned. Be humble and recognise that there may be possibilities you haven't seen; give yourself the opportunity to be positively surprised by your team.

DELEGATION

Which decisions can you delegate to others? Are there things you can have oversight and sign-off on but not control? Which projects could other people manage? One of the main things that stops people delegating is that they are worried that those they delegate to will make mistakes. To get over this, it's helpful to reframe your attitude to the costs of decisions. Jeff Bezos at Amazon points out that there is a difference between *reversible decisions* and irreversible decisions. Most decisions fit into the reversible category. While there may be some time and resources wasted in a decision you reverse, your reward is that by delegating this sort of decision to others you remove yourself as a bottleneck, speeding up your team's capacity to innovate. Which reversible decisions could you give to others?

The measure of a good leader is how many other leaders they create. People need to be free to make mistakes in order to figure out how to correct them. It is this that teaches them how to think and eventually to lead. Spoon-feeding and micromanaging people is a short-run solution that creates dependents, not leaders. Just as we spoke of having an 'investment in loss' as an individual in the previous chapter, you need to have an investment in loss for the people you manage too.

HAVE LOTS OF REGULAR CHECK-INS

Delegating doesn't mean it's sink or swim for your team! As Barrett puts it, you need a balance between freedom and vigilance. You need to give people the freedom to take the initiative and make creative decisions. But this must be matched with regular check-ins on their progress to ensure their projects are fitting with the activities of the rest of the team. Even more than that, check-ins are important because freedom can be intimidating. You need to ensure your people feel guided, coached and supported – not left to drown in ambiguity.

They'll need lots of encouragement to get up the steep learning curve if the project you've given them is a stretch. In your feedback, focus on their individual strengths. We always say in improv that a good team needs a mix of pirates, hearts and heads. A head brings great logic and structure to the show; a heart brings emotional grounding; and pirates get in there and shake things up so it never gets stale. Bear in mind that your team needs a similar mix of people and give feedback accordingly. Round pegs are good at being round pegs; they can do without being criticised for not fitting into a square hole.

DISCRETIONARY TIME

Taking an improvisational approach to management is not about totally ripping up everyone's job descriptions. Much of people's time will still be spent on the usual mix of everyday essential tasks and long-term initiatives. But why not add some 'discretionary time' into the mix – a small amount of time every week for that person to pursue a work project of their choosing?

For example, 3M allow employees to spend 15 per cent of their time on pet projects. Google similarly has a '20 per cent rule' with innovative results. AdSense, Gmail and Google News are just three products that have emerged from this discretionary time. A good way to elicit suggestions for what this might be from someone you manage is to ask them: 'What sort of thing would you love to work on here?'

CREATE THE RIGHT EMOTIONAL CULTURE

In a complex, fast-moving world, creating the optimal environment for innovation and agility is increasingly the role of the leader. We'll turn to how to create this environment now.

BUILDING THE RIGHT CLIMATE

In 2012 Google were curious. They wanted to discover what it was that made the most successful Google teams great. What was the secret sauce? If they could find out what their best teams had in common, they could then roll it out across all the teams at Google and raise performance across the board. It was a heady goal. The investigation was to be called Project Aristotle and, like most research projects, it began with a hypothesis. They supposed that the best performing teams would be made up of the most talented individuals. It seemed like common sense. But when they examined the data it turned out they were completely wrong. Why?

The idea that shoving together the most talented individuals you can find will be enough to make a great team has a strong and resilient heritage. In 1990 the evolutionary biologist William Muir conducted an experiment with chickens in which he aimed to produce a flock consisting of only the most productive birds. Over six successive generations, Muir took the most productive hens – the ones that laid the most eggs – from each cage and used them to breed the next generation of hens. But the resulting 'super flock' of high-achieving birds didn't achieve highly at all, nor did they outperform the average control flock. In fact, these super chickens ended up pecking their competitors to death, leaving only three survivors.[51]

Studies of high-performing human teams show that talent and competition are insufficient outside of the coop too. For example, researchers at MIT studying high-performing teams realised that they had three things in common. First, they showed high 'social sensitivity': being present and empathetic to another's feelings and then regulating your behaviours in light of this. Second, there was equal conversational turn-taking, with all group members participating equally. And finally, successful groups contained more women than less successful teams.[52] It was turning to research such as this that made Project Aristotle's researchers realise that 'group norms' of behaviour might provide the solution to their puzzle.[53]

When they re-examined their data, they realised that when it came to a high-performing team at Google, who was on the team mattered less than how the team worked together. They identified five elements of a successful team, the most important of which was 'psychological safety'. A term borrowed from Professor Amy Edmondson's research into the subject at Harvard Business School, the Google researchers described it like this:

> 'Psychological safety' refers to an individual's perception of the consequences of taking an interpersonal risk or a belief that a team is safe for risk taking in the face of being seen as ignorant, incompetent, negative or disruptive. In a

> team with high psychological safety, teammates
> feel safe to take risks around their team members.
> They feel confident that no one on the team will
> embarrass or punish anyone for admitting a mis-
> take, asking a question or offering a new idea.

It's clear then that, when we talk about 'culture' in our teams and organisations, we tend to mean what might be described as 'cognitive culture'. It's the intellectual stuff, like the 'mission statement', or the values, or the sort of rituals that are part of the workplace. (Bring your dog to work day, anyone?) And while this stuff is undoubtedly important, what is also crucial is the *emotional culture* of a place. Emotional culture is enacted in the 'micromoments' of daily life. It is the realm of small gestures rather than big declarations of feelings. Because it is the small acts of support, how we receive other people's ideas verbally and non-verbally, that add up to an emotional culture of psychological safety.[54] But how do you foster this sort of emotional culture in your own team?

FOUR IMPROV COMMANDMENTS TO HELP BRING THIS CULTURE TO YOUR ORGANISATION

1. Support other people's risks

A fundamental belief of improvisation is that fearlessness is a group function, rather than just an individual attribute, as is commonly thought. While clearly there are brave individuals in the world, groups can make the people within them braver based on how members behave towards one another. Fundamentally it comes down to two things. First, how I respond to the risks you take. And second, how I respond to your mistakes as and when they occur. We'll look at mistakes in a moment, but let's begin by looking at how we should respond to risks.

As an improviser, I am much more likely to take a risk onstage if I know that the risk will be supported by my fellow players. If I go out on a limb and I am left hanging, that is going to make me fearful next time – fearful enough for me to probably not follow my impulse and take the risk. The consequence is that I learn to contribute less and the group suffers. So, if we want our colleagues to be fearless in putting forward their ideas or in trying something new, we need to support them by taking a 'yes, and' approach when they do, rather than simply staring at them blankly as if to say: 'Yeah, good luck with that!'

▶ Exercise

WHAT I LIKE ABOUT THAT IS ...

This exercise can be used as an icebreaker before your next brainstorm to get everyone in the right mindset. The game is pretty simple. It involves two or more people who, for the sake of the exercise, are in a product design team. You'll also need a flipchart and pen, but A4 paper will do if you are in a pair. It works like this:

1. **The facilitator of the exercise should give the product design team a product to design.**
   It can be anything at all, for example: 'Design a new toaster.'

2. **The participants then take it in turns to pitch ideas for features of this new toaster, drawing them on the paper as they do.**

For example, they might say: 'This toaster has an extra-long power cord.'

3. **The important thing is that the next person has to respond to this feature by saying what they like about it, before they go on to add another feature of their own.**

For example, if the person before you had added four bread slots to the toaster, you might say something like: 'What I like about that is the whole family can toast their bread at the same time.' And then you would add your own, new feature.

4. **Carry this on for a few minutes until you have a product that is ready to be launched.**

This is an exercise that is about 'yes, and' thinking. You can see that having to reflect on a positive aspect of the last contributor's feature slows your brain down, stopping you getting lost in your own thoughts as so often happens in creative meetings. This way you don't just pitch your own ideas but also connect to and feed off of other people's ideas too. Another important thing to emphasise in this exercise it that it's not just about saying the words, 'What I like about that is ...,' it's about *how* you say them. We want to maintain a positive energy in terms of body language, tone of voice and our general engagement in the process. These small gestures contribute to the overall emotional culture.

▲ ▲ ▲

Central to our attitude to our colleagues' risks is delaying judge-ment of their idea in a spirit of trust. After all, creativity is not just about people coming up with great ideas, it's about the team recognising them as such (or at least committing unconditionally to exploring how they might become great ideas in time). To see how we might adopt this spirit of trust, let's turn to Del Close. A seminal figure in the Chicago school of long-form improv, Close is responsible for maxims that improvisers all over the world still use to this day. One is particularly relevant here:

> If we treat each other as if we are geniuses, poets
> and artists, we have a better chance of becoming
> that onstage.

Close's point was twofold. First, if I expect your idea to be genius, then I am more likely to see the genius in it when you share it. Second, and more subtly, people behave as we expect them to behave. If I expect you to be a genius, then soon enough you'll rise to the challenge. Isn't that a pretty inspiring idea?

▶ Exercise

STRETCH ASSIGNMENT

How would you manage someone if you believed them to be intel-ligent, responsible and creative? Imagine giving someone you manage a project that they think is too big for them to chew. Can you try this out in real life? When you do, check in with them regularly but don't micro-manage. Most of the time people respond to this sort of trust and rise to the challenge, growing their skill set and self-confidence as they do.

Our attitude to risk taking is not just shown in how we support our colleagues' ideas, it can also be shown in little rituals before the risk is taken. Before shows improvisers go around every player on the team, look them in the eyes, pat them on the back and say: 'I've got your back.' In The Committee, there's another simple phrase we're fond of too. Borrowed from a brilliant Chicago-based improviser called Holly Laurent, we say to each other: 'If you do something weird, I'll do something weirder.' This custom is a way of communicating to each other: whatever you do onstage, I'll support it. But more than that, it's a licence we give ourselves to push boundaries and take a risk. These might seem like little gestures, but an emotional culture is exactly that: an ecosystem of little gestures.

▶ Exercise

ADD INFORMATION, DON'T JUST ASK QUESTIONS

If you take an improv class, the coach will tell you not to ask questions in scenes because when you ask questions, you put all the pressure on your scene partner to create the scene, rather than sharing the responsibility for it, as you should if you are genuinely supporting them. For example, you often see beginner improvisers acting like Player B here:

> **A:** 'I came to the hospital as quick as I could.'
> **B:** 'Why are we at the hospital? And WHO ARE YOU?'

Instead of questions, improvisers are taught to make statements. By making statements you add information into the scene and help out your scene partner by embellishing their offer. For example:

> **A:** 'I came to the hospital as quick as I could.'
> **B:** 'We had a boy! He's beautiful, Derek.'

216

In this version of the scene, both players are moving the actions forwards. When applying this principle offstage, it's helpful to be aware of when you're asking questions as a way of slowing down or blocking an idea because you don't like it. Instead of asking questions, try to add a 'yes, and' style response which affirms your colleague's idea and then adds information from your own perspective. That's not to say that questions can't be gifts, though. Questions can be constructive as long as they are framed in a way that encourages exploration and not just paralysis by analysis.

▲ ▲ ▲

CASE STUDY: Simon Gomes, lawyer

Improv has helped me in how I manage my team. It has especially improved my listening skills. Whereas before, if I was in a meeting, I'd be obsessing about the agenda, trying to keep everything on track and not really listening, now I am in the room, engaging with people's ideas so I can understand and respond to them.

Also, I've removed 'but' from my language. Rather than responding to someone with 'Yes, but ...', now, I'll say: 'That's really good, AND have you thought about this?' The idea is that we are building something together as opposed to competing over who is right. I am acutely aware now that the language you choose has an impact on others. If you use 'but', all you think about is the next bit that follows. The person just hears 'no'.

But improv is not saying 'yes' to everything. I understand 'yes, and' as about building a better version of what either of us has separately. It's still disagreement, but it's productive. It's a healthier way of sharing your perspective with others. Since I've made this simple change, people feed back to me that I am much more collaborative than I used to be. ■

2. Don't humiliate, ideate

The legendary improviser and founder of The Annoyance Theatre in Chicago, Mick Napier, once said: 'If you do a shit on the floor, my job is to pick it up and squeeze it until it becomes a diamond.' Imagine the risks you'd be willing to take if your colleagues had the same mindset. When I step out onstage with my teammates in The Committee, I know that if I make a mistake, they will try to turn it into something useful. I also know that if I am drowning in a scene, someone in the team is going to dive in and help me out. After all, they've got my back. If I make a mistake, or do a bad scene, I am never blamed for it.

That's the thing with risk taking, you have to support it when it comes off *and* when it doesn't. You don't get to choose. The nature of risks is that they will sometimes fail. How you react to my error will determine if that error is stigmatised or not. Yet it goes beyond blame. Reacting well to a colleague's mistakes is not just about not throwing him under a bus when it happens. It's about empathy, about realising that he probably doesn't feel great, that he probably wants someone to put their arm around his shoulder and say: 'It's OK,' but more than that: 'I'm really glad you took that risk. Please do it again.'

▶ Exercise

THE GOOD, THE BAD AND THE UGLY

At your next team meeting, get every person sat around the table to share something positive that they've done or had happen to them at work recently. Maybe it's a positive update on a project? Then get them to share something that didn't go to plan and what they learned from it. And have the room literally applaud it. This little ritual is a great way to get people into the habit of reflecting on and learning from failure. Most of all, it has the effect of destigmatising mistakes and therefore changing people's attitudes to risk.

▲ ▲ ▲

Most people aren't dicks. No one is reading this and thinking, 'Wow. *Don't* humiliate someone for making a mistake?' Most of us know better than to do that. But there is often something more insidious at play in teams. There's an archetypal guy, let's call him 'Sarcastic Kev'. Sarcastic Kev is basically a nice bloke, but he's world weary and is always the first to gallows humour. It's fine sometimes – after all, we don't want to take ourselves too seriously. Kev is a funny guy, and he doesn't mean anything by it. He's just messing around. But what Sarcastic Kev doesn't realise is that his incessant piss-taking makes his colleagues anxious about making a mistake, lest they become the butt of his next joke. And so everyone on Kev's team becomes more timid and risk-averse.

Organisational psychologist Edgar Schein suggests that you can divide an organisation's culture into three distinct levels: artefacts, values and assumptions.[55] *Artefacts* refer to the overt and obvious bits of an organisation that even outsiders can see, for example, the stuff on the wall in reception, the ping-pong tables, the free breakfast in the canteen. The *values* of an organisation are those the company publicly declares, for example, in the flowery company 'purpose' or when executives say things like 'We are customer-obsessed.'

Then, finally there are the shared basic *assumptions* of every-one who works at the organisation. These are the bedrock of a team or organisation's culture. They are what people actually think and do – the beliefs and behaviours so deeply embedded that people in the organisation don't notice them. These shared assumptions are not necessarily the same as the company's arte-facts or the espoused values. In fact, often they are in conflict. If you want people to 'think outside of the box', then it's not enough to graffiti it all over the wall in a sexy font, install 'think-ing pods' in the office or put out a press release. You have to walk the walk. You have to be the ally of those people who take the interpersonal risks that thinking outside of the box actu-ally involves. And you have to hold people like Sarcastic Kev to account.

3. Stop competing, start co-creating

In improv 'we' trumps 'I'. Given the complexity of the world, and the speed of change, it's the same offstage too. The visionary who hoards his idea, like Gollum and the ring, is a thing of the past. The 'ideas guy' who is actually the 'my ideas' guy can't get the job done anymore. No idea exists as an island; to think it does is delusional. Ideas that work are networks, as Pixar's Ed Catmull writes in his brilliant memoir *Creativity, Inc.*:

> Too many of us think of ideas as being singular, as if they float in the ether, fully formed and inde-pendent of the people who wrestle with them. Ideas, though, are not singular. They are forged through tens of thousands of decisions, often made by dozens of people.[56]

In improv, it's not about forcing through your idea; it's about finding 'the' idea. To do this you need to drop your ego. When you collaborate in a team, it is not a battle to the death to see which person's idea wins the day. It's about finding the best solution to the problem you are trying to solve. This requires everyone involved to listen deeply, give up control of their ideas, and let go of their need to emerge as the smartest person in the room.

While you are letting go of your plan (the script in your head of what you think should happen), you are not letting go of your expertise and experience. You can still offer your perspective at every step of the process. However, you are surrendering the belief that there is one, perfect solution. In truth there are often many versions of an appropriate solution. What we can normally agree on is the outcome we are all trying to achieve. In improv our outcome is that we want to make a funny scene. That is non-negotiable. But we are willing to be flexible on the journey towards that outcome. How often have you been in a disagreement with someone because they need you to agree not only with their basic idea but also with all of the specifics of it too? You can often get the outcome you want if you are willing to give up control of the means to get there. As improvisers say: *Hold on tightly, let go lightly*.

There is another benefit to dropping your ego to collaborate in this way, which is that if you co-create your idea with other people, they are much more likely to get behind it subsequently. After all, it's easier to support an idea that you thought was yours in first place. They are also more likely to champion it with others. It's a win–win scenario. And while you might not get 100 per cent of the personal credit for the idea you co-created, you can take satisfaction from your contribution to the team effort. After all, when the team wins, you win too.

▶ Exercise

THREE-SECOND PAUSES

Research suggests that while we openly talk about valuing creativity, we will often reject creative solutions when they are put forward by others, which is clearly not ideal when it comes to collaboration.[57] This bias against creativity is not overt but may be down to an unconscious motivation to avoid uncertainty (a motivation we explored in depth in Chapter 1). To avoid this knee-jerk rejection of other people's ideas, it helps to slow down our thought process slightly so that, rather than *reacting* to others emotionally and instinctively, we *respond* to them mindfully.

There is a simple exercise we do with beginner improvisers to teach them how to do this onstage. In this exercise they are tasked with improvising a two-person scene, for which they will be given a location and the relationship between their characters. The twist is that, during the scene, before they can respond to the last person's line of dialogue, they have to take a three-second pause. In corporate workshops I often use a version of this exercise, designed to be done in pairs. So find a friend to work with.

1. **Your task is to have a creative conversation of some sort. For example: 'How might we improve collaboration in our team?'**
The specific brief doesn't really matter here; it just has to be a conversation where you engage with the other person's point of view.

2. **Before either participant responds to their colleague's line(s) of dialogue, they must take a pause of three seconds.**

During this pause, ask yourself these three questions internally before responding:

- What have I learned?
- What haven't I learned?
- How can I move what I have learned forwards?

▲ ▲ ▲

Notice how the questions in the exercise are not about judgement. The whole point of pausing is to avoid the instinctive 'yuk' reaction we often have to other people's ideas in the moment, in order to allow us to respond in a more collaborative way. This approach is inspired by Daniel Kahneman's magisterial book, *Thinking Fast and Slow*, in which the behavioural economist explains how human thinking works. Kahneman reduces it to a mercifully simple metaphor. Predominantly, he argues, people use two cognitive systems: 'System 1' and 'System 2'.

System 1 relies on familiar patterns in order to make quick judgements. It's automatic and effortless. System 2 requires effort, focus and operates more methodically than System 1. This is the sort of thinking we're using when we're *aware* that we're thinking, such as when we solve a maths problem. It is when using System 1 thinking that we are vulnerable to cognitive biases because when we make decisions quickly, we take shortcuts.

Shortcuts work most of the time, but sometimes they lead to inconvenient outcomes and, occasionally, absolute disasters. Scientists have identified more than 200 separate cognitive biases that affect us. According to Kahneman, we are more susceptible to these biases when we are already involved in another 'effortful task', such as listening. This is why we have to be extra alert to the risk of cognitive bias in meetings with colleagues.

4. Manage team energy levels

Our energy level as a team has a huge impact on our ability to collaborate well. When you are in an energised, positive headspace, you are much more likely to see opportunities rather than problems. On the other hand, when you are in a flat, negative headspace, you are more likely to be creatively blocked, risk-averse and to get into conflict. We experience this reality every day. It's why when you're hungover even the idea of getting out of bed to put the kettle on seems an impossible task. Yet, when you are juiced up on New Year's Eve, with one gin and tonic in you, you're certain that you are going to launch that start-up, lose three stone and learn the clarinet, all in the same month.

A good group energy level doesn't happen by accident. We have to facilitate it deliberately. We'll get on to how you can do that as a team leader in a moment, but managing the energy level in a group isn't just the responsibility of the leader. Every single member is accountable for it. You choose your level of engagement, energy and general attitude. In an improv troupe, we share responsibility for the show equally. Everyone needs to contribute at the top of their intelligence; we shouldn't have to carry anyone. If you turn up distracted, surly and flat, that puts more pressure on me. It's not fair. So when you show up for a meeting, actually show up and be in the room.

This is crucially important because whatever energy level you choose will tend to be mirrored by others. It's social psychology 101: our behaviours tend to conform to whatever is occurring in the group. For example, if during an energy slump you 'check out' of the meeting and pick up your phone or cross your arms and stare out of the window, this is the green light for others to do the same. The good news is that, in a similar way, positive behaviours can also become normalised. Your good energy levels and attitude are infectious too.

Let's turn our attention now to how to facilitate meetings and create a climate which encourages people to contribute. Here's a quick guide to eliciting and maintaining a good energy level at any team meeting:

- **Ask people to put their phones away and state the rules of the game.**

  Mobile phones are bad news for collaborative environments. One intriguing study has suggested that merely having a mobile phone present on the table, let alone in use, significantly degrades the quality and depth of our social interactions.[58] To get around this, politely ask people to put their phone on silent and away from view. Say that phones aren't to be used in the meeting, but that there will be an opportunity to check for urgent emails during breaks.

  Stating this rule on phone use is part of telling people how you want them to participate in the meeting generally. Active listening, give and take, energetic engagement and 'yes, and' behaviours are the order of the day. When you've done this, pose the direct question: 'Do you think you can do that?' This may seem patronising, but by setting out the ground rules and getting verbal buy-in from attendees, you will boost accountability and have a much more productive meeting.

- **If you are in a brainstorm situation, start the meeting with an energising icebreaker.**

  A warm-up exercise gets everyone's blood going, allows them to shake off any distractions or stresses

they brought with them into the room, and gets
them connected with other members of the team.
Plus, it puts everyone in a more playful headspace.
This is especially important if the ambient energy
level of the group at this particular time of day is
low.

- **Variety is important.**
  Another thing to bear in mind is the variety of
  tempo and content in a meeting. Vary the length
  of different sections. Vary the tone and the type
  of task engaged in. For example, not everything
  should be a discussion; try making some elements
  experiential too. For optimal energy, we want a
  good balance of doing versus talking. Rather than a
  simple brainstorm, can you use some of the ideation
  techniques from the spontaneity chapter?

- **Keep the meeting only as long as it needs
  to be.**
  Longer is not necessarily better, amen.

- **If the meeting is longer than twenty minutes,
  don't have everyone sat down throughout.
  Mix it up.**
  Get participants on their feet, being physical. A
  simple way of doing this is to have standing-up
  meetings. Or break the team into sub-groups
  and get them to break out with a task and then
  return back to share what they've come up with.
  A simple version of this is to set a team 'brief' and

then get every sub-group stood around a flipchart using Post-it Notes to come up with ideas. There is something about using your hands that gets the creative juices going. And, as IDEO say, 'the room remembers': making the brainstorm process visual makes it easier to capture and share ideas later.

- **Make room for introverts.**
Clearly, though, what constitutes a good energy level is nuanced. While we don't want to be flat, we don't want to be manic either. Energy levels that get too high can become dysfunctional. We want a playfulness that gets people out of their heads, but this must be balanced with focused attention on others. When energy levels get too excitable, we can stop listening to our colleagues. When you have a room full of passionate, extroverted people, their energy can crowd out the more introverted types, meaning we risk losing their contributions.

  As a way around this challenge, it's useful to provide some structure to the meeting to ensure that everyone has space to contribute. This can be as formal as going around the room one by one and getting everyone individually to share their thoughts. Or, if the group is too big for this to be workable, try using some 'liberating structures'.[59] The simplest version of these is known as 1-2-4-all. Here's how it works.

▶ Exercise

1-2-4-ALL

This little exercise is about collecting the thoughts of everyone in the room in a way that isn't just them thinking out loud, which can get repetitive and is also biased towards extroverts and higher-status people.

1. **Set them the task.** For example: 'What are the most important takeaways from this meeting?'

2. **Start with solo work.** Everyone has one minute for solo reflection on the task.

3. **Move to pair work.** Each individual then joins with a colleague for two minutes of sharing and discussion.

4. **End on group work.** Finally, each pair groups up with another pair for three or four minutes to discuss what both groups have created. The idea is to quickly synthesise learnings and make sure everyone has a chance to contribute. To end the exercise, a spokesperson from each group of four then shares their key points with the rest of the room.

▲ ▲ ▲

CONCLUSION

This chapter has been about the behaviours that – when adopted by everyone – can unlock and multiply the collective intelligence of a team. If we follow a few simple practices, we can be smarter, more creative and more agile together. As individuals, we don't know what we don't know. Bringing our colleagues into conversations – and being open to their ideas – provides all of us with an important check and balance to our inevitable human fallibilities. As venture capitalist Morgan Housel puts it: 'Your personal experiences make up maybe 0.000000001 per cent of what's happened in the world but maybe 80 per cent of how you think the world works.'

We are all too biased, we are all too limited in knowledge and expertise, and the world is simply too complex for us to do it alone. Way back in 1624 John Donne wrote that 'no man is an island'. And never has this been more true. Of course, most people get the importance of collaboration *theoretically*. But effective collaboration is first and foremost an emotional and a communication challenge. We've already explored the centrality of listening in Chapter 2, and we get deep into other elements of communication in the next chapter.

Here, let's reflect on the emotional difficulties manifest in collaboration. It's easy to get to defensive when we collaborate, to hold our colleagues (and our direct reports) at arm's length. To collaborate is to make yourself vulnerable. It is to admit, 'I don't have all the answers,' and, 'I need some help.' To make statements like these, whether explicitly or implicitly, takes great self-confidence – not to mention humility.

It requires great agility too. Because when you give up control of a process or an idea, you don't know where people are going to take it. True co-creation requires you to be willing to go there, wherever that may be. This requires a flexibility of mind, and a tolerance of ambiguity, that can be hard to achieve. It is to agility we turn for our final chapter, where we explore how we might better respond to the curveballs that are constantly thrown at us by others and by life. Because if there's one thing improvisers are good at, it's thinking on our feet.

Chapter 6

AGILITY

'You don't learn to walk by following rules,
you learn by doing and by falling over.'[60]
—Sir Richard Branson

This is the greatest moment of their lives, but the weather is closing in. It's 1985 and climbers Joe Simpson and Simon Yates have just done what no climbers have done before and ascended the imposing West Face of the Siula Grande peak in the Peruvian Andes. As a violent storm wails, they now have no choice but to begin their descent. This should be the easy bit. But Simpson suffers a fall and badly breaks his leg. Miles from help, with limited supplies and in life-threateningly cold temperatures, they have no choice but to keep going down the mountain.

Yates decides to lower his old friend down the steep, snow covered face using ropes, bit by agonising bit. The storm continues to rage. Yates can barely see beyond the end of his nose, and the wind is too loud for him to hear his partner's screams, as he unintentionally lowers Simpson over the edge of a large cliff, leaving him suspended in mid-air, swinging in the gale.

Unable to pull Simpson back over the cliff edge, and gradually losing traction in the loose snow himself, Yates realises that there is no other way out. Faced with the possibility of them both dying on that mountain face, Yates makes the agonising decision to cut the rope.

After surviving another night on the mountain in sub-zero temperatures, Yates descends the face and returns to base camp to recover. He assumes his friend is dead. But Simpson has miraculously survived the fall and lies trapped on a ledge deep in a giant crevasse.

If you were Simpson, what would you do next?

* * *

Agility is our capacity to flexibly and quickly respond to change. It is a capacity that we use every day when we encounter the unexpected, both the good and the bad. Examples abound: we have a conversation with a client and they react in a way we hadn't anticipated. We have people over for dinner and only find out when they arrive that one is vegetarian. We share a report with our manager and receive some critical notes. We go to give a presentation to the board and our laptop breaks two minutes before it's meant to start. In life we are constantly having to rip up our plans. The question is, what do we do *next*?

Improvisers are faced with this challenge in almost every moment of every show. To be successful in such an uncertain environment, you have to learn to thrive despite the constant rug pulls. In fact, you have to learn to make them work in your favour. The world of onstage improvisation offers a great methodology that we can learn from to be more agile in our daily lives. In fact, this methodology can be reduced to a simple four-step loop. Before we explore exactly how it works, I'd like you to try an exercise.

▶ Exercise

SWEDISH STORY

Even Swedes haven't got a clue why this game is called Swedish Story! Regardless of its etymology, this is a great exercise to train your mental agility because as soon as you've responded to one change, another comes along seconds later. In order to be successful, you need to keep changing direction as and when required. Agility isn't a destination, it's an ongoing approach. To give it a go, first find a partner to work with.

1. **Decide which person in the pair is going to tell the story and which person is going to be the 'word generator'.**

2. **The storyteller begins improvising a story.** The story should be inspired by a particular location. For example, it might happen in the desert. If you are the storyteller, take all the pressure off yourself to be funny or interesting. Trust me, your story will get interesting soon enough.

3. **Every fifteen seconds or so, the 'word generator' throws in a random word.** It doesn't have to make obvious sense in terms of the story told. In fact, it's more fun if it doesn't.

4. **The storyteller's job is to incorporate the word into the story in some way, allowing it to change the narrative.** For example, the exercise must go like this:

   A: 'One day in the desert was an explorer, making his way across the sand on a camel.'

B: 'Raspberry.'

A: 'This explorer was looking for the tomb of the Raspberry Pharaoh, a legendary figure from Ancient Egypt.'

B: 'Worm.'

A: 'Who once put a spell on all of Egypt that turned all those who would not obey him into worms.'

B: 'Papyrus.'

A: 'The explorer was carrying an ancient map, scrawled on papyrus.'

And so on!

▲ ▲ ▲

THE NLDC LOOP

Let's analyse what this exercise requires of you. Like many improv exercises, it's a microcosm of scenarios we encounter every day in life. In this game, you have a plan, a script in your head about where things are going, and then you are suddenly forced by events to react and adapt to a curveball. In order to deal with this change and carry on moving successfully towards the outcome you want, you have to cycle through a loop I call 'NLDC': notice; let go; decide; communicate. The quicker and more accurately you can cycle through this loop, the more agile you'll be in any scenario. Let's explore in more detail what each stage of this loop involves.

- **NOTICE**

    The first step in the loop involves observing what has happened, or is happening, as accurately as possible. It's an obvious thing to say, but we cannot react to change if we don't notice it first. You need to notice the facts as they are. This requires us not to be stuck in our heads but to be present to the moment. In this exercise the noticing part is pretty simple; it's just listening to a word. In real life it's likely to be more complex, of course, such as noticing an emerging trend or spotting the manoeuvrings of a competitor.

Why don't we notice change when it occurs? Perhaps we don't bother to look for it in the first place. (Maybe we're too busy, too complacent or too afraid of what we'll find.) Or perhaps we do notice things, but we then ignore or deny them – again, out of fear or overwhelm at the consequences that the change implies. Or perhaps we're blinded by cognitive biases. For example, we all possess a confirmation bias that means we're more likely to see evidence which confirms what we already believe than we are to see evidence which contradicts it.

Noticing change is also a matter of expertise and experience. The more expertise and experience you have, the more detail and nuance you'll notice in any situation. For example, if you go for a walk with a botanist, they will see a lot more of the surrounding nature than you will. Perhaps most crucially, expertise allows us to better determine what the most important and relevant aspects of the situation are. For instance, a new improviser and a great improviser might notice the same offers in a scene. But the great improviser will choose to build on the offers with the most potential and to ignore the rest. The same principle is true offstage too.

● **LET GO**

Noticing a change is not enough. You must also remain calm despite it. If we panic, we lose the emotional balance required to adapt to it successfully. On top of staying composed, there are two other aspects to being adaptable. First we must *surrender* our current idea or plan in order to choose a response that fits the facts we've just observed. This requires courage and flexibility, as often we are giving up the certainty of what we're currently doing in exchange for the uncertainty of a new approach – not to mention giving up all the resources, social capital and emotional investment we may have poured into an existing plan.

Second, we need to *reframe* this change as an opportunity, in order to prevent fear paralysing us. We must ask ourselves: 'Where's the offer here?' In short, we say 'Yes, and …' to the change and not 'Yes, but …'. We haven't fully accepted a new reality until we've let go of an old plan. For example, in this exercise the storyteller repeatedly has to throw away her story's plot with every new word the generator throws at her. Offstage this is about abandoning an approach that it isn't going to get the job done given the new facts you've acquired. This is an emotional challenge as much as it is a mental one.

- **DECIDE**

  Next, we have to decide what to do from the various
  options available to us. The important thing here
  is to make this decision quickly. We can't know for
  certain what the outcome of our decision will be,
  so we need to act without full information. That
  doesn't mean that this decision is random though.
  We use what might be termed *informed intuition*,
  which means that, having observed the situation as
  well as possible, and bearing in mind the principles
  we've internalised from past experience about what
  works, we make a sensible guess.

  Improvisers say that the only bad choice you can
  make is no choice. Because even when we make a
  bad choice it means that something is happening.
  If something is happening, then we are getting
  feedback. If we are getting feedback, then we are
  learning. Remember, we can always adjust our
  course if that choice turns out to have been wrong.

  Improvisers call the human propensity for
  analysis paralysis 'negotiation'. Beginner improvisers
  are expert at it. The classic example goes as follows.
  If you get two beginner improvisers onstage in a
  scene and tell them, 'OK. So ... you're in a boat
  rowing to a desert island,' the improvisers will spend
  the entire scene talking about what *might* be on the
  desert island, or what they *could* do when they get
  there. But they never actually get there. We always
  say in improv: make the active choice. In other
  words, stop wimping out and get to the island!

- **COMMUNICATE**

  Finally, having made a decision, we act on it –
  which in improvisation, and so often in life, involves
  communicating this choice clearly and persuasively
  to others. We need them not only to understand it
  but to buy into it too.

  We'll turn to how you can communicate like
  an improviser soon. Before we do, it's important to
  recognise that this process is a loop. As soon as we
  have decided and acted, we zip right back to the
  first step because we need to notice the effect of
  our action in case we need to change our approach
  again. You can see that agility it not a destination we
  reach but a state we constantly inhabit.

THE NLDC LOOP OFFSTAGE

Let's return to the dramatic story of the climber Joe Simpson from
the beginning of the chapter. We left him lying on a ledge, deep
in an icy crevasse, with a broken leg and apparently no hope. I
asked you what you would hypothetically choose to do next in
Simpson's position. Here's what he did in real life: he decided to
throw himself off the ledge. In his own words:

> Short of dying on the ledge, my only choice was
> to lower myself deeper into the crevasse. You've
> got to make decisions; you've got to keep making
> decisions – even if they're wrong decisions. If you
> don't make decisions, you're stuffed.

Joe landed 80 feet down, at the bottom of the crevasse. As he gathered his senses, struggling to stay conscious amid the searing pain from his broken leg, he saw a slim corridor of light leaking in from one side. He'd found a way out. Simpson then spent days dragging himself back to base camp, traversing fathoms of glacier and rock, frostbitten and severely dehydrated. Totally exhausted and near delirium, Simpson arrived back at base camp mere hours before Yates was due to be picked up. If he'd missed this pick-up, he would have been condemned to death. His incredible true story can be seen in the powerful documentary film, *Touching the Void*, or read in his book of the same name.

The fact that Simpson survived can be traced back to his ability to make decisions under conditions of uncertainty and change. He says:

> I really struggled to make that decision. I was so
> scared of going deeper. The other option was just
> to sit there, blindly hoping it might get better, and
> I just knew it wasn't going to get better.

Simpson observed the reality of his situation, calmly facing the hardest of facts. He threw away his original plan. And he quickly made a decision before acting on it. Inadvertently, he had cycled through the improviser's NLDC loop. Of course, you are highly unlikely to be in a situation like Simpson's in your own life. So let's apply the improviser's NLDC loop to one of the offstage scenarios from the chapter's introduction: turning up for a presentation only for your laptop to fail.

NOTICE: Sarah is the marketing director at a health and beauty brand. She arrives at the quarterly board meeting where she is about to give a presentation updating everyone on her strategy for the following year. But when she goes to plug her laptop into the projector, she realises it has totally died. She is distraught because she has spent weeks on the presentation and she is going to look unprofessional to the board members who are about to shuffle into the meeting room.

LET GO: Despite the shock, Sarah stays calm. She realises she isn't going to be able to make the presentation she intended and that this means she'll have to do something unorthodox. She asks herself: 'Where is the offer here?' And she realises it is a great opportunity to show vulnerability, prove she can think on her feet, and connect in a much more human way to members of the board. She decides to say 'Yes, and …' to the mishap.

DECIDE: It's two minutes before the board members are due to come in, so Sarah grabs some paper and a pen and lays out five headlines that she'll use as the structure of her talk. She tells herself that what she lacks in slides she'll make up for with eye contact and energy.

COMMUNICATE: When everyone is sat down around the meeting room table, Sarah breaks the news with a big smile on her face. Rather than thinking she's unprofessional, many of them look relieved that they don't have to sit through yet another load of boring slides. Sarah makes all her main points but, because she has to be more spontaneous, she tells them in a more informal and relatable way than she would have done with her deck. Without slides she has more time for questions at the end, and her answers to these questions show everyone in the room her depth of knowledge. Despite the setback, Sarah's presentation is an enormous success.

IMPROV YOUR COMMUNICATION

Communicating is a central part of the NLDC agility loop because in any stressful context this is what often goes missing first. As we explored in depth in Chapter 2, when it comes to communication in improvisation, it all begins with listening. Here we will look at the other side of the coin: how to speak with impact. Improvisers fall back on two fundamental principles to do this:

- **The responsibility for the message belongs to the sender**. If your communication is not received or understood, that's on you, not your conversational partner. Speaking is not enough, what's important is what they actually hear.

- **Don't talk *at* the other person, relate *to* them instead.** When you speak you should be focused on what the other person knows, thinks and feels, and not just on what you know, think or feel.

Here are some practical tactics you can employ to bring these principles to life in your communication at work and at home.

BE DIRECT AND CLEAR WITH YOUR OFFERS

One of my earliest experiences in improvisation was a series of workshops with Canadian improviser David Shore. The tenet he drilled in to us in every class was: '*Be super fucking clear.*' It's a tactic and a phrase that I've used every day since, both on and offstage. It represents the key difference between scripted drama and improvised drama. In a scripted drama, the subtext is what makes the drama so compelling, but in improv, if my intention exists only behind my words, there is a big danger my scene partner will miss it entirely. After all, people aren't psychic.

But how often do we behave as if they were? Too often we communicate in subtext and then get disappointed or irritated when we aren't understood. Relationship therapist Esther Perel put it astutely when she said: 'Behind every criticism is a veiled wish.'[61] Most relationship problems occur because of this sort of asymmetric information: when we don't have full information about each other's thoughts, feelings and needs.

Marshal Rosenberg, a psychologist and conflict resolution expert, understands this intimately. According to Rosenberg, in his brilliant book *Non-Violent Communication*, there are four elements of effective communication:

1. Observations (you observe what's going on).

2. Feelings (you share how this makes you feel).

3. Needs (you state what you need based on this feeling).

4. Requests (you ask for something specific that the person can do to help you meet this need).

For example:

> 'When I come home and see that you haven't cleared up after you've made yourself dinner, [1] I feel frustrated because I have to clear it up if I want a clean kitchen. [2] Which is important to me, because mess makes me anxious and I can't

relax. [3] So would you be willing to clear up after yourself in future? [4]'

Notice how direct and yet non-confrontational that is. It doesn't attack the person, but the explanation of the precise behaviour and the request to fix the grievance are specific and clear.

But being direct and clear is not enough. When I say a line in an improv scene, my job isn't finished until I can see in my scene partner's eyes that it has been received. This is important, because what is obvious to me might not be obvious to them. So I need to see my offer land and, if it hasn't, repeat it until it has – only this time more clearly. This ensures that we are on the same page and not talking about two different things.

CASE STUDY: Mark Rawle, doctor

A cardiac arrest is about the most high-pressure situation in medicine. When someone's heart stops beating, every second counts. They can often be chaotic affairs, with doctors, nurses and allied health professionals rushing round the patient, all trying to work toward the common goal of restoring life. As a medical registrar, you find yourself in the role of leading these arrests: coordinating the team from the foot of the bed, providing oversight. Obviously we practise these situations frequently, and the clinical knowledge is drilled in through learning and simulation; yet leading a cardiac arrest in the real world is something completely unique. When faced with such pressure, needing to consider multiple aspects of care all at once, there is a risk of tunnel vision. You need to develop a strategy for ensuring individuals involved in care co-ordinate their actions as a team. For me, the unlikely source of that strategy has been improv.

In an improv scene, being clear with your offers and suggestions makes everyone's life easier. Demanding your scene partner 'Get in!' is vague enough to be interpreted in many ways; 'Get in the boat!' provides a huge amount more information. It's this same strategy that works well in a cardiac arrest situation. I've been involved in arrests where the co-ordinator shouts to the room: 'Get an ABG!' A good five minutes might pass before they realise that no one has followed their command, as they either didn't understand it or thought someone else was doing it. By making sure context and definition are present in your instructions, like in your scenes, people respond far more quickly. 'Steven, could you take an arterial blood gas sample from the patient and then take it to the lab for analysis? Let me know as soon as you get the result,' is infinitely clearer and means everyone knows exactly what needs to be done and who is doing it. ■

AVOID THE CURSE OF KNOWLEDGE

When you know something, it becomes very hard to imagine what it's like to not have that knowledge. Actor, science communicator and improviser Alan Alda calls this 'the curse of knowledge', and it prevents us from fulfilling our number one role when we communicate, which is to relate to the person in front of us. As Alda puts it: 'Communication doesn't take place because you tell someone something. It takes place when you observe them closely and track their ability to follow you.'[62] This is especially important when it comes to persuasion, because when people don't understand something, they tend to say no.

A classic example of the curse of knowledge is the use of jargon. Jargon may be OK when we are chatting to the in-crowd, but outside of this close circle jargon can be alienating and even baffling. As Alda writes:

> Jargon is dangerous because it usually buries the very thing you most want the other person to understand. The insidious thing about jargon is that we know how beautifully it expresses precisely what we want to say, and it simply doesn't occur to us that the person we are talking to doesn't have a clue as to what we are talking about.

Onstage, while jargon is rarely an issue, using overly flowery language to say something simple often is. In an improv scene, to paraphrase Mark Twain, we don't use a $50 word when a $5 word will do. We want to keep the language obvious because, again, our aim is to be *super fucking clear*. For example, we don't want the show to get confused just because our scene partner has never heard of the word 'obsequious'. The curse of knowledge is why we're often worse at communicating about the things we are the most familiar with, such as our jobs. Try this exercise below to see how you can be more engaging the next time someone asks you: 'So, what do you do?'

▶ Exercise

JARGON BUSTING

You can do this with a colleague, but it also works as a solo exercise. Just grab a pen and paper.

1. **Think about your job and write down as many buzz words, jargon terms and acronyms related to it as you can.** Make a list so you've got them to hand.

2. **Try explaining your job using as many of these phrases as possible.** If you are doing this alone, record yourself on your phone so you can listen back to what you sound like. Although clearly exaggerated, is it really that different to how you've heard other people talk about what they do?

3. **Now, explain your job to my mum!** My mum is in her late sixties (your secret is out, Mum!), so bear that in mind. As smart as my mum is, she isn't down with much business gobbledygook. Your task here is to put your list of bullshit away and see if you can get her to understand what you do and why it's important. Again, if working solo, record yourself and listen to it back.

4. **Half-life.** Half-life is an improv exercise where you first tell a story as it naturally comes to you and then tell it again but in half the time. It's a great tool to get you to cut out any non-essential words or concepts. So, let's apply the same idea here. Now you've explained your job to my mum, do it again but this time in just twenty seconds. By the end of this exercise you should have a good, punchy description ready for any networking event.

▲ ▲ ▲

USE 'WE' AND AVOID 'I'

In the next conversation you have, check how many times you start a sentence with the pronoun 'I'. The trouble with using 'I' is that it automatically sets you up to give your perspective on things.

Because we filter so much information about the world through our own reality, it is second nature to do this. But it can make you sound self-absorbed. In your next conversation, try shifting to the pronouns 'you' or 'we' instead. Not only are they more inclusive and persuasive, they have another benefit too. It slows you down, forcing you to consider that there might be another point of view. It's a small step to more empathic communication. For example, don't say: 'I think we should do this …' Instead, say: 'We should think about doing this …'

KEEP IT SHORT AND SIMPLE

In an improvised scene, the first few lines are called the 'initiation'. Improvisers are taught that the initiation is only the first offer and should not necessarily be a map for what should happen in the rest of the scene. But sometimes, by making a long and detailed initiation, a fearful or arrogant improviser tries to control the scene by telling their scene partner absolutely everything. For example:

> **A:** 'Thank you for joining me in my office here at the Council, Perkins. As you know, I am your boss. You have been late three times this week. I imagine this is because you still live with your mother and she is ill at the moment. But I wanted to let you know, as a former army general I am a hard taskmaster, and I won't stand for it!'

Imagine being the other person in this scene. Not only is there no room left for your ideas, but that is also a lot of information to take in and remember in one go. Therefore, offers are likely to go astray and things will quickly get confused. Onstage, rather than clarifying things, adding too much information can be a serious roadblock to communication. This is true offstage too.

If you want to communicate clearly, less is more. Be concise, be precise and get to the point. Remember, you don't have to say everything all at once, and this is true in both our verbal and written communication. Let's be honest for a moment, *NO ONE IS READING YOUR LONG EMAILS.* At best they are skimming them. By saying too much, you are communicating less efficiently than if you'd said almost nothing at all.

▶ Exercise

JUST SEVEN WORDS

This is an improv exercise that perfectly embodies the short-and-simple principle; it works like this.

1. **Find a partner to have a conversation with.** This also works in groups of up to five.

2. **Your task is to have a conversation about anything at all.** Sometimes this works best when you provide a specific brief. For example: 'What are the secrets to having a fulfilling career?'

3. **The twist is that you are only allowed to use a maximum of seven words each time you speak.** Take the pressure off yourself to speak in elegant sentences and focus on hitting the word count. Just as in a normal conversation, you are still trying to get

your meaning across and connect with others. But this constraint forces you to clarify, simplify and prioritise what you want to say. Obviously you won't have to do anything so exaggerated in the real world. However, this exercise illustrates how unnecessarily convoluted a lot of our communication is.

▲ ▲ ▲

MAKE THE AUDIENCE THE HERO OF THE STORY

A central part of relating to the person you are communicating with is to speak to what's in their head, rather than what's in yours. In this sense, the old improv adage of 'start where they start' refers not just to the amount of knowledge the audience has about the topic but also to what they care about. When you communicate it's helpful to imagine the other person has the question in their head, 'So what?', or more precisely, 'What's in it for me?'

How exactly do you make them care? You tell them a story.

There have been thousands of books written on storytelling, and improvisers will tell you that the art of narrative can be complex and nuanced. But storytelling for the purposes of communication is actually pretty simple. At a basic level, a story is a hero's journey containing three things:

1. a hero

2. who wants something, but

3. there's something in the way of them getting it.

If you understand those three elements, you can tell a powerful story. The trouble is, when we do reach for a story to persuade others, we often pick the wrong hero – and are less influential as a result.

Everyone is the hero of their own story. They have their own goals and their own conflicts that they have to overcome to reach these goals. If you can show the person you're speaking to how your project helps them achieve what they want, or overcomes their points of conflict, then they'll be ready to buy into it. In order to do that, rather than making yourself the hero of the story (as we often instinctively do), you need to make the person you're trying to persuade the hero instead. To show you how, let me take you to Ancient Greece.

There are a few versions of the myth of Theseus and the Minotaur, but the specifics are less important than the overall structure. It goes a bit like this: King Minos of Crete was an unpleasant man who kept ordering his navy to attack Athens on the other side of the Sea of Crete. The King of Athens, defenceless due to his relatively weak navy, resolved to do a deal with King Minos to stop the conflict. The agreement was that in exchange for a ceasefire, Athens would send seven men and seven women every year as a sacrifice to the Minotaur.

The Minotaur was a half-man, half-bull creature, the son of an affair Minos' wife had with an actual bull. (This aspect is left out of the kids' version.) Anyway, this beast was now kept trapped in the middle of a labyrinthine maze, to stop him attacking innocent passers-by. This Athenian sacrifice continued for years until finally, Prince Theseus resolved to put an end to the bloodshed. One day, Theseus volunteered to be one of the Athenian offerings and set sail for Crete with the other men and women. They were met on the beach by King Minos and his beautiful daughter

Princess Ariadne, who fell in love with Theseus as soon as she saw him – as women often do in stories written by men.

When her father's back was turned, giddy with love, Ariadne provided Theseus with a sword, a shield and a ball of yarn to help him on his mission. Theseus entered the labyrinth, unravelling the yarn as he progressed into the heart of the maze. Using his sword and shield he slayed the Minotaur and followed the trail of yarn to escape the labyrinth unharmed. Before King Minos could stop them, Theseus and his beloved Ariadne set sail and arrived back in Athens to live together happily ever after. The end.

Let's analyse this story for a moment. The hero is clearly Theseus. But his heroism would have been impossible without Ariadne, and especially without the tools she gave him. To pull this back to everyday life, if you want to persuade someone to buy your product or support your initiative, they should be playing the Theseus role in the story you tell. *They should be the hero.* Where do you or your company fit in? You would play the role of Ariadne (i.e. you *help* the hero by proving the resources) and your product or idea are the resources (the sword, shield and yarn).

This sort of swapping of the hero is the difference between the following job pitches:

1: 'We are trying to improve our social media marketing in order to hit our growth targets for next year, and we'd like you to join the team to help us do that.'

2: 'I know you enjoy the creative side of the job the most, and what this role will allow you to do is to have the freedom to create our whole social media strategy. We need some help here, and I think this would be the perfect

environment for you to spread your wings and
do more of what you love.'

Which one would you find more persuasive?

BRING THE (RIGHT SORT OF) ENERGY

Our energy level – and the quality of that energy – is an important part of communication. The sort of energy we bring to a conversation or meeting affects how willing other people will be to listen to and absorb our message. Will they be inspired, or will they zone out? More broadly, this energy with which we carry ourselves tells a story about the meaning of a change or situation to others on our team. When we have positive body language, an upbeat mood and a calm demeanour, it tells everyone that the change is no big deal. It says: 'Guys, we've got this.' But if we are irritable and downcast, it tells the opposite story, and this negative energy is infectious.

Our energy level can be thought of in terms of both intensity and charge. The intensity is the amount of energy we have in a particular moment: we may be high energy or low energy. The charge of this energy is to do with emotional mood: is it positive or negative? We might combine low energy with positive mood, such as being laidback and cheerful. Similarly, we might combine high energy with negative mood, such as when we fly off the handle. It's clear that when we think of our energy levels, we need to consider both aspects, intensity and charge. As we explored in the previous chapter, both are matters of choice and, therefore, personal responsibility.

Our energy shows up in how we use our voice, our body and our face. If you want to make people feel inspired, this emotion needs to show up energetically across all these channels.

Enthusiastic words aren't enough; the energy you bring to any communication more generally must be congruent with your message. As a rule of thumb, people with a charismatic presence match and then raise the energy in any meeting or conversation they are in. Think of the people in your life who you most look forward to being around. You'll find they almost certainly fit this rule.

Just as we have a habitual status in life, we also have a habitual energy level. It might be said that we fit into one of two broad camps: 'cats' or 'dogs'. Dogs bound around, full of enthusiasm and excitable energy. They are always coming 'at' you. Conversely, cats are stiller, precise and gentle. They are happy in their own bubble. As a disposition, being a cat or dog is neither positive nor negative.

While we'll fit more comfortably into one camp than the other, there's a caveat: we need both these energy modes when we communicate. We can't just stay in a comfort zone of our natural energy type. Dog energy is useful for when you want to inject passion into a room or a conversation. Cat energy is useful when you want to appear credible or bring some calm introspection to a conversation. It's horses for courses: we choose the best energy level and type according to the situation and the outcome we want to pursue. We need to be flexible.

COMMUNICATE MINDFULLY

This principle follows directly on from the one above. If we can choose our energy level and mood, and if it's important that this choice be relevant and specific to the scenario we're in, then we need to make sure we *do* make that choice. In practice, mindful communication means that we are aware of our current energy level. We then consider what energy level and tone is most suitable for the situation at hand. And finally, we take steps to bridge that gap. These steps are a process I refer to as 'checking in'.

Without having the presence of mind to check in with where we're at physically, mentally and emotionally, we let the vagaries of life set the tone of our interactions rather than ourselves. Communication goes wrong when it just 'happens' to us, when we stumble into meetings or interactions without a sense of how we want to behave. Checking in helps us to be at our best more often, and helps us to avoid sleepwalking into difficult conversations when we're not in a good place to have them. When you have this sort of self-awareness, you are more likely to be inspiring and less likely to get into conflict.

You bring a mindfulness to your communication by answering these questions:

1. Where am I at in this moment in terms of the intensity and charge of my energy?

2. What does this person need from me here in this respect?

3. Given (1) and (2), what do I need to change?

By deliberately checking in with yourself, you are more likely to communicate with intention and, therefore, to achieve the outcome you want. There is freedom in self-awareness.

FINALLY, REMEMBER THE LOOP

No matter how good a communicator we become, our words and gestures don't always land in a way we hoped they might. As well as making sure we start where our audience start, we also need to make sure we stay in sync with them throughout the conversation. Our communication can't be 'set it and forget it'. We need to react and adapt to the person we are speaking with in real time. This requires us to notice how our words and gestures are landing (or not). As the philosopher George Herbert Mead put it: 'The meaning of a gesture is in the response.'

This takes us back to the agility loop from earlier: notice, let go, decide, communicate. During a conversation we need to keep moving back through the loop to ensure that we are always relating to the person in front of us. Our communication doesn't always have the desired effect because there's a gap either between our intention and what we've said or between what we've said and what the other person has heard. We need to pay attention to these gaps by being as present as possible to the other person, all the while, moment by moment, asking ourselves the following questions:

- **How is what I am doing and saying affecting the other person?** Are their eyes glazing over? Are they looking around the room for someone more interesting to talk to? *If you are not achieving the desired impact, then check in with the offers you are giving off.*

- **What am I doing physically?** Is my body language suitable? Is my energy too low or too high? Am I making eye contact? What's my facial expression?

- **What am I saying and how am I saying it?** Do I need to get to the point? Is my tone of voice engaging? Do I need to give a different example?

- **Is there anything I need to change in my approach?** If your first approach doesn't work, then you need to change it and try something else; don't just carry on doing the same thing in the hope that it will connect eventually. By making these adjustments in real time, you are more likely to achieve the outcome you want and to communicate effectively.

SOLVING COMPLEX PROBLEMS

At the beginning of the chapter, I defined agility as *our capacity to flexibly and quickly respond to change*. In this final section of the chapter we will expand that definition slightly. Rather than just responding to change, people and organisations who are agile *expect the unexpected* and build it into their process for creating anything. This method for solving complex problems is inherently improvisational in nature, and it's important to learn because, as I laid out in the Introduction, the World Bank and the World Economic Forum both rate complex problem-solving as the most important skill for workers in the future.

I appreciate the term 'complex problems' can feel a little abstract, so to understand what they are, it helps to contrast them with their siblings: simple problems and complicated problems. Simple problems are ones with a straightforward technical solution that we've handled before. For example, submitting your expenses is a simple problem. Complicated problems are problems that we've handled before but that require a higher level of analysis and expertise to solve. Again, with these problems there tend to be proven procedures to fall back on – even if they might only be available to certain experts. For example, preparing your company accounts statement is a complicated problem.

What counts as a complex problem?

- Starting a disruptive new business.

- Responding to a client brief.

- Bringing up a child.

- Maintaining a long-lasting romantic relationship.

- Learning any new skill.

You can see from the examples above that, unlike with simple and complicated problems, in order to solve complex problems knowledge alone is not enough. This is because there are no simple sets of steps, no models of best practice, that we can rely on entirely to solve them. Complex problems are neither fully visible nor defined. We only find out about the demands of the problem in the process of solving it. For example, when bringing up a child, while you could read various books to help you parent, there are too many unknowns and interrelated factors at play for off-the-shelf solutions to be adequate. There are no right answers, only best attempts, and you often only know if you've found an effective strategy in retrospect.

Crucially, complex problems are not problems you can solve once and for all. They are always a work in progress because the context in which they exist is constantly shifting. For example, if you launch a new business, your products and marketing – and pretty much everything else – have to continually change to keep up with evolving customer tastes and the unpredictable behaviour of competitors. So, what can we do when we don't know what to do? We've got to improvise! And the improviser's 'learn-by-doing' approach can help you to:

- Waste less time and fewer resources on any project you are involved with.

- Stop procrastinating on the things you've always wanted to do.

- Learn any skill quickly (and on the job).

Let's look at exactly how.

LEARN BY DOING

Onstage, improvisers solve a very complex problem indeed. In an improvised show, everything is completely uncertain and ambiguous. When it begins, the cast don't know who the characters will be or which roles they'll play. They don't know the story. They don't how many scenes there will be or what they'll be about. They don't know any of the dialogue or any of the jokes. They don't even know what the first line of the show will be. Their only option is to begin the performance and pay attention to what emerges.

As Keith Johnstone writes: 'The improviser has to be like a man walking backwards. He sees where he has been but pays no attention to the future.' By moving through each scene – and therefore the show – in this way, slowly the boundaries of this particular performance become apparent. The characters solidify, the themes emerge, and we stumble across the outlines of a story. The point is, as with other complex problems, we can only discover the rules of the game by playing it. And it's futile to try to predict how the game will end before you start.

Offstage, in the world of start-ups, this sort of learn-by-doing approach is often described as 'validated learning'.[63] It relies upon a strategy of moving from problem to solution by making little bets which allow us to test our assumptions about our ideas at every step. The goal here is fast cycles of learning. We want to cram in as many loops of real-world feedback as we can, making lots of iterations as we go.

The first step is to build a 'minimum viable product': the simplest version of whatever your thing is (an app, a website landing page, etc.). Then you release it to see how real end-users interact with it. The aim is to answer some key questions: *Is anyone interested? What specifically do they like about it? What isn't working?* You gather this feedback and then decide whether to stop doing what you are doing entirely, continue to do it while expanding on certain aspects, or 'pivot' from your original idea towards something different and, hopefully, better.[64] Then the cycle begins all over again.

SAVE YOURSELF TIME, EFFORT AND MONEY

What we are trying to avoid with a learn-by-doing approach is investing precious resources into something that no one wants. To show you what I mean, let me give you an example of the opposite approach.[65] Say you are a wedding planner and you get approached by a couple to organise their wedding. You have a meeting with them at their home and, although they are good at saying what they don't want, they are vague about what they *do* want. However, you're experienced. You've seen couples like this many times before and, having spent some time with this particular couple, you're pretty sure you know what sort of thing they'll like.

You set about creating this amazing plan. Venue, catering, decoration, flowers, band: the whole shebang. It takes you a week of work. You travel back to the couple's home to proudly present your masterpiece, only to be met with awkward silence and furrowed brows. You've totally missed the spot. Not only have you now lost their trust – and their business – you've also wasted a week of your life.

This sort of frustrating and demoralising situation is easily avoidable if we use a more agile process. Offstage this is often referred to as 'rapid prototyping'. Making a rough early prototype of your idea aids collaboration with others. As innovation guru Michael Schrage puts it in his book *Serious Play*: 'Prototypes can be more articulate than people.' In life, we often know more than we can articulate, and prototyping helps us express these ideas in response to something concrete. Prototypes can therefore be massively useful in gauging what your client wants at the start of a project. This isn't always clear, as our poor wedding planner discovered. As Schrage writes:

> 'It's far easier for clients to articulate what they want by playing with prototypes than by enumerating requirements. People don't order ingredients from a menu, they order meals.'

Doing this early in the process can avoid a huge amount of wasted effort because, more often than not, the client responds: 'Well, you've given us almost exactly what we discussed. But now we've seen it, we realise it's not what we really want. We really need you to do something different. How about …?'

Prototypes help us to collaborate with others by creating what Schrage calls a 'shared space' for communication. This is because a prototype ensures that everyone has something specific to react and refer to. Abstract ideas, like what you want or think is beautiful, are much easier to elaborate on when you reference something solid rather than simply conceptual. Prototypes, therefore, ensure that everyone is talking about the same thing and not at cross purposes. When someone says, 'This is wrong,' it gives you more clarity as to what it would mean for this project to be 'right'.

To use this principle offstage ask yourself: *What's the earliest I can share some work with a client? What's the simplest version of my idea I can produce? How quickly can I get their feedback?* The key thing to make clear to the client is that things will change and quality will improve from this early prototype, but that it would be enormously helpful for them to give you input at this nascent stage.

GREASE THE WHEELS OF CO-CREATION

As well as clients, prototypes can help us capture feedback from our colleagues too. Their input and ideas can be a key ingredient in helping us solve complex problems, providing a fresh perspective. As Ed Catmull writes about Pixar:

> Candour could not be more crucial to our creative process. Why? Because early on, all our movies suck [...] I'm not trying to be modest or self-effacing by saying this. Pixar films are not good at first, and our job is to make them so – to go, as I say, 'from suck to non-suck'.

This journey from bad to great requires lots of candid feedback, and prototypes can both help make this feedback meaningful to the creative and easier for everyone else to give. For example, at Pixar, in the process of creating a movie, story artists repeatedly pitch storyboards of short sequences of the film to the story team, the director and often the wider creative team in a constant stream of feedback and re-working.

When it comes to solving complex problems, conflict in teams can be a good thing. After all, we don't want 'group think', the sort of collective blindness where everyone agrees with each other either because they're too scared not to, or because they've all been 'drinking the Kool-Aid'. The aim, remember, is to test our assumptions about our ideas.

But while diverse and opposing points of view should be celebrated, opposing goals or agendas should not. Therefore, for disagreement to be productive, leaders needs to create a respectful and psychologically safe environment for these discussions. They need to structure the debate so that it is organised and contained. Here's a suggestion for how you might do that.

▶ Exercise

RED TEAMING

One of the secrets of managed conflict is to make clear to people what sort of meeting they are attending and how you want them to communicate inside it. With red teaming, the idea is for the group to take a deliberately adversarial or disinterested perspective and to rigorously challenge whatever idea is at hand. When people understand it's a thought experiment – and about criticising the idea and not the person who created it – the aggression is directed towards a positive end.

Another thought experiment you can try is a 'pre-mortem'. Imagine you have launched your product (say) and it was an absolute disaster. Why did it happen? What went wrong? Why did people not like it? This exercise helps bring to the surface criticisms or worries people may have had for a while but have been unwilling to put forward, lest they be thought of as not a 'team player'. When the worries have been aired, you can then take positive steps to address them before it's too late.

▲ ▲ ▲

Finally, we can also use prototypes to collaborate with our customers. For improvisers, feedback from our audience is absolutely crucial. We create out shows in dialogue with them. When they laugh at something that's been said onstage, they are saying: 'We like this. Do more of it.' When they don't laugh, they are saying: 'Not for us, please try something new.' What they find funny defines the content of each scene and therefore the show as a whole. In a very real sense, the audience help us write the script. We co-create the comedy with them.

Offstage, the same principle holds too. If you don't listen to your audience, you are ignoring a huge resource. If you offer a new product on your website and nobody bites, it's a sign that you might be barking up the wrong tree. Similarly, if a customer sends you an inquiry for services you don't yet provide, it is a sign from the market that there is demand for a new service. Patterns of feedback from customers are also signs to how you could adapt your offering. For example, if you consistently get praised for a certain element of your product or service, it is a signal that you should double down on it. Negative feedback also helps you find solutions to problems you weren't aware you had. Customer feedback is an incredible gift if you are willing to listen to it.

When was the last time you spoke in depth to a customer? What if you brought them into the development of your product, service or idea? How might you use social media, surveys and other digital tools to do that?

The process of learn-by-doing is simple to learn, but that doesn't mean it's easy to do. The difficulty comes in having the mental strength to cope with the frequent bouts of failure this inevitably involves. When the focus is on releasing a rough prototype and getting feedback as quickly as possible, the chances are that you'll often receive a critical response. The key to becoming more agile, therefore, is to change your relationship to 'not perfect'. This doesn't mean you lower your standards of performance, just that you see the bigger picture. Being intermittently imperfect is an intrinsic part of the package of solving complex problems.

You need to move from seeing everything as an exam on whether you are good or clever enough and instead see everything as an experiment. When you learn to see feedback as information and nothing more, it releases you from what can be its suffocating grasp.

CASE STUDY: David Simpson, software start-up founder

One of our founding tenets at Beacon is 'Move fast and humbly'. It's a play on Mark Zuckerberg's famous 'Move fast and break things' line. For us, the 'humbly' part is really important, and I borrowed it straight from my experience in improv. You are moving humbly when you believe that *it's OK to change your mind*.

Our approach when we develop anything is: 'OK, let's come up with something, take a stab to the best of our knowledge, then see how it works out. But if it doesn't, then *be prepared to drop your shit.*' It's the improviser in me again: don't hold on to things too tightly! We need to change our mind as soon as new information arrives.

The willingness to change your mind is such a crucial tool onstage and offstage. It's way more important than having everything figured out – because everything is going to change anyway. The world is too chaotic, too unpredictable for you to wait 'til you have 100 per cent of the answer. Instead, make decisions quickly and then be prepared to change your mind.

And start small! It's improv again: bring one brick, forget about the cathedral. We are creating our software in collaboration with the customer. For example, we might have a new feature we want to build. But we think small and we think quick. Rather than get this feature 100 per cent perfect, we'd build 10 per cent of it and then get in out in the wild, in front of customers as soon as possible. *What do they think?* If it doesn't work, we just throw it away and try something else. If you want to be agile, you've got to be prepared to let go. ■

STOP PROCRASTINATING

Having an improviser's learn-by-doing approach can also stop you procrastinating over doing the things you've always dreamed of. As David wrote above, the key thing is to focus on starting small. Improvisers are biased to action over preparation. That isn't to say that preparation isn't important. It's just that improvisers have learned that the best way to understand a problem – and therefore to learn how to solve it – is often to make a start. Being biased in the other direction, towards preparation over action, is paralysing. It leads to the perennial thought: *I'm not ready yet.*

You don't need all the knowledge, skills or resources required to finish a project in place at the start of it. While of course we need some entry-level knowledge and resources, the most important thing is our overall approach: which is to try stuff, get feedback and then try again; this time only better, by both pivoting out of our mistakes and noticing our successes so we might double down on them.

Act before you are ready. It kickstarts you, attracting other related ideas, resources and opportunities like a magnet. Before you know it, you are off and running, excited about what you could build. To put this principle into action in your own life, give up the idea of ever being 'ready' and instead ask yourself the following question:

> *What is the smallest step I can take right now*
> *but still learn from?*

For example, I have always wanted to learn how to make curry-house quality Indian food at home. I love it, but I had always put off learning because it just seemed so complicated and involved. There were too many ingredients, techniques and cheffy gizmos. But then one lazy Saturday morning I asked myself: *What is the most basic curry recipe I could try today?* And I looked it up online.

I didn't *try* to do it badly, but I gave myself permission to be crap. Under my logic, if I did it badly and the next time made it just 5 per cent better, I would only have to make the dish ten times to be 50 per cent better. And 50 per cent better than bad is pretty good! Now, I regularly host dinner parties where I make a plethora of different Indian dishes. I'm not curry-house level yet, but I'm getting there. Anything worth doing is worth doing poorly.

The ability to start our most meaningful projects is not a question of resources, despite what we often tell ourselves. In this modern age you have almost any resource you need to start almost anything you dream of, right at your fingertips – whether it be the ability to make websites, access to relevant freelance experts, or even full blueprints for success from other already established projects. Seek inspiration everywhere. As coders are fond of saying, why can't part of your recipe be 'Proudly Found Elsewhere'?

Once you've taken the first step, you might ask: *What do I do next?* When we improvise, we don't need a map; we just need a compass. The learn-by-doing process is our compass. You just need to be brave enough to start, and the feedback will tell you the rest, if you are willing to listen and be changed by it.

RECAP: AN IMPROVISER'S GUIDE TO COMPLEX PROBLEM-SOLVING

Assume failure and build it into the process.
- Share your work as early as possible for feedback. Don't wait until it's perfect.
- Leave time for a few drafts.
- Say yes to the mess: rather than seeking to avoid failure, capture its learning power through rapid prototyping.

Open up your process: collaboration makes ideas stronger and speeds up the journey from problem to solution.
- Co-create solutions by pulling clients, customers and colleagues into your idea generation and development.

Be prepared to humbly change your approach.
- Pivot without shame.
- Notice and double down on successes.

Go offer-by-offer: you don't need to have the right answer straight away.

- Start small.
- Iterate, iterate, iterate.

Good ideas are more important than who came up with them.

- You don't have to be the smartest person in the room or have all the answers. Be willing to use and celebrate ideas that aren't yours.
- Practise divergent *looking*, not just divergent thinking. Cast a wide net and borrow winning ideas from everywhere and anywhere.

Agility is not a destination; it is a way of being.

- Always stay present to feedback so you can adapt as required.
- Mix optimism with brutal realism.
- Measure the important things and regularly check in with your results.

LEARN IN AN AGILE WAY

Having a learn-by-doing approach can also help us quickly build skills in both ourselves and those we manage – if we have the right attitude to feedback. Samuel Beckett famously wrote: 'Ever tried. Ever failed. No matter. Try again. Fail again. Fail better.'[66] The most crucial part of this (frequently misquoted) mantra being fail *better*. Failure is only valuable if we learn from it so that we can do better next time. And feedback is the mechanism through which we do it. This is the expertise of the coach. But the power of feedback can be leveraged by all of us with a few simple hacks. It is to these hacks that we turn as we hurtle towards the end of our time together.

Most of what is taught about feedback in the workplace is how to *give* feedback. But how you receive feedback is at least as important. Improvisers must get very good at receiving notes. They get them after every performance; they get them in every rehearsal. Receiving this volume of feedback is not emotionally easy, but if you to learn to do it well it can become an enormous competitive advantage, simply because most people don't learn from their mistakes. Below is a simple guide for how you can both give and receive feedback, so that you can learn new skills in a more agile way.

HOW TO RECEIVE FEEDBACK AT WORK

1. **Say 'thank you'.**

Improvisers are taught that the best response to any note is 'thank you'. Even if you don't agree with it, you should listen attentively with a mindset of gratitude. If you want to be agile you must be teachable, so *take the note*. It is still your decision whether or not to act on it. But remember that feedback is very difficult to give and, considering how valuable it can be, saying 'thank you' encourages that person to keep giving it to you in the future.

2. **Don't get defensive.**

It's easy to have a strong emotional reaction to feedback that manifests as aggressiveness or defensiveness. This is another big reason why it's so difficult to give feedback: we're afraid of retaliation from the person that we're actually trying to help. Try to stay calm during feedback, discuss it to ensure you have clarity on what they are trying to say, and, where appropriate, admit to any mistakes you might have made. This doesn't just make the conversation easier. It also allows you to own any errors, which is a crucial first step in fixing them.

3. **Deliberately seek it out.**

Because feedback is so valuable, you should try to make feedback easy to give. You achieve this through how you respond to it when it is given but also by proactively seeking it out. For example, ask for feedback after projects, presentations or even meetings by asking specific questions to elicit it – 'specific' being the watch word. Feedback-givers can get overwhelmed if asked broad questions like: 'Can you tell me how I'm doing at the moment?' It's better to give a clearly defined request such as: 'I am worried that my writing style is a little dry. Can you feed back on how I might make this report more engaging?' This sort of request is likely to give you some specific information that you can put into action straight away and which, therefore, will be more useful to you in the long run.

▶ **Exercise**

STOP. START. CONTINUE.

This is a useful structure you can use to guide others in giving you feedback. Simply ask them: 'What is one thing you'd like me to stop doing, one thing you'd like me to start doing and one thing you'd like me to continue doing?'

▲ ▲ ▲

4. **Ask clarifying questions.**

While we can help people give us specific feedback by making specific requests, sometimes the feedback we get is vague and a little woolly. If this is the case, try asking questions that clarify what they've said. For example: 'Would you mind sharing an example of when you've noticed me do this?'

A related issue here is receiving a response that crams several different notes into one giant iceberg of feedback. This can obfuscate things if you aren't careful; so in this instance you might ask: 'What's the one big thing you'd like me to be doing more of?' Remember the point of feedback is to change and improve behaviour, so leaving with a clear and actionable takeaway is important.

HOW TO GIVE FEEDBACK

1. **Be specific, clear and timely.**

The trouble with most feedback is the timing, frequency and specificity of it. If we get feedback at all, it tends to be a long way after the incident we are receiving feedback on. For many people it happens once a year as part of their performance review, and when they get it it's often vague. This is not an agile way to learn. The improv model of feedback is what we call 'side coaching'. During rehearsal, a coach will interrupt a practice scene to feed back on a bad choice that the improviser has made so they can correct it in context. Similarly, after shows feedback is given when the performance is fresh in everyone's minds.

So, while you don't want to do it mid-meeting, try to ensure the feedback you give is as close as possible to the moment in which the negative behaviour occurs. Therefore, rather than storing feedback up for occasional check-ins, try to give it consistently in small dollops throughout the year. And, if possible, give this feedback privately: one-on-one and face-to-face. For a method of how you might do this, try the exercise below.

▶ Exercise

I LIKE. I WISH. WHAT IF?

This is a useful feedback framework borrowed from design thinking. When you give someone feedback you offer three bits of information: first, something you like about a project or behaviour; second, something you'd like to see be different; and third, a suggestion for a correction or something new that could be added.

▲ ▲ ▲

2. **Give both negative and positive feedback.**
   While we want to correct unhelpful behaviours, we also want to build on helpful behaviours too, in order that they can become super-strengths.

(Remember what we spoke about in Chapter 4: notice and double down on the good stuff.) So, make sure you mention the good and not just the bad stuff when you feed back.

This is also about tone. Many people use the 'shit sandwich' approach to feedback, which is bad feedback wedged in between two bits of good feedback. This is a useful tactic because receiving negative feedback is so difficult that sugaring the pill is an important step in boosting their resilience.

▶ Exercise

BREAKFAST OF CHAMPIONS

A team of psychologists was able to make feedback 40 per cent more effective by framing it with these twenty words: 'I'm giving you these comments because I have high expectations of you and I am confident you can reach them ...'[67] As Kim Scott observes in her book *Radical Candor*, people will accept direct feedback if you show them you personally care. This sort of framing is a great way to do this.

▲ ▲ ▲

3. **If you find a problem, suggest a fix.**

A good debrief doesn't focus on the outcome. It doesn't say: 'That wasn't funny and therefore it was bad.' Instead it focuses on the process that led to the bad outcome. If you want someone to stop a behaviour you need to give them something to replace it with. When an improv coach side-coaches an improviser, she won't just point out the bad choice the improviser made, she will offer one or two better choices that the improviser could have taken instead. By doing this the coach makes it less likely that the mistake will be repeated in the future and mixes negative feedback with an empowering tool.

4. **Give feedback for the right reason.**
Before rushing into giving feedback, it's important to reflect on why you are giving feedback in the first place. Are you genuinely doing it for the person's benefit? Or are you trying to get something off your chest? It's important with feedback to assume positive intent on behalf of the person you are feeding back to. Make sure to show that you know that person is doing their best to perform their job well, despite their imperfections. This ensures that the feedback is helpful and not just a release valve for your own frustration.

CONCLUSION

At the start of the chapter, I defined agility as our capacity to flexibly and quickly respond to change. This is the pivotal skill of the improviser, and it centres on our acuity to feedback. We've explored how feedback doesn't just inform our next moment; its effects are deeper, richer and longer-term than that. Feedback transforms our experience into knowledge and expertise, which in turn informs our intuition, so that our spontaneous decisions in the future are more likely to be intelligent. Each journey around the loop of notice, let go, decide and communicate gives us new information that is useful next time.

We can see that agility is built around two central paradoxes. First, in order to be agile, we need a process that constantly tries to test and disprove our knowledge, yet through this same process our knowledge and expertise also constantly expand. Second, executing this agile process requires us to plan, yet the reason we plan is to give ourselves the opportunity to throw the plan away. We are back to that balance between freedom and structure, between order and chaos. Improvisation exists in the interaction between our knowledge, our actions and the world. The loop never stops – which is why it's so interesting.

An improvised show is about as uncertain as life gets. But improvisers are comfortable in this environment. Why? Because they have accepted their lot and with that comes peace. If we are to find similar equanimity offstage, we must surrender to the complexity of our environment in the same way. Don't fight it, use it. *Everything is an offer*.

But peace of mind doesn't just come from accepting our environment. It also comes from knowing that we are not alone in it: change is less scary when someone has got your back. Beyond having teammates that you trust, you can also find calm in having a process: a toolbox of techniques, skills and mental models with which to respond and adapt to change. Although improvisation is the art of acting without a plan, it doesn't mean you act without a method. Like all arts there is a craft to it, and it's less scary when you know how. My purpose over the past six chapters has been to share it with you.

Finally, improvisers have an optimism that everything will work out in the end. They've learned from experience that there are lots of opportunities in change. When you move through the world with the same belief, it's amazing how many more opportunities you notice in the world. Suddenly the constant disruption which is now part of our everyday lives isn't so intimidating. In fact, you might even decide to deliberately disrupt *yourself*. It is to this last thought that we turn in our final moments together.

CONCLUSION

'I'm not mad! I've just read different books!'
—Ken Campbell

Sat on the tube on the way back to my grubby little flat in Stockwell after my first improv class with Stirring Steve I felt an exhilaration I hadn't felt in years. The closest thing I can equate it to was how I felt after I went cold water swimming one Christmas Eve at Parliament Hill lido. There I was, stood almost naked in the freezing cold December air, and yet warmth jetted out of every pore. *I felt alive.* Of course, I'd been alive before the improv class too – biologically speaking. But it turns out I wasn't really, not in the sense that matters: the emotional sense, the spiritual sense. The sense that makes you want to dance, do shots and look up in awe at the bright full moon.

I was always the sort of person who thought life was two to one against, but now I had a giddy optimism that was so unusual it was actually making me feel self-conscious. I couldn't wait to go back the next week and do another class. That presence, that connection with others, that spontaneity: it was addictive. It's like that feeling when you're in a long-term relationship that hasn't really worked for a while, but you think you still love them anyway, and then you accidentally happen to meet someone else and realise you don't love your partner at all, because *this* is what love is and how did you ever forget? I was having an affair with improv.

CASE STUDY: Chrissy Williams, comic book editor

Improv has massively helped me work on my confidence through differentiating between 'you're bad' and 'your idea was bad'. For example, last week I cooked possibly the worst soup of all time for my partner. (How can you burn something that's largely made of water?) Ordinarily I'd be berating myself and apologising, completely lost in my own guilt and shame. Instead, I said: 'This soup is really fucking terrible.' We both laughed and ate something else, and it was no big deal. There's something so empowering in improv about just saying 'the thing' out loud instead of worrying about it. It's rewired my brain to fret less about unimportant stuff and has freed up lots of anxious energy for better things. I have no idea how I managed to function before improv! Ashamed of soup? WTF? ■

Improv and I are now life partners, but it's an open relationship. Improv still sees other people and that's OK. I would dearly love you to be one of them. If you're wondering what an improv class is like, let me bring it to life for you a little here. Improv is traditionally taught experientially in workshops. These workshops normally last two or three hours and you do a bunch of exercises in pairs and in small groups. Classes tend to consist of around fifteen people, and they're facilitated by a coach who introduces the games and side-coaches you so that you learn loads but most importantly enjoy yourself as much as possible.

If you're shy and worried that improv classes will be full of extroverts: don't worry; there will be tons of people like you. There are always some extroverted types too, but it's good to be around different sorts of people. One thing that improvisation has ideologically built into its culture is that it's an inclusive, safe space that celebrates the individuality of everyone in the room. Most schools offer a variety of levels of training so you can begin your journey with people who are beginners just like you. The make-up of classes varies depending on where you take them, but most of the time there is a real mix of folks. So it won't be you and ten other wannabe West End stars in tap dancing shoes and shit-eating grins. You'll have a lovely time.

There are improvisation schools all over the world now, and so there's a good chance there might well be classes near you. I am co-director (with Stirring Steve Roe) of an improv school and theatre in London called Hoopla. We've been going for fifteen years now and if there is a friendlier place in the world to learn improv I would be amazed. We'd love to see you there, but if you don't live nearby, get in touch with me and I'd be happy to recommend somewhere closer to home.

I appreciate that, regardless of your personality type or confidence level, signing up for a class is an intimidating thing. It feels like you are taking a big risk. But the rewards in terms of your self-confidence are enormous. Improv begins from the assumption that human beings are absolutely amazing. Based on this fundamental belief, improvisation is not about reinventing the wheel. Improv is about augmenting our natural capacities for generosity, spontaneity and storytelling with small tweaks of behaviour and mindset to allow us to be at our best more often. Doesn't that sound like a fair swap for feeling a bit nervous once a week?

CASE STUDY: Pete Kinsella, rail engineer

Improv has changed my life in every single way. The concept I most often use is 'yes, and', which is especially helpful with my mother. She has dementia and spends a lot of time feeling very distressed, believing all sort of things are going to happen to her. I've found that outright denying her fears does little to ever calm her and will often make her worse. Employing the principle of 'yes and' allows me to enter the perceived situation she finds herself in and steer it along another path to a happier place.

One time she wouldn't take her medication, believing that the drink it was in had been poisoned. My father had been trying for a while, telling her she was okay and there was nothing wrong with it. I chose a different tack. I accepted the offer. I said I was appalled that someone had poisoned her drink. I said it was not good enough and I was going to sort it out, and listed what I was going to do. I then diverted down a different route and asked her what her favourite drink was and got her talking about that. After a while I said I'd fetch her whatever drink she liked. I went out with the glass, came back in and said: 'Here's the drink you wanted, mum.' And she finished it off in one. ∎

Beyond confidence, the biggest thing I've got from improv is the ability to do what Harvard Business School professor Ron Heifetz describes as 'get off the dance floor and onto the balcony'. This is the mental activity of stepping back when you're in the middle of the action in order to ask yourself: *What's really going on here?* By stepping 'onto the balcony' you are capable of seeing your life and your behaviour for what it is. You are able to *notice what you notice*, as in, you become aware of what you are paying attention to. When you notice what you notice you can ask yourself: *Is what I am currently paying attention to getting me what I want? If not, what would I have to pay attention to in order to get it?* There is freedom in self-awareness.

The writer and futurist Alvin Toffler once wrote: 'The illiterate of the 21st century will not be those who cannot read and write, but those who cannot learn, unlearn and relearn.' Let alone questions of literacy, our capacity to unlearn is central to our growth and happiness. But we cannot unlearn anything unless we are capable of getting onto the balcony and noticing patterns in ourselves. Patterns of thinking, feeling and behaving can trap us where we are in life, and trap us in dysfunctional relationships too, stuck in the same old scripts. As Arthur Miller wrote: 'The present is merely that which the past is capable of noticing and smelling and reacting to.'

How do we break out of these patterns? We need to deliberately challenge ourselves, to disrupt our routines so that we are forced to pay attention in new ways. Taking an improv class may be that disruption for you, but it doesn't have to be. You just need to say 'Yes, and …' to something that scares you. One of Del Close's favourite improvisation maxims was to *follow the fear*. What he meant by this was that in order to use fear, you first have to admit that you're feeling it. Then, when you've noticed that you're feeling scared, you should follow it. For Close, fear was a sign you should do something. Onstage, when I am scared to enter a scene, it is normally because I know that this scene needs me. And offstage, in life, fear is a signal that I am risking something important. Fear, paradoxically, often shows us what we love. So we need to learn to follow the fear. We get scared when we care. What a wonderful privilege to have things that are so important to us.

NOTES

1. We found out only after calling ourselves this that 'The Committee' happened to be the name of improv legend Del Close's original team in the 1960s! Vainglorious or what?! Total mistake, I hasten to add.

2. Bob Kulhan, *Getting to 'Yes And': The Art of Business Improv* (Stanford University Press, 2017).

3. Check out this article from the World Economic Forum summarising their *Future of Jobs Report 2018*: '5 things to know about the future of jobs', Vesselina Stefanova Ratcheva & Till Leopold, 17 September 2018, https://www.weforum.org/agenda/2018/09/future-of-jobs -2018-things-to-know.
    The World Bank's *World Development Report 2019: The Changing Nature of Work*, p. 20, http://documents.worldbank.org/curated/ en/816281518818814423/pdf/2019-WDR-Report.pdf.

4. Thank you to the future-of-work consultancy Hot Spots Movement for their insight here and in other chapters. Their cutting-edge research was formative in my thinking when writing this book. https://www.hotspotsmovement.com

5. Mihaly Csikszentmihalyi, *Flow: The Psychology of Happiness* (Rider, 2002).

6. Keith Johnstone, *Impro: Improvisation and the Theatre* (Methuen Drama, 1981, 2007).

7. Giles Story, 'Anticipating Pain Is Worse Than Feeling It', *Harvard Business Review*, March 2014, https://hbr.org/2014/03/anticipating -pain-is-worse-than-feeling-it.

8. The website BehaviouralEconomics.com provides a tidy summary of this bias on their site: https://www.behavioraleconomics.com/ resources/mini-encyclopedia-of-be/status-quo-bias. If you'd like to dig deeper, check out: W. Samuelson & R. J. Zeckhauser, 'Status

quo bias in decision making', *Journal of Risk and Uncertainty*, 1, 1988, pp. 7–59.

9. An amazing new piece of research suggests a causal link between doing improv and tolerance of uncertainty: Felsman, Gunawardena & Seifert, 'Improv experience promotes divergent thinking, uncertainty tolerance, and affective well-being', *Thinking Skills and Creativity*, Vol. 35, March 2020. https://doi.org/10.1016/j.tsc.2020.100632

10. The study was discussed in an article for *Psychology Today*: Christopher Bergland, 'The Neuroscience of Social Pain', *Psychology Today*, 3 March 2014. The study: Giovanni Novembre, Marco Zanon and Giorgia Silani, 'Empathy for social exclusion involves the sensory-discriminative component of pain: a within-subject fMRI study', *Social Cognitive and Affective Neuroscience*, Vol. 10, Issue 2, February 2015, pp. 153–64, https://doi.org/10.1093/scan/nsu038

11. George Land & Beth Jarman, *Breakpoint and Beyond: Mastering the Future Today* (Harper Collins, 1992), p. 153. You can also watch Land's TEDx Talk 'The Failure of Success' in which he reflects on the study: https://www.youtube.com/watch?v=ZfKMq-rYtnc&t=528s

12. Adam Grant on research showing the link between volume and originality in: 'How to Build a Culture of Originality', *Harvard Business Review*, March 2016, pp. 86–94, https://hbr.org/2016/03/how-to-build-a-culture-of-originality.

To read more about the serial order effect, see: Roger E. Beaty & Paul J. Silvia, 'Why do ideas get more creative across time? An executive interpretation of the serial order effect in divergent thinking tasks', *Psychology of Aesthetics, Creativity, and the Arts*, 6(4), pp. 309–19. http://psycnet.apa.org/journals/aca/6/4/309

13. Daniel J. Simons & Christopher F. Chabris, 'Gorillas in our midst: sustained inattentional blindness for dynamic events', *Perception*, Vol. 28, 1999, pp. 1059–74. You can find the test itself here: http://www.theinvisiblegorilla.com/gorilla_experiment.html

14. Shunryu Suzuki, *Zen Mind, Beginner's Mind* (Weatherhill, 1970).

15. Aaron E. Carroll, 'To Be Sued Less, Doctors Should Consider Talking to Patients More', *The New York Times*, 1 June 2015, https://www.nytimes.com/2015/06/02/upshot/to-be-sued-less-doctors-should-talk-to-patients-more.html

16. Ronald B. Adler, Lawrence B. Rosenfeld & Russell F. Proctor II, *Interplay: The Process of Interpersonal Communication*, 12th Edition (Oxford University Press, 2012).

17. Douglas Heingartner, 'Now Hear This, Quickly', *The New York Times*, 2 October 2003, https://www.nytimes.com/2003/10/02/technology/now-hear-this-quickly.html

18. T. J. Jagodowski, David Pasquesi & Pam Victor, *Improvisation at the Speed of Life* (Solo Roma, 2015), p. 39.

19. Edgar H. Schein, *Helping: How to Offer, Give, and Receive Help* (Berrett-Koehler Publishers, 2009).

20. From his book with Tahl Raz, *Never Split the Difference: Negotiating as if Your Life Depended on It* (Random House Business, 2017), and discussed in an interview of Chris Voss by Eric Barker, 'Hostage Negotiation Techniques That Will Get You What You Want', June 2013, https://www.bakadesuyo.com/2013/06/hostage-negotiation

21. Sir John Whitmore's renowned GROW coaching model uses great open questioning: https://www.performanceconsultants.com/grow-model

22. C. J. Limb & A. R. Braun, 'Neural Substrates of Spontaneous Musical Performance: An fMRI Study of Jazz Improvisation', *PLoS ONE* 3(2), 2008, https://doi.org/10.1371/journal.pone.0001679

23. Check out this interactive piece based on the research: Sarah L. Kaufman, Jayne Orenstein, Sarah Hashemi, Elizabeth Hart & Shelly Tan, 'Art in an Instant: The Secrets of Improvisation', *Washington Post*, 7 June 2018, https://www.washingtonpost.com/graphics/2018/lifestyle/science-behind-improv-performance/.

    Here's Charles Limb talking to Patrick Cox on 'This is your brain on improv', *The World in Words*, 24 May 2018, https://www.pri.org/stories/2018-05-23/your-brain-improv

24. Sarah Valencia Botto talks about her research at TEDxAtlanta, 'When Do Kids Start to Care About Other People's Opinions?', TEDxAtlanta, March 2019, https://www.ted.com/talks/ sara_valencia_botto_when_do_kids_start_to_care_about_other_ people_s_opinions?

   Or you can check out the study: S. V. Botto & P. Rochat, 'Sensitivity to the Evaluation of Others Emerges by 24 Months', *Developmental Psychology*, 54(9), 2018, pp. 172334. https://doi. org/10.1037/dev0000548

25. R. A. Beghetto, 'Creative mortification: An initial exploration', *Psychology of Aesthetics, Creativity, and the Arts*, 8(3), 2014, pp. 266–76. https://doi.org/10.1037/a0036618

26. As Keith Johnstone says, if we can learn not to judge our ideas, imagination becomes as effortless as perception. See: *Impro*, p. 80.

27. Johnstone, *Impro*, p. 80.

28. Steven Johnson, *Where Good Ideas Come From: The Seven Patterns of Innovation* (Penguin, 2010).

29. Sir Ken Robinson's talk on 'Changing Paradigms' was animated by the RSA. 'RSA Animate: Changing Education Paradigms', The RSA, YouTube, 14 October 2010, https://www.youtube.com/ watch?v=zDZFcDGpL4U

30. The principles of design thinking are mapped out by David Kelley, IDEO founder, and Tom Kelley, IDEO partner, in their book *Creative Confidence: Unleashing the Creative Potential in Us All* (William Collins, 2014).

31. 'Brainstorming – Rules & Techniques for Idea Generation', IDEO, https://www.ideou.com/pages/brainstorming

32. Kirby Ferguson, 'Everything is a Remix', YouTube, 16 May 2016, https://www.youtube.com/watch?v=nJPERZDfyWc

33. Jake Swearingen, 'An Idea That Stuck: How George de Mestral Invented the Velcro Fastener', *New York Magazine*, November 2016, https://nymag.com/vindicated/2016/11/an-idea-that-stuck-how -george-de-mestral-invented-velcro.html

34. Rob Fitzpatrick, *The Mom Test: How to Talk to Customers and Learn if Your Business Is a Good Idea When Everyone Is Lying to You* (Founder Centric, 2014).

35. Mark Twain, *Pudd'nhead Wilson* (Charles L. Webster & Co., 1894).

36. Amy C. Edmondson, 'Strategies for Learning from Failure', *Harvard Business Review*, April 2011, https://hbr.org/2011/04/strategies-for-learning-from-failure

37. Matthew Syed, *Black Box Thinking: Marginal Gains and the Secrets of High Performance* (John Murray, 2016).

38. Theresa Robbins Dudeck, *Keith Johnstone: A Critical Biography* (A&C Black, 2013), p. 161.

39. J. R. Hayes, 'Cognitive Processes in Creativity', in: J. A. Glover, R. R. Ronning, C. R. Reynolds (eds), *Handbook of Creativity. Perspectives on Individual Differences* (Springer, 1989).

40. Aneeta Rattan, Catherine Good & Carol S. Dweck, '"It's ok – Not Everyone Can Be Good at Math": Instructors with an Entity Theory Comfort (and Demotivate) Students', *Journal of Experimental Social Psychology*, 48(3), May 2012, pp. 731–7. https://doi.org/10.1016/j.jesp.2011.12.012

41. Holly A. McGregor & Andrew J. Elliot, 'The Shame of Failure: Examining the Link Between Fear of Failure and Shame', *Personality and Social Psychology Bulletin*, 1 February 2005, https://doi.org/10.1177/0146167204271420

42. Read about Stefan's project here: Melanie Stefan, 'A CV of Failures', *Nature*, 468, 2010 doi:10.1038/nj7322-467a, as published online on 17 November 2010 at: https://www.nature.com/naturejobs/science/articles/10.1038/nj7322-467a. Check out Stefan's CV of failures here: http://melaniestefan.net/Mela_24Nov2017.pdf

43. Steve Peters, *The Chimp Paradox: The Mind Management Programme for Confidence, Success and Happiness* (Vermillion, 2012).

44. Rob Cross, Scott Taylor & Deb Zehner, 'Collaboration Without Burnout', *Harvard Business Review*, July–August 2018, https://hbr.org/2018/07/collaboration-without-burnout

45. Rob Cross, Reb Rebele & Adam Grant, 'Collaborative Overload' *Harvard Business Review*, January–February 2016, https://hbr.org/2016/01/collaborative-overload

46. Susan Cain, *Quiet: The Power of Introverts in a World that Can't Stop Talking* (Penguin, 2012).

47. Fritz Strack, Leonard L. Martin & Sabine Stepper, 'Inhibiting and facilitating conditions of the human smile: A nonobtrusive test of the facial feedback hypothesis', *Journal of Personality and Social Psychology*, Vol 54(5), May 1988, pp. 768–77, https://doi.org/10.1037/0022-3514.54.5.768

48. See: Frans Johansson, *The Medici Effect: Breakthrough Insights at the Intersection of Ideas, Concepts, and Cultures* (Harvard Business Review Press, 2004).

49. This idea isn't just bound up in improv but is borne out by prevailing management theory. Check out Douglas McGregor's model of Theory X vs Theory Y, as first introduced in *The Human Side of Enterprise* (McGraw-Hill, 2006, 1960); Daniel H. Pink's book on motivation *Drive* (Canongate, 2011); and Abraham Maslow's hierarchy of needs, first proposed in his 1943 paper 'A Theory of Human Motivation'.

50. Frank J. Barrett, *Yes to the Mess: Surprising Leadership Lessons from Jazz* (Harvard Business Review Press, 2012).

51. As told in Margaret Heffernan's TED talk 'The Pecking Order'.

52. Anita Williams Woolley et al., 'Evidence for a Collective Intelligence Factor in the Performance of Human Groups', *Science*, 29 October 2010, vol. 330, issue 6004, pp. 686–8.

53. You can see what the aims of their study was and how they went about it at re:Work, 'Guide: Understand team effectiveness'. https://rework.withgoogle.com/print/guides/5721312655835136/

54. Sigal Barsade and Olivia A. O'Neill, 'Manage Your Emotional Culture', *Harvard Business Review*, Jan–Feb 2016, pp. 58–66. https://hbr.org/2016/01/manage-your-emotional-culture

55. As quoted in 'How to Tell if Your Company Has a Creative Culture' by David Burkus, *Harvard Business Review*, 2 Dec 2014. https://hbr.org/2014/12/how-to-tell-if-your-company-has-a -creative-culture

56. Ed Catmull, *Creativity, Inc.: Overcoming the Unseen Forces That Stand in the Way of True Inspiration* (Transworld, 2014), p. 90.

57. Jennifer S. Mueller, Shimul Melwani & Jack A. Goncalo, 'The Bias Against Creativity: Why People Desire But Reject Creative Ideas', 2011, Retrieved 3 Feb 2020 from Cornell University, ILR School site: http://digitalcommons.ilr.cornell.edu/articles/450

58. Andrew K. Przybylski & Netta Weinstein, 'Can you connect with me now? How the presence of mobile communication technology influences face-to-face conversation quality', *Journal of Social and Personal Relationships*, 20(3), 2012, pp. 237–46.

59. There are over 30 liberating structures, developed by Keith McCandless and Henri Lipmanowicz. You can check them all out here: http://www.liberatingstructures.com

60. Richard Branson, 'You learn by doing and by falling over', Virgin website, 27 October 2014, https://www.virgin.com/ richard-branson/you-learn-doing-and-falling-over

61. Perel tweeted this on 9 August 2016, and also talks about it in her appearance on the Scandinavian talk show, *Skavlan*, 5 Dec 2018. https://twitter.com/EstherPerel/ status/763058633269706755?s=20; https://www.youtube.com/ watch?v=5CnxqgVZJm4&feature=youtu.be

62. See his brilliantly titled book, *If I Understood you, Would I Have This Look on My Face?* (Random House, 2017).

63. This improvisational process is well established in the start-up world, where it is variously referred to as a 'sprint', 'scrum' or 'hackathon'. Eric Ries in his influential book *The Lean Startup* summarises the method simply as build–measure–learn.

64. A classic example of a pivot is YouTube. It launched on Valentine's Day in 2005 as a video dating site with the slogan 'Tune in, hook

up'. It bombed. Soon the creators of YouTube decided to lift restrictions on what videos could be uploaded to the platform, believing that the scope for user videos was much wider than naff dating vlogs. The rest, as they say, is history.

65. In software development this is known as the 'waterfall approach'.

66. In Beckett's 1983 story 'Worstward Ho', in *Nohow On* (1989).

67. David Scott Yeager et al., 'Breaking the cycle of mistrust: Wise interventions to provide critical feedback across the racial divide', *Journal of Experimental Psychology: General*, 143(2), 2014, pp. 804–24. https://psycnet.apa.org/doi/10.1037/a0033906

Thank you to academic and improviser Clay Drinko for all his help in the research on the science of improvisation.

ACKNOWLEDGEMENTS

There's a story about the late Peter Cook, surely one of the best comedic improvisers who has ever lived. He's cornered at a drinks party by a dull man who eventually tells him, 'I'm writing a novel.' 'Oh really?' replies Cook. 'Neither am I.'

Writing a book is hard. The hardest bit is probably starting in the first place. Then finishing it is pretty tricky. Oh, and the bit in the middle is dreadful. *The acknowledgements though!* Now, here's fun.

Like performing improv comedy, the writing of a book is a team sport. This surprises some people. They imagine the author, in their grotty bunker somewhere, hacking at their keyboard with nothing but a tea-stained mug for company. And there is a lot of truth in that. But the DNA of a good book contains chromosomes from a big family of forebears. I'd like to thank them now.

First, thank you to my editor Kiera Jamison at Icon. You saw the potential in this book when it was just an idea in my head. More than that, you gave me a kick up the arse when I needed it, and you puffed up confidence when I needed that too. Thank you for teaching me to put the audience first in everything. Most of all, your assiduous and generous notes have made me a better writer. I will remember that forever.

Of course, Kiera is part of big gang at Icon Books. Others I must thank for their tireless work include Andrew Furlow, Ruth Killick, Rob Sharman, Lydia Wilson, Duncan Heath and, of course, Philip Cotterell. Like the best improvisers, I know you all do your best every day to make me look good. I am so grateful that you've got my back. Shout out to Luke Bird for the striking cover design. And let's hear it for Conor Jatter for his help with the diagrams too.

Second, I need to thank my partner Naomi Petersen. Not only for being a crucial sounding board on innumerable occasions, but

291

also for putting up with me when I was a total fucking misery. Writing a book makes you self-absorbed – especially when a deadline looms. Thank you for being kind and forgiving when I wasn't great company. You don't know how much that helped me get this over the line. Thank you also to my parents, Belinda and Jonathan Dickins, for being unbreakingly supportive of my totally mental career choice.

Then there are those who have contributed so much insight to the content of this book. The brilliant people who agreed to let me use them as case studies. The clients who teach me as much as I teach them. The people who read and offered notes on the first draft: Phillipa Berry, Katy Schutte and Liam Brennan. Thank you to Emma and Harriet at Hot Spots Movement for their expertise on the future of work. Thank you to my researcher Michelle Cook. And thank you to my brave soldiers on The Committee: Kayleigh, Freya, Sally, Nick, Adam, Clare, Maddy, Monica, Kat and Ivan. Long may we play together.

I wrote in the Introduction that I stand on the shoulders of giants. This book would not have been possible without the seminal work of Viola Spolin, Keith Johnstone and Del Close. I hope I've done your ideas justice – wherever you are. I've also had so many great teachers along the way in my improv life. Too many to name here, but I'd like to give a special shout out to David Shore, Maria Peters, Lauren Shearing, Chris Mead, Holly Laurent and Mike Orton-Toliver. Plus, all the amazing performers I've had the pleasure of both watching and playing with over the years. I learn from you in every show. Improv is the most amazing community to be part of and one of the great joys of my life.

Finally, I'd like to thank Steve Roe at Hoopla. You were my first teacher. Then you took a gamble on me and let me teach. I was in a bit of a hole before you and improv came along. 'Yes, and' saved my life. And, thanks to you and all the other wonderful improv teachers, performers and applied practitioners out there, it will save a lot more yet.

APPENDIX
IMPROV WARM-UP EXERCISES
TO TRY IN THE OFFICE

Pass the clap

This is not what it sounds like! This is a great exercise for focusing everyone; it gets people out of their seats and it's weirdly addictive.

1. Everyone stands in a circle.

2. Someone starts by looking at the colleague to their right or to their left, engaging them with proper eye contact.

3. When they've done so, the aim is then for both of them to clap at the same time.

4. The person who has 'received' the clap (ahem), then passes it on to the colleague to their right or left and the clap is passed around the circle.

5. To increase the difficulty, you can increase the speed. But remember the aim is to clap at exactly the same time!

6. For higher level clapping, you can allow people to pass the clap to colleagues across the circle too.

Red ball

This simple icebreaker is good for getting everyone to shake off their day and be present with one another.

1. Get the group into a standing circle.

2. The facilitator of the exercise mimes passing a red ball to someone else in the circle. When the ball is thrown, the thrower says, 'Red ball'. When the ball is caught, the catcher also says, 'Red ball'.

3. This person then passes it to someone else in the circle and the game continues. Coach participants to maintain eye contact in order to make sure that their 'offer' is being received. This ensures that no balls are dropped.

4. As the game continues, add in different colour balls to make things harder. For example, after a minute or so you would have a red, blue and green ball all being simultaneously passed among the circle.

Crazy 8s

This is a very high energy warm-up that is useful to use when a group is a flat and you want to quickly get the blood flowing.

1. Get the group into a standing circle. In unison, everyone lifts their right hand above their head, shakes it quickly, and counts to 8 with each movement. For example: (flick) 'One!'; (flick) 'Two!'; (flick) 'Three!' and so on.

2. Next, they repeat this with the left hand ...

3. Then they repeat it with their right foot (flicking it in the air while maintaining balance on their left foot).

4. And then finally with their left foot.

5. Now, everyone immediately repeats this pattern, beginning with their right hand, except this time the players only count up to 7.

6. In each round, the players count up to one number less and make one fewer action on each limb, until everyone is quickly waving their entire body shouting '1! 1! 1! 1!'

7. When this is finished everyone shouts: 'CRAZY EIGHTS!'

APPENDIX
HOW TO IMPROVISE ONLINE

Virtual communication is a massive part of our working lives these days. But how can you apply everything in this book to Zoom calls and other online platforms? That's what we'll explore in this bonus guide.

It's handy to start with a definition. Communication is getting what is in your head and heart into the head and heart of another. The goal is mutual understanding and, often, to get them to take action or change their behaviour in some way.

Effective communication is a dance between you, your audience, and the context. Like any good dancer, sometimes you need to take the lead, sometimes you need to follow. Like any good dancer, you turn any stumbles into part of the dance. You may have choreography but remain open to the inspiration of the moment. Communication is an improvisation: it may have an intention, it may have a message, but it does not have a script. Crucially, communication is a two-way, dynamic process: a dialogue.

It can go wrong in a number of places: at the level of the sender, the medium, or the recipient. We can see that the so-called 'new normal' has presented new challenges at all three levels.

At the level of the sender, we are now having to communicate in a different way. Virtual mediums are less forgiving when it comes to an audience's attention: they are likely to have their email application flashing, a tab for their favourite sports site or shopping portal open, and their phone vibrating next to them. Not to mention their kids running around next door and the doorbell going.

At the level of the medium, clearly only one person can speak at a time. On top of that, we are usually represented onscreen as a stamp-sized image, therefore losing a lot of the non-verbal information we would normally have access to. People's internet bandwidth is of variable quality. Let's not even get started on dealing with people who haven't worked out the mute button!

At the level of the recipient, it's easy to feel ignored and that interrupting to ask questions or make points is awkward. More than that, people report having more 'performance anxiety' on virtual platforms. Suddenly what would be an informal contribution in a face-to-face meeting becomes a speaking event with all eyes on you. No wonder we are Zoom-fatigued!

We can't do much about the medium. We can only play to the conditions we find ourselves in. But it's worth reflecting also on what hasn't changed. The fundamental aspect of our communication remains the same: the human being(s) on the other side of that screen. As we explored in Chapter 6, the foundation of all good communication is R&R:

- **Relate**: Don't talk at the other person, relate to them instead. When you speak you should be focused on what the other person knows, thinks and feels, and not just on what you know, think or feel.

- **Responsibility**: The responsibility for the message belongs to the sender. If your communication is not received or understood, that's on you. What's important is not what you say, it's what they hear.

These basics apply as much online as they do offline. The following six principles will help you put them into practice.

SIX PRINCIPLES FOR OUTSTANDING VIRTUAL COMMUNICATION

1. IT ALL BEGINS WITH LISTENING

You may recognise this as the title of Chapter 2. Listening is as important online as it is offline, perhaps even more so, as there are so many more opportunities for distraction and taking in the non-verbal communication (i.e. the emotional subtext) of other people on video-calls requires more focus. The fundamental approach remains the same: we want to play the scene we are in (not the one we want to be in). To do that we need to listen with intent. Here are some listening tips as applied to online mediums:

- **Turn everything off.** Get your phone off or at least on airplane mode. Shut down your email application. And resist the temptation to change your fantasy football team. Remember, when your camera is on, *we can see you when you are doing something else!*

- **Make notes as people speak.** Studies suggest this a great way to boost your listening, especially during longer calls.

- **Beware the chat function.** If you're typing into the chat function you are thinking about what *you* want to say and not what *the speaker* is saying.

- **Activate the speaker view function.** This will stop you looking at Siobhan's new hairdo in window number eight and focus you on the presenter.

2. BE INCLUSIVE

Being inclusive is about having empathy for other people's way of communicating. It requires you to understand that different people have different personalities and different communication styles, and so we need to be adaptable in how we communicate. This is true offline too, of course, but online it's even more important because of the 'monologue effect'. This is the phenomenon that virtual calls and conferences often result in individuals speaking for long periods of time without stopping, simply because they aren't picking up on a lot of non-verbal signals that they would normally notice in a face-to-face meeting.

As well as fitting somewhere on the continuum between the two main personality types, 'introvert' and 'extrovert', we all also have our own unique communication style. Communication styles have been broken down in various ways by different experts, but often the differences in the taxonomies are small. The breakdown I prefer is based on an oft-quoted theory by management psychologists David Merrill and Roger Reid. In short, as a communicator you probably fit into one of four camps:

- **Analytical:** passive in meetings; highly detail-focused. (Likes to be slow and methodical)

- **Amiable:** passive in meetings; relationship-focused. (Wants to avoid conflict)

- **Driver:** assertive in meetings; outcome-focused. (Gets to the point but can be tactless)

- **Expressive:** assertive in meetings; energetic and emotional. (Often thinks out loud)

No one style is better than the others, necessarily, but if a colleague or client has a style different to yours it means you'll need to flex your style when you communicate with them. This flexing begins with self-knowledge. When you are aware of your own style or pattern of communication, you now have a choice: Is this the best way of communicating in this context and to this person? Or do you need to try a different approach?

You can see that Analytical and Amiable styles can easily be crowded out in virtual meetings by the monologue effect, more likely to be inadvertently delivered by the natural Drivers and Expressive communicators. What we explored in the collaboration chapter with regards to status offers the fixes you can make to your approach here:

- Proactively seek people's opinions and bring introverts (and Amiable/Analytical communicators) into the conversation.

- If you are not the one speaking, be the ally of those who haven't been given the opportunity to share yet. For example, 'Jim, you haven't had a chance to speak, really interested to hear your views on this …'

3. WATCH YOUR ENERGY

If the camera adds ten pounds, then our webcams take away 10 per cent of our energy when we speak. There is a dilution effect. If you want to sound passionate, think how passionate you would be face-to-face and then exaggerate it. It will feel odd as you sit alone in your kitchen, but it will look about right to your audience. Much of this is to do with the tech, which cuts off most of your body and therefore loses a lot of your emotional meaning. Instead, it's got to show up in your voice and face.

Also, it's easy to forget that there is a human being on the other side of that screen. Research shows that people in online communication are often more brusque and even rude than they would be in face-to-face conversation. Generally, we perceive other people as less friendly on Zoom calls. Therefore, we need to be more proactively warm than we think we need to be. Don't forget to smile, make jokes, show up with enthusiasm. Here are some tips to maintain the energy through a video call:

- **Focus on *very* active listening.** Listen visually: nod, smile, make affirmative noises.

- **Watch your posture.** Being slumped at your desk, resting your face on your palm not only reduces your energy, it saps energy from everyone else.

- **Take the meeting standing up if you are feeling lethargic.** Obviously adjust where you place your laptop, so it remains at roughly eye level.

- **Be an involved audience member.** This is not Netflix! We need you to be active, not just passive. Energy is contagious, remember.

- **Use your voice as an instrument.** Our voice is the main way we can add energy on a video-call. So, be loud and proud. Don't rush. Use pauses. And don't forget to have some light and shade in your voice: just think how you would read a children's book. You wouldn't read that in a flat monotone, so why deliver your presentation like that?

I appreciate that this all seems exhausting. And one of the main challenges with virtual communication, as the research attests, is that it's exhausting for all concerned. So think about how you replenish your energy after an online meeting:

- **Move around.** Don't just jump straight to the next call if you can avoid it.

- **Recentre yourself with some deep breaths.** In through your nose, out through your mouth. Keep your eyes shut and focus on how the air feels entering and leaving your diaphragm.

- **Take a micro-digital detox.** Don't just hop from Zoom to Slack to your text messages.

4. BE A 'YES, AND' SORT OF PERSON

We covered this in depth in Chapter 1, but it bears repeating as 'yes, and' is an even more essential tool online where we lose the micro-gestures that normally show cooperation and rapport. As 'yes, and' is a way of showing you have heard, understood and are explicitly building off the last person's suggestion, it goes a long way to establishing these signals in a virtual space. Saying 'yes, and' is a tangible demonstration that you are collaborating with your colleagues and clients.

5. TAKE UP SPACE

We explored how you might take up space in a room earlier in the book. A similar principle applies in virtual communication, but here we need to think about how we look onscreen.

How often have you seen this on a Zoom call: the person with their laptop on their thighs, so they loom over it, their jowls lit up but the rest of their face in almost darkness. Is this a sort of person you would trust?

Clearly the content of your presentation is important. If you want your audience to trust you, you have to be credible – and that's about *what* you say and *who* you are. However, trust is also based on congruence between your message and *how* you deliver it. If you're not confident in your presentation, then how can you expect your audience to believe in it?

A crucial part of projecting confidence is strong body language: chest out, shoulders back and your head level (as if it's held up by a bit of string). A quick hack to get into this position is to tuck your bum in under your spine: you'll notice your posture changes automatically. These body language pointers also apply when sat down for virtual presentations. It helps here to get a cushion behind your back to support your posture (it forces your back into an S shape.) When you've sorted out your posture, think about how to set-up your space:

- **Have your laptop so that the camera is at eye level.** The easiest way to do this is to prop it up on something. Some people use books, I use a full A4 ring binder. (When you speak to your audience, *look at the camera* and not their face on the screen.)

- **Have your laptop screen just over an arm's length away from you.** This means you are nicely framed without being too close or too far away. Plus, people will be able to see your gestures – a crucial part of communicating your emotional content.

- **Sort your lighting out.** It's not vain to be well-lit. In fact, it makes you look more professional and allows you to communicate more meaning with your face. Here are the basics: you want light from at least two different sources. Ideally some sort of natural light and then a form of artificial light. I use the window next to my desk, the overhead bulb on the ceiling, and a twenty quid ring light I bought on Amazon. (The sort that YouTubers use – trust me, it's magic!)

6. REMEMBER THE ELEPHANT

The elephant, the rider and the path is a metaphor created by NYU social psychologist Jonathan Haidt. It's all about how we get people to change their behaviour. According to Haidt, there are two systems in the brain: the rational system and the emotional system. Think of your brain as a human rider on top of an elephant. The rider represents the rational system. That's the part of us that plans and solves problems. The rider might do some analysing and decide: 'I want to go that way.' But it's the elephant – the emotional system – that provides the power for the journey. The rider can try to push or drag the elephant in the direction she wants to go, but if these two disagree: the elephant will win. After all, it's massive!

This power imbalance between reason and emotion makes adopting new behaviours hard. And it is this power imbalance we need to consider with our communication. Too often in business communication we default to logical argument and data. And, of course, these are important in making a case for anything. But as people have their minds changed by emotion, we need to address this in how we present our ideas. If we want to appeal to the elephant, we need to tell stories.

As I wrote earlier, attention is a scarce resource on virtual platforms, and stories are the best technology we have to hook and hold our audience's attention.

Your stories don't need to be long: 30 seconds will do. The best way is to think of them as another form of evidence. Shown a graph? Great, now give an example showing this principle in action. You'll have your audience in the palm of your hand.

While we're at it, we should also consider Haidt's third element: the path. In his metaphor, the path represents the external environment that the elephant will travel down. The elephant and rider duo are more likely to complete their journey if you can: (a) shorten the distance of that path; and (b) remove any obstacles in their way. This is crucial in virtual communication. We need to take care to communicate with brevity and with clarity. *We need to treat words as if they are gold.* If you waffle, your audience will be on their Facebook pages in no time. We've all been there …

ABOUT THE AUTHOR

Max Dickins is co-director of Hoopla, the UK's first improvisation training school and London's first dedicated improv comedy theatre. Offstage, as a coach and business speaker, he has brought improvisation into workplaces across the world, with clients including Facebook, Google and Unilever – even teaching candidates on *The Apprentice*. As a comedian and writer, he has had his own Sony Award-nominated show on Absolute Radio, appeared numerous times on *Michael McIntyre's Big Show*, and taken critically acclaimed shows to the Edinburgh Festival and on tour in the UK. His book *My Groupon Adventure* was described by the *Irish Examiner* as 'full of heart'.

@maxdickins
www.maxdickins.com

WORK WITH MAX

BOOK MAX AS A SPEAKER

Max has worked with clients all over the world, bringing improvisation concepts to life in keynote speeches, workshops and executive coaching sessions. To find out more about how to book Max for your event, please visit **www.improvisethebook.com**.

BRING MAX INTO YOUR OFFICE

Since 2005, Hoopla have been market leaders in improvisation for business. We've trained upwards of 25,000 people, across four continents, taking improv concepts offstage to help people solve real-world problems. From global accountancy firms like Grant Thornton, through to disruptive tech giants like Amazon and Google, through to upmarket fashion brands like Chanel: we've worked with them all.

Hoopla run a range of in-house workshops on topics including:

- Leadership and agility
- Creativity and innovation
- Collaboration and communication skills
- Presentation skills and storytelling
- Diversity and inclusion
- Psychological safety and feedback

You can find more details at **www.hooplaimpro.com**.

'I thought this workshop would be good, and helpful in some areas of work. But it was applicable in every single part of what we do. I thought it was fantastic.'
— Katharine Newby Grant, brand director, P&G Northern Europe

FURTHER LEARNING RESOURCES

The learning doesn't stop here! You'll find lots of extra free content on the website for this book **www.improvisethebook.com**.

You can find Max on Twitter: **@maxdickins**